PENGUIN BUSINESS
WHO CHEATS AND HOW?

Robin Banerjee is the chairman of Nucleon Research Pvt. Ltd, a global clinical research organization. He served as the managing director of Caprihans India Ltd between 2012 and 2022, and has held senior management positions at Hindustan Unilever, ArcelorMittal Germany, Thomas Cook, Essar Steel and Suzlon Energy.

Robin is a chartered accountant (FCA), cost and management accountant (FCMA), company secretary (FCS) and master of commerce (MCom). He is the recipient of two lifetime achievement awards from *CFO India* (Feb 2023) and Manufacturing Today (Oct 2023).

Robin holds board positions at several companies, chambers of commerce and business schools. He is a much-sought-after keynote speaker, a popular columnist, a business coach, a philanthropist and a gym enthusiast.

Praise for the book

'This book is a succinct warning on the frauds occurring in some parts of the corporate world. It argues forcefully to lift the veil of the corporate structure in order to fix accountability for poor corporate governance. The minority shareholders with virtually no power to run the affairs of the corporation actually pay for the sins of promoters—directors and top management who effectively run the corporation. Manipulations in companies' accounts and share prices may increase the wealth of the top management. However, it is the general public and the minority shareholders who ultimately pick up the bills resulting from frauds and mismanagement in the corporate world. Values that serve society are integral to good corporate governance as much as in the public sphere.'

—**Dr Ashok Khemka**
IAS

'The book is a well-researched compilation of the large number of crimes committed by corporates over the last many years; it covers them all, not just once but many times over, in various situations and contexts. Not only a "must-read" but a "must-be-kept" in one's personal and professional library!'

—**Ashok Barat**
Ex-CEO and MD, Forbes & Co Ltd; Ex-President of Bombay Chamber of Commerce and Industries

'[The] author's understanding of the subject and the ability to communicate it crisply is a highlight of this book. This book is a welcome addition to my bookshelf. It can be read over time and you can dip into any page.'

—*The Hindu Business Line*

'The book is a myth-buster for the lay reader who may discover that many of the corporations they held in high regard have feet of clay. What makes the book connect with readers is that most of the cases covered have surfaced in the past decade and a half. Banerjee's research is thorough.'

—*Week*

'Cyber-fraud, insider trading, tax avoidance—there are any number of examples of companies and executives who have succumbed to the temptation of shortcuts in business. The book draws on these examples to talk about how they can be checked and what shareholders can do to protect their interests.'

—*Mint*

'The book decodes the metaphysics and cheating mechanisms corporate companies often resort to.'

—*Dignity Dialogue*

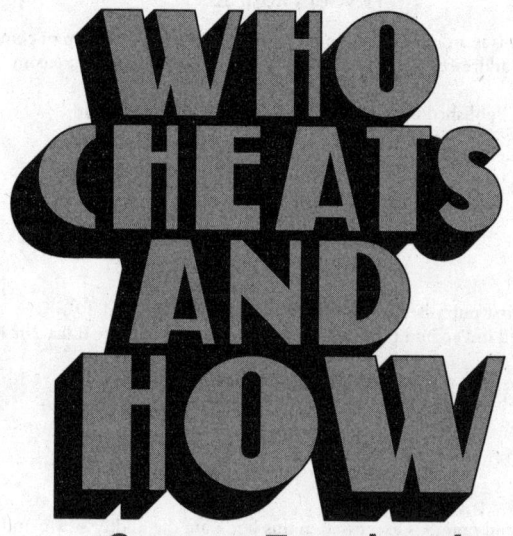

WHO CHEATS AND HOW

Scams, Fraud and the Dark Side of the Corporate World

ROBIN BANERJEE

PENGUIN BUSINESS

An imprint of Penguin Random House

PENGUIN BUSINESS

Penguin Business is an imprint of the Penguin Random House group of companies whose addresses can be found at global.penguinrandomhouse.com

Published by Penguin Random House India Pvt. Ltd
4th Floor, Capital Tower 1, MG Road,
Gurugram 122 002, Haryana, India

First published by Sage Publications India Pvt. Ltd 2015
Published in Penguin Business by Penguin Random House India 2024

Copyright © Robin Banerjee 2015

All rights reserved

10 9 8 7 6 5 4 3 2 1

The views and opinions expressed in this book are the author's own and the facts are as reported by him which have been verified to the extent possible, and the publishers are not in any way liable for the same.

ISBN 9780143464600

Typeset in 11/13 pt Berkeley by RECTO Graphics, Delhi
Printed at Replika Press Pvt. Ltd, India

This book is sold subject to the condition that it shall not, by way of trade or otherwise, be lent, resold, hired out, or otherwise circulated without the publisher's prior consent in any form of binding or cover other than that in which it is published and without a similar condition including this condition being imposed on the subsequent purchaser.

www.penguin.co.in

To the three most beautiful women in my life—
My mom, the reason for my existence; my significantly better half,
Ananya; and my heart and soul, Roshnai, our daughter

Contents

Acknowledgements	xi
Introduction	xv
Fraud and Scams: Mode and Style	xxv

Chapter 1: Corporate Charlatans — 1
- The Greedy Corporates — 3
- Contract Rigging, Bribery and Kickbacks: A Way of Life — 5
- Theft: Route to Instant Gratification — 12
- 'Lies, Damn Lies and Statistics' in Disclosures — 15
- Bypass Rules—A Shortcut to New Business — 18
- Taking Labour for a Ride — 19
- Extortion Provides Easy Money — 21
- Who Bothers about Conflict of Interest? — 24
- Collusion — 29
- Price Fixing, an Easy Way Out — 32
- Making Top Management Rich: Backdating of Stock Options — 34
- Fleecing by Buying Back Shares — 39
- Taxes Too Taxing: Let's Go to Tax Havens — 40
- Too Much Tax? Plan, Avoid or Cheat — 43
- Privacy Can Become an Open Book — 46
- Why Bother about Political or Economic Sanctions? — 49
- Press Can Impress Fraudulently — 51
- Food Not Excluded from Fraud — 54

Chapter 2: Can We Trust Our Banks? — 57
- Even Banks Commit Fraud — 58
- The LIBOR Scandal: Banks Can Fix Anything — 59
- Money Laundering — 64
- Miss-selling by Banks — 69
- Dangerous Banks: Uninsured or Unlicensed — 76
- Sham Deals — 78
- Fraudulent Loans — 79
- Camouflage and Concealment: Disguising Debts — 82

- Endless Possibilities: Miscellaneous Banking Fraud — 83
- Banks Are Victims (Fraud in Banks) — 85
- Even Banks Are Fallible: Failures in Internal Controls — 89
- Banks Can Be Vulnerable (Fraud Perpetuated *on* Banks) — 91
- Tricking Banks to Obtain Debts — 96
- Why Pay Back Loans? — 97
- Making a Fool of Banks through Faulty Security — 98
- Itsy-Bitsy Bank Fraud: Miscellaneous Causes — 99
- Banks' Fraud Stories — 101

Chapter 3: Quick-Rich Financing Schemes — 108
- King of the Moneymaking Racket: The Ponzi Scheme — 108
- Selling Dreams through Falsehood: The Pyramid Scheme — 116

Chapter 4: Stock Market Swindles — 121
- The Insidious Insiders: Insider Trading — 121
- Brokers: Banned and Discredited — 127
- When Brokers Cheat — 128
- Rapid Trading for a Fast Buck — 129
- Deceitful Listing — 131
- Clever North America-Listed Chinese Companies — 134

Chapter 5: Crime in Our Wired World — 142
- How Cyber Goons Operate — 143
- What's Next? — 145
- Who Commits Cybercrime? — 146
- What Are Cybercrime Fallouts? — 146
- Cyber Security World: A Glimpse — 147
- The Originators — 149
- Corporate Organisations under Attack — 150
- What Are the Preventive Actions That Can Be Taken? — 151

Chapter 6: Accounting: Cheating and Creativity — 154
- Tricky Sales Revenue Booking — 155
- Creating Sales Out of Thin Air — 175
- Booking False Vendor Rebates — 182
- Tinkering with the Past: Retrospective Changes in the Sales Recognition Policy — 184

- Manipulating Profits with One-Time Events — 186
- Fudging Operating Income and Losses — 191
- Subsidiaries, JVs and Affiliates: An Option to Hide Problems — 194
- Hiding Problems by Understating Costs — 197
- Playing with Inventory to Generate Profits — 208
- *Cookie Jar* Reserves and Illusory Profits — 210
- Who Knows the Future: Writing off Future Costs in Current Year — 216
- Deceitful Accounting of Derivatives — 217
- Bluffing through Off-Balance Sheet Financing — 219
- Creation of Non-existent Cash-in-Bank — 227
- Boosting Operating Cash Flow to Give a Rosy Picture — 232
- Manipulating Reporting on Business Segment to Camouflage Poor Performance — 233
- Who Wants to Pay Tax? Manipulate to Avoid — 234
- Manipulation of Accounts Prior to M&A — 235
- Shoddy Accounting — 239
- Lax Internal Controls — 241
- Accounting Red Flags: All Is Not Well — 243
- Non-Accounting Red Flags: Poor Corporate Governance — 247

Chapter 7: Checkers Could Be Cheaters — 251
- KPMG — 254
- E&Y — 256
- Deloitte & Touche — 257
- PwC — 260
- 'Selfie': How Can Corporates Detect Fraud? — 263

Chapter 8: Do Pharma Companies Care? Do Medicines Heal? Are Doctors Concerned? — 265
- I Scratch Your Back, You Scratch Mine: Doctors, Drug Makers, et al. — 266
- Fraudulent Marketing of Drugs — 270
- Marketing Trial on Humans Going Wrong — 276
- Tampering with Drug Test Trial Data — 276
- Drug Trial Without Long-Term Patient Trial — 279
- Lack of Humane Treatment of Humans in Testing Drugs — 281
- Bad Advertisements for Drugs — 282

xii | WHO CHEATS AND HOW?

- Wrong Pricing of Drugs   282
- Investors Can Sue   283
- Are Irresponsible Executives Not Responsible?   284

Chapter 9: 'The Last Word' on Fraud Yet to Be Revealed   **285**

Index   292

Acknowledgements

It is difficult to jot down the names of all those numerous individuals and corporations who helped me weave my thoughts on ethics, understand the black and white of business management and sift through shades of grey to detect the curvatures of crooked behaviour in seemingly straight business dealings.

On a lighter vein, this book owes its origin to those who cut many-a-corner to do business, jump rules to make that extra buck and play truant to fool others. This book would not have seen the light of the day if the business world only comprised sages and saints! However, since time immemorial, cheats and charlatans have prowled the earth and will continue to subsist as long as man exists.

Seriously speaking, I owe much to Hindustan Unilever, where I spent the first two decades of my work life and got to know how business can be run with scruples. It has been an amazing experience of running an organisation of mammoth proportions with integrity and honesty.

Information available in public domain on the darker sides of corporate life is sketchy. Much of my research is based on news items and articles appearing in various newspapers and magazines, especially *The New York Times*, *Financial Times*, *The Financial Express* and *The Economic Times*. I have also got valuable input from articles in *The Economist*, *The Wall Street Journal*, *Forbes*, *The Huffington Post*, *The Independent*, *CFO Innovation Asia*, *China Daily*, CNN.money, NDTV Profit, *Asia Africa Intelligence Wire*, *The Week*, *Business Standard* and *The Times of India*.

Fraud-related reports published by the big four—PwC, E&Y, Deloitte and KPMG—have been relied upon to take help of their research in the domain of human and corporate behavior on fraud and scams.

The Forbes Book of Business Quotations was handy in several instances.

My mentor, guide and uncle, Debu Bhattacharya, one of the most successful corporate executive in recent times, illustrated to me what rectitude, dedication, sincerity and hard work means. I have learned so much from him that it is almost impossible to summarise my indebtedness to him in this meagre space.

Ruben, my brother and senior editor at *Al Jazeera*, went through the first draft of this book. He chipped, chopped, changed and challenged almost everything I had written. Without his guidance and advice, this book would have just remained an incomplete manuscript.

'Thank you' seems an inadequate expression to convey my deepest gratitude to all who took so much trouble to go through my manuscript and give me invaluable feedback. I would like to thank Ashok Barat, Asok Chattopadhyay, Aashutosh Akshikar, Akshay Kumar, Abhishek Ghatak, Dr Asha Naik, Anupam Dasgupta, Debabrata Mukherjee, Gautam Sircar, Saibal De, Sanjay Kapoor, Sandeep Banerjee, Dr Subhasis Ray, Soumitra Panda, Sudipto Panda and Tapash Bhattacharya for their invaluable contributions.

From time to time, as I wrote the chapters of this book, I needed a sounding board. Ananya, my wife, kindly consented to go through bits and pieces of my writing, mostly at odd hours, and made extremly useful suggestions.

Dr Roshnai, our daughter and a medical professional, went through the chapters on medical fraud in detail. The portion would not have taken the shape it has without her input, correction and clarification of various medical nuances and terms in common man's language. I am grateful to Abhishek, our son, for being steadfast behind me in all my endeavours.

No book can come into existence without the active intervention of the editing team. Savitha Kumar and Saima Ghaffar played a very involved and active role in giving this book its shape and form. And my final words of gratitude. I owe this book to Sachin Sharma, the dynamic, young commissioning editor at SAGE Publications—my publisher. In the early days, when I had only written the chapter headings and a brief synopsis, he and the AVP of SAGE (Commissioning), R. Chandra Sekhar, placed their trust in me by sending me a contract immediately after I presented my idea for the book to them. I have heard of authors struggling over long periods, hunting for good publishers. I have been singularly lucky in not trudging that dreary path of disappointment. Not only did Sachin guide and encourage me from day one, he (along with his colleague Rudra Narayan Sharma) even named my book.

I know I have missed many names—*gurus*, guides, relatives, colleagues and friends who moulded, directed, advised and encouraged me in my quest to articulate my beliefs, knowledge and experience. I beg their forgiveness.

My obeisance to all of you!

Introduction

To cheat is an instinct that some find irresistible.

The legendary seven-time winner of the toughest cycling race on earth, Tour de France, and a cancer survivor, Lance Armstrong, practised deceit. He not only doped by removing his blood, storing it in the fridge and then transfusing it back into his body during races, but he also tricked his opponents by fitting a motor on his bike. Even Tiger Woods, Golf's most celebrated player, cheated while playing the 2013 Masters by surreptitiously shifting his golf ball.

The world's most popular athletics event is the men's 100-meter dash and only nine men have ever run it in less than 9.8 seconds, of which six have cheated and failed dope tests—starting with Ben Johnson at the Seoul 1988 Olympics final, followed by household names and world champions like Tyson Gay of the USA and Asafa Powell of Jamaica.

Simona Halep of Romania, the former world No. 1 tennis player and two-time Grand Slam champion, got caught in 2023 for taking banned drugs to stimulate her red blood cell production to enhance endurance. Similarly, the five-time tennis Grand Slam champion Maria Sharapova, one of the world's highest-paid female athletes, was suspended for two years in 2016 when she was found to have taken banned heart medication that helps to improve blood flow and allows athletes to recover faster.

These famous names in sports chose deception over dedication to achieve what they had set out for. While fame was what they sought, what they ended up embracing was infamy. Considered champions at the peak of their careers, they later turned out to be cheats.

DECEPTION DEMONSTRATION AND DELIGHT

So why did these acclaimed people cheat?

The lines between right and wrong have indeed become hazy. For many, dishonesty is a shortcut to success. While some tricksters are ambitious and want to win by hook or crook, many cheat because others are cheating.

Some cheat as no one presumably is watching. In 2014, the Russian Olympic Committee enhanced its medal haul by having doping experts collaborate with the country's intelligence services to switch out urine samples of its players through a hole in the testing laboratory's wall.

Conning also could be a matter of habit—Bernard Madoff, the perpetrator of the largest and most widespread Ponzi scheme in the world, enjoyed tricking the gullible and popularized the Ponzi way of making money. This involves structuring an investment scam that pays existing investors with funds collected from new investors.

Several cheat as they can do nothing else. Consider the sea pirates in Somalia. With nothing much else to do, they con others of their fortunes by seizing hostages and seeking ransom.

Some cheat for the thrill of it—the illegitimate office affair, the illicit kiss, the casual sex, et al. Consider Silvio Berlusconi, the media baron and ex-Prime Minister of Italy, who was found guilty of having paid sex with a minor girl and then abusing his office to cover it up. A habitual cheater, Berlusconi had also been convicted of tax fraud.

There are so many who swindle. Even judges cheat—60 experts taking the test for becoming official judges in the 2016 Olympics rhythmic gymnastics event cheated; Harvard University students cheat—100 students cheated in 2012, with another seventy found cheating the year before; teachers cheat—some allotted higher grades to students for upgrading their schools' league table positions; international committees cheat—the allocation of 2022 World Cup Football by FIFA to Qatar was marred by cheating allegations.

But not all cheat. All champions are not crooks, not all judges are corrupt, all teachers are not partial and not all financing schemes are pre-meditated. But a few are. The challenge is to sift the bad from the good, the egregious from the ethical.

CORPORATE CHEATING CULPABILITY

Let me now shift gears and move to another domain. Can a business firm cheat?

A corporation is an artificial legal entity—it can buy, sell, borrow, lend and produce. But can it deceive? Is it not the people from within who lie? If the employees of a company cheat, can the corporation's responsibility be far behind?

Be it by choice or compulsion, some of the corporate world has not been immune to cheating. Businesses are a microcosm of our society, comprised of people like you and me. It would display the same strengths and weaknesses that we all have. No wonder many in the corporate world have feet of clay.

When a corporation commits fraud, who should be held responsible? Is it the company management or the shareholders?

Several companies have repeatedly been penalized, taken to task and admonished for wrongdoing. But the top management, who masterminds the trickery, generally gets away rather lightly. Take the example of Jeffrey Skilling, the ex-CEO of Enron Corporation, who spearheaded one of the worst accounting frauds in history, destroying the company, but got away with a relatively lighter punishment. Initially jailed for 24 years, his term of imprisonment was reduced by 10 years, and he walked away free in 2019 after paying some penalties.

In order to examine whether the shareholders, the ultimate owners of a company, are at all responsible or not, it is necessary to raise the veil of corporate structure and take a peep.

Who owns a company? In theory, it is the shareholders. But in reality, the controlling shareholders, directors, and top management run a corporation. They decide on their own sweet will, how much dividend to declare, and how many stock option shares to be allotted to themselves.

The concept of stock options, created to encourage employees to enhance shareholder wealth, has been horribly misused in several instances. This led some management to take short-term measures, doctor books of accounts, and manipulate share prices to enhance their coffers.

Who should be held responsible for poor corporate governance when practised?

Not all the shareholders—the owners—may have little power to run a corporation, especially when the company has minority shareholders. It is the motley crew of controlling shareholders and the top management who conducts the corporate show. Are the shareholders not akin to the creditors, the contractors, or the suppliers? Not at all.

What say does a shareholder have in these decision-making processes? The majority or controlling shareholders (holding more than 50% of the shares) will have a say in the company's strategic intent and may sometimes even be involved in the day-to-day management. But when it comes to the minority shareholders, it is usually a fait accompli. This provides an immense opportunity for the corporate head honchos to play foul for self-aggrandizement at the cost of the often-powerless minority 'owners' of corporations. The form and structure of corporate management is, in a way, a fraud on the multitude of small and marginal shareholders!

Short-term myopic view of the management often results in long-term value erosion.

This whole issue of short-term versus long-term sometimes makes things go awry in the corporate world. Frauds and scams get committed to fulfil the ever-growing desire to win for the immediate instead of the longer-term reward. And the owners—especially the minority shareholders—have been able to do very little to stop the rot.

Let me cite a story. The largest corporate fraud in India has been committed by ABG Shipyard Ltd. Once among the largest players in the Indian shipbuilding industry, having made over 165 vessels in about 16 years, killed the company through their myopic views. The company borrowed from 28 banks and defaulted to repay about Rs 23,000 crore ($3.5 billion). The company kept lying and showed fudged contracts, drawing loans between 2005 and 2010 and only to money launder a large chunk between 2012 and 2017. This sort of episode cannot happen unless both the lenders and the borrower were hand-in gloves. Due to their short-term greed and corrupt practices, the duo killed a solid business venture. The company has since been declared bankrupt.

Should the whole of management be held responsible for any fraud?

Sometimes, deceptions are committed only by a few, keeping many from within in the dark. General Motors fraudulently sold cars with defective ignition keys for 10 years since 2004, resulting in 13 deaths and 54 crashes. Though some engineers knew about the defects, the top management remained blissfully ignorant. In a contrary scenario, the French bank BNP Paribas conducted the business of clearing billions of dollars illegally for over a decade since 2002 with Sudan, Iran and Cuba, countries subjected to the USA sanctions, with the full knowledge of the top management.

Do people who are seemingly doing well in the corporate world cheat?

Yes, many play the con game. Ramalinga Raju started Satyam Computers in India, dreaming of capturing the software market using Indian engineers' gift of computer-related skills. As he progressed distinctively well with his strategy, greed got the better of him. Mid-way, he cooked books and falsified bank statements. And then the rest is history, with Raju confessing that he ran one of the largest scams in the Indian history of over a billion dollars.

Numerous other instances exist when the well-heeled and famous play the con game.

One way is through 'insider trading,' dealing in shares with non-public confidential information obtained from known sources, usually an insider. Look at the lifestyle iconic figure Ms. Martha Stewart, a Forbes billionaire. She wished to just make an additional $51,000 (Rs 24 lakhs) on the sly through advance insider information on the developments in a friend's company. She played in the market by selling her shareholding in that company before others got to know the news she knew. She got jailed, fined, and barred from directorship for five years.

Rajat Gupta, the retired Chairman of McKinsey and the former director of Goldman Sachs, fared little better. He passed on boardroom secrets to his friend Raj Rajaratnam, a hedge-fund titan so that he could deal in shares with insider information. Gupta broke the trust that the corporate world reposes on its board members. The gross impropriety earned him a 2-year jail term.

Numerous corporates have cheated over time; many famous names have played foul with our trust; loads of super-rich have cut corners; and the rogue show keeps rolling with impunity.

DIPPING HUMAN MORALS

In view of the regularity in which fraud cases are hitting news headlines, has the morality of mankind gone down? Is it on a decline or was it always this way?

The issue of integrity becomes more profound when one sees the names of those involved in the sleaze; many are supposedly considered to be the very best in their class: McKinsey, FTX, Wirecard, Siemens, Microsoft, GE, Merck, Goldman Sachs, Barclays, HSBC, Walmart, IBM, AIG, Jet Airways and Larsen & Toubro.

The list of misdeeds by the big names is equally long: making false promises of medications launched, stealing customers' money routed through trading platforms, pocketing people's money raised for charity, showing non-existent cash balance on the balance sheet, bribing government officials for favours, and sucking out bank money through related party transactions. The unethical games played make for a bottomless pit.

Obnoxious behaviours—including cheating—are sometimes displayed by corporations, despite the high horses they often ride in preaching morality and value systems. Let me cite an example of Hewlett-Packard (HP), the global technology giant. The company spied on journalists, board members, and employees in 2005 under the order of the then Chairperson, Patricia Dunn. Sometime later, in 2010, Mark Hurd, the former CEO was sacked as he falsified expenses about a female consultant on contract, who incidentally filed a suit of sexual harassment against Hurd. These are instances of deception at the highest levels of the corporate echelon.

As so many corporate frauds take place, are corporate executives psychopaths?

A study reported in June 2021 by Fortune magazine states that 12% of corporate senior leadership displays a range of psychopathic traits. This is against 1% found among the general population. The psychopathic persona displays egocentricity, greediness, recklessness, lack of empathy, manipulativeness, and exploitativeness. It is but natural that psychopathy in senior management could lead to all kinds of problems, including the destruction of shareholder value.

Open a newspaper or watch a TV show containing global news any day, and chances are that you will find the news of some cheating or fraud occurring somewhere in the world. Be it a bribery and corruption scandal, Ponzi game, cybercrime, product safety violation, toxic dumping, banking scam, tax evasion, money laundering, or bid rigging—the world of skulduggery is ever active.

Behind these tales of duplicity and deception lies the interesting stories of scammers' true skills. Psychologically, they can sense the precise outlines of what others aspire for. Fraudulent acts are like magic mirrors for other people's real desires, showing things they cannot refuse.

Scammers can sense other people's insecurities and use them to make promises that others would believe. Think of the quick-rich Ponzi schemes where defrauders make other people trust that hefty returns can be made if money is deposited in some make-believe schemes. Many business executives play this game.

Ultimately, the public must pick up the bills to clean up the mess created by the so-called white-collared, super-intelligent, debonair corporate directors and managers.

Philanthropy is often used as a veil for fraud. Many rich people who cheat carry out big charity. Philanthropy often makes the rich look better and helps them to conceal their crimes—it is a scam. The friendly face of generosity may not be as saintly as it may seem. While half of the world lives on $7 a day, globally, over 2,50,000 philanthropic foundations own a combined wealth of $1.5 trillion, not necessarily spending on the causes that would uplift the downtrodden.

The infamous Sam Bankman Fried, the owner of the cryptocurrency marketplace FTX, was the face of philanthropy in the USA in 2019. While he had donated over $80 million, he ran away with

$8 billion of FTX customers' deposits. Bankman-Fried used altruism as a cover while conducting a fraudulent business [FTX went bankrupt in 2022].

Philanthropy can never be used as justification for dishonest business practices. Principles of morality are often getting compromised for the gain of a few – is the unfortunate truth.

BLAME GAME

Who should be blamed for the sorry state of business affairs with business executives scheming to scam?

Is the education system to be blamed? Is the business education a matter of farce and hype? Is it the decay of societal values? Or is it none of these, but a basic human trait to make money by hook or by crook?

Numerous studies have been undertaken at various points in time, under various geographical and social conditions, to determine why corporate leadership and their managers cheat. But the jury is still out, with no clear answer forthcoming yet. Understanding the human mind and what makes it take some time, the devious route defies any particular trend, pattern, or rationale.

But one aspect is time and again proven. It is greed among some, which often favours commercial transactions over general-good, and profit over business purposes. A report on Barclays Bank's business practices affirmed that top executives' focus on short-term return on equity led to a vacuum in culture and values, and its elevated pay policies reinforced that.

The other reasons for poor human behaviour to scam others include rationalizing fraudulent actions, opportunities available to cheat, ulterior mindset, and peer pressure for better performance. However, no one needs to be blamed for these traits except for the perpetrators themselves.

There are numerous ethical businesses, people and managers. But the existence of some bad eggs within a basket is making things baffling and complex. This makes society, and especially the business world, sometimes a bad place to live and work. It is the presence of self-interest over the common good, which is creating the lopsided experience of ethics.

The asymmetrical approach to morality may be due to the unequal distribution of global wealth in spite of the growth in the overall wealth of economies. A good moral stance and sound corporate governance are being sacrificed at the altar of personal gains. Unless the matter of fair distribution of wealth is addressed, and where there is yet no clear agreed method to do so, one is afraid that the world will continue to see the practice of unethical demeanour. The degree, value, quality, and type of unprincipled behaviours may vary from time to time and from region to region, but the end is not near yet.

Frauds and scams damage corporate reputation and dent a company's brand image. It is common knowledge that the Board and the senior management are usually hawk-eyed on profit fulfilment targets. With differing purposes and intent, strong ethics enforcement is not often on their 'things to do list.'

Whoever is to be blamed, the absence of ethics is a recipe for poor corporate governance. This leads to a dent in the corporations' hard-earned goodwill.

TECHNOLOGY TRICKS

Technological developments of the modern era have made fraudsters happier, making lives for you and me more challenging.

The recent trend of our growing dependence on networked technologies and the increased outsourcing of computer systems to cloud-based outfits have provided an exceptional opportunity for cybercriminals.

Cybercrime comes in two distinct forms. One is cyber-dependent crime, like hacking, and the other is cyber-assisted crime, which is merely traditional organized crime made through the use of computers.

The Internet has become a den for prospective swindlers. The use of email and online messaging services to dupe victims into sharing personal data, login credentials, and financial details is rather common. Stealing confidential, protected, or sensitive data is a risk we live with.

The use of malicious software (malware) to damage or disable users' devices or steal personal and sensitive data is often practised. Ransomware use has become rampant. It is a type of malware that prevents users from accessing critical data and then scamsters demand payment to restore access. Business email compromise is a sophisticated form of attack targeting e-payments and engineering techniques to make unauthorized payments. And the risks are almost endless.

The recently developed and fairly popular—digital currencies have created another haven for fraudsters. Enough evidence proves that cryptocurrencies now play an active role in organized crime. Drugs, guns, terrorism and girls are usually being transacted through these new means.

With time, the cheats have become savvier, and duping has become an art.

With the internet forming an integral part of our daily lives, cyberattacks are occurring with increased frequency and severity. To cite a recent instance, MGM, one of the biggest hotel-casino operators in the USA, suffered a massive blow in 2023 when its slot machines and digital hotel room keys stopped working. Online reservations and credit card systems failed.

Stealing credit card numbers and passwords has almost become a child's play for professional hackers. We keep hearing bouts of stolen credit card numbers, causing huge losses to bank customers. The bad news is that in 2022, India became the most targeted country by hackers. How can you even think your bank account and credit cards are safe from fraudsters?

Things have come to such a pass that even one of the world's biggest cyber security companies – FireEye – had its defences breached and its system hacked in late 2020. This adversely affected thousands of companies. Just imagine the horrible situation when the specialists on whom the business world is counting for protection are themselves vulnerable.

Not to have finished with their tricks, the hackers have now turned their attention to destabilizing the broader financial markets, including hacking into servers of stock exchanges like Nasdaq, the global electronic marketplace for securities trading.

Technology has moved into an extreme zone. Hackers and cyber-fraudsters can remotely stop a car while it is running, break into hi-tech homes, and even stop a heart implant from functioning. There is currently no system in the world that is 'un-hackable'. With the internet, Bluetooth and mobile smartphones in use everywhere, just imagine our vulnerability to crooks and cheaters!

Cyber fraudsters earn a gargantuan $1.5 trillion every year. Small businesses account for almost half of the cyber-attacks. Phishing (attackers tempting users to do wrong stuff) is one of the top assaults, accounting for almost one in six cases. Will these noxious practices end soon, with police and government actions? Improbable is the answer.

COMMODITY CONS

Unlike manufactured products like laptops, mobiles, soaps, and shampoos, commodities are usually subjected to wild price fluctuations. And these price swings in food, fuel, minerals, and metals lead to scams and swindles. Commodity trade generally involves traders who could have shady and opaque ownership structures, including tax haven location and shell company involvement.

The machinations of the scandal-plagued world of commodity trading are plentiful. In early 2023, it transpired that China's largest bank, ICBC, released export documents of $170 million to Maike, China's biggest copper trader, without first collecting payment owed to ING, the Dutch lender to Maike. It so happens that Maike declared a cash crisis shortly after this episode, sinking ING's hopes of recovering the money.

In September 2023, Aurubis, Europe's largest copper producer, was hit by a large-scale €185 million fraud. The suppliers of scrap material and the Aurubis's sampling division's employees are suspected of colluding, leading to missing precious metals such as gold, silver, and palladium.

The saga of stolen commodities is unending. In 2022, global trading groups, including Glencore, cut ties with a Chinese metals merchant after $500 million of copper went missing at a warehouse. In other commodity-related scandals, supposed bags of nickel at a London Metal Exchange warehouse were found to be full of rocks, while US trading company Gerald Group bought tin concentrate in Brazil that was found to be just sand.

Cheating in the commodity business primarily occurs from the structure of its business model. Credit is increasingly given on a corporate basis rather than individual transactions, and lenders inability to inspect traders' activities visibly. The problem is accentuated through lax governance on the part of the traders, including insufficient due diligence of the party on the other side of the transaction, inadequate audit inspections of shipments, and the inability to detect rogue employees.

There are more reasons for the commodity sector to be targeted by scamsters. As commodity prices fluctuate, and when prices are on the upswing, more banks chase the sector, leading to potential fraud. A vulnerable sector is scraps and their quality, especially in the recycling industry, where visual inspections still dominate over technology. Plus, the business often relies on paper-based systems that are susceptible to manipulation.

Impregnable commodities are often the soft target for hardened criminals!

FIND FRAUD FAULTS

How does one identify that frauds are occurring or could occur?

Several things can be done to identify deceits and duplicity within an organization.

It's the top management mindset that helps to prevent this scum of the modern society. Apart from creating a culture of integrity within an organization and a strong internal control system, fraud 'risk assessment' is the most important tool that any management should implement against economic fraud.

You may note, however, that not every organization has the adequate bench strength to carry out such an assessment nor the requisite skills. The help of outside specialists should be sought in such cases. Organizations that carry out fraud risk assessments can identify potential risks better.

With the changing times and enhanced technological prowess, fraudsters will continue to upgrade themselves to be in business, but organizations need to try and keep a few steps ahead. It is a growth business and recession-proof for scamsters; please remember. Things are unlikely to get better but may only get worse. Beware!

DEPICTING DUPLICITY

Is the world flat when it comes to ethical values across geographies?

Differing cultures, values, customs, and traditions drive and guide various nations. Giving occasional expensive gifts is gratitude and deference in Japan, but bribery in the USA and the UK. Cash is king in China with bag loads of currency brought to buy a car or a house, but it is an unheard-of practice in Germany or France. Mafia management is part of Italian business practice, but in Russia, one is better off if they are kept in abeyance. Mistresses yield immense power in China, rate cards are available in Thailand for bribing government officials to get things done within time, linkages with politicians will help business in India, and physical safety possesses great premium in Nigeria; the list is unending. International businessmen and executives are often exposed to the vagaries of inconsistent ways of doing cross-country business.

Hence, what is bribery in one geography could be normal corporate behaviour in another. All types of cheating cannot be considered conning activities in every part of the business world.

Deceit has taken gigantic proportions globally, with companies losing about 5% of revenues or $3.5 trillion annually due to frauds. Accounting frauds, which form about one-tenth of all frauds, have the highest median loss at $1 million.

While the Almighty is omnipresent, the fraudsters are all pervasive nowadays!

ARTIFICE AND AUDITORS

Whenever corporate fraud happens, the first question is: what were the auditors doing?

Contrary to popular belief, auditors are not responsible for fraud detection. They are not policemen or detectives. When accounts are audited, it implies a reflection of the 'true and fair' view of the financial transactions.

Just because a company's accounts are audited, it does not assure that no fraud or cheating is going on within the company or that their financial statements are fully trustworthy.

The auditors would sign off accounts after obtaining reasonable assurance that the financial statements are free of material misstatement, whether caused by error or fraud. While conducting audits, they would continually assess fraud risks. For instance, when performing analytical procedures, auditors would assess whether some unusual transactions or relationships may indicate fraud or probable risk.

Looking at another way, the auditor would report any fraud when he figures out that there is 'reason to believe' a fraud has been committed.

Historical evidence shows that external auditors have been able to detect only about 3% of the reported frauds.

While most auditors are trustworthy, not every auditor is squeaky clean. There are loads of instances where ineptness or collusion with auditees existed.

Flaky corporate governance continues to exist worldwide, whether the accounts are audited or not. It will always be a challenge to identify black sheep within a flock.

WHY THIS BOOK

Corporates have cheated in plenty over the years. Some have supplied you with below-par products not matching their original promise; a few have assured you great returns if you kept money with them, only to shatter your trust; many have run away with bank money borrowed, ultimately leading to the loss of your money kept with your bank; and the swindle stories are endless.

Names involved in corporate cons often make a who's who listing, sometimes leading to disbelief when recalcitrant labels are heard.

Frauds and scams in the business world come in various shapes, shades, and sizes, and unfortunately, there are no one-size-fits-all formulae to identify them.

It is good to be aware of the corporate world's behind-the-scenes machinations—which businesses structured them, how they practised, what their nuances are—and hopefully prevent their recurrence.

Knowledge of how numerous human minds have worked in the past to perpetuate some of the gravest economic crimes will help you to fight them better, or will it just spark the desire within yourself to make a fast buck? This book will go a long way to help you pull up your socks and be ready to take guard against the deceitful world's possible onslaught.

Corporate 'fraudtainment,' like any entertaining show, keeps the drama theatrical, however large or small, senseless or terrifying the themes could be. While the curtains may fall on some, some other compelling episodes will pop up elsewhere. The fraudtainment shows just go on.

The book you are holding will provide broad insights into the murky world of corporate deceit, deception and dishonesty!

Awareness helps avoidance, and prevention is better than cure.

Fraud and Scams: Mode and Style

Cheaters are on the prowl! 'Fraud on the rise' claims the 2013–14 Global Fraud Survey of the Economist Intelligence Unit (EIU). And the worst is overall 70% of companies reported to have suffered from at least one type of fraud in 2013. This is a horrendous development.

Who commits fraud? What are the key trends in fraud and scams? Why is fraud committed? What motivates people to commit fraud? Which geographies are more vulnerable to it? Are men more prone to commit fraud than women? Are poor people more susceptible to it? The questions go on and on. One wishes there were clear answers to these and also that a clear trend had emerged. Unfortunately, this subject is rather abstruse and contentious, where it is difficult to derive consensual answers.

WHO IS A TYPICAL FRAUDSTER?

Is it possible to paint a picture of a typical fraudster? Would it not be wonderful to be able to determine potentially greedy and deceitful people?

According to a KPMG study conducted in 2011, a typical fraudster is usually a male between 36 and 45 years old who commits fraud against his employer, works in a finance-related role, holds a senior management position, has been employed by the company for more than 10 years and works in collusion with another perpetrator. Many fraudsters work within their organisations for several years without committing fraud before an influencing factor makes them succumb to temptation.

IS THERE A RATIONALE FOR FRAUD?

It is usually the desire for personal gain that is the greatest motivator for fraud. The possibility of fraud being committed increases during economic downturns or difficult times. Setting of stiff targets, attempts to conceal poor business performance and safeguard bonuses are some strong motivations for people to commit fraud, especially in accounting, as observed during KPMG's survey.

Companies that are victims of misreporting and falsification of accounts by members of their staff must examine whether the targets they have set are reasonable because if they are not, this will encourage camouflaging of accounting information—to the ultimate detriment of the enterprise. Concern over disgruntled employees committing fraud is also on the rise.

What is really disturbing is that there seems to be general acceptance of unethical business practices a fait accompli.

WHAT FRAUD IS COMMON?

Asset misappropriation—theft—belongs to the top slot in all types of fraud.

The ACFE 2012 Global Fraud Survey puts theft being at 87% of all the fraudulent incidents reported. Corruption and financial statement fraud follow in the second and third positions. The EIU study in 2013–14 confirms that misappropriation of assets takes the top spot and accounts for 69% of the most commonly reported types of economic fraud. Procurement fraud (at 29%) comes next, followed closely by bribery and corruption, cybercrime and accounting fraud.

It is clear that misappropriation of assets is fairly easy, since it provides immediate gratification by stolen assets being sold. The other primary areas of risks include corruption and bribery, and doctored financial accounts. Cybercrime has been posing a serious challenge of late.

MIND THE GAP

One of the significant findings of KPMG's survey includes the large 'internal control' gaps (up from around 50% in 1997 to around 75% in the firm's 2011 survey) that are being increasingly exploited by fraudsters. Cost-cutting exercises, leading to fewer resources monitoring controls in organisations, are perhaps encouraging fraudsters to be more active than earlier.

According to a Deloitte's survey in 2010, there are some interesting and very apparent contradictions between the perception of senior management and the practical realities of how fraud is controlled. For instance, during 2009 and 2010, there was a significant increase in board-level discussions on introduction or improvement of fraud monitoring in companies, but there has been no actual improvement in their monitoring activity, which emphasises the fact that organisational fraud is not yet a risk that is adequately understood or covered by enterprises.

What is more disconcerting is that most respondents feel they do not have adequate staff to identify financial fraud risk areas, and furthermore, that their employees' skills are inadequate in context of their knowledge and expertise.

ARE FRAUD AND CORRUPTION THE SAME?

Fraud and corruption are words that are often used interchangeably. However, these two are different although similar in some aspects.

Fraud uses deceit or misrepresentation to obtain an unfair advantage. Examples of fraud include falsification of account holders' signature to withdraw money from their bank accounts or submission of false invoices to obtain payments.

Corruption, on the other hand, is the illegal use of an official position to secure an advantage through breach of trust. Examples of corruption include government officials unduly favouring particular people or organisations on receipt of unlawful payment in cash or kind.

The bad news, however, is that the geographical spread of fraud and corruption goes hand in hand, as indicated by EIU's Global Fraud Survey.

GETTING TO KNOW ABOUT FRAUD

How does one get to know of existence or likelihood of fraud?

KPMG's study revealed that 15% of companies' knowledge of fraud is derived from anonymous tip-offs (and a similar number from accidental discoveries) and 10% from whistle-blowers. They seem to increasingly depend on employees or third parties to report wrongdoing, accidental discovery or in a few cases confessions to identify potential fraud.

Therefore, providing individuals a means to report suspicious activities is crucial for the success of organisations' anti-fraud programmes. The 2012 ACFE Survey reports that since its initiation in 2002 till date, the most common method of initial detection of fraud is from 'tips' and 40% of fraud was reported in 2012 through tip-offs.

WHISTLE-BLOWING

Employees of organisations seem reluctant to report their colleagues or complain about outsiders' irregular activities. This leads to known instances of fraud remaining unreported. Many employees feel that it is not their job to provide tip-offs to their companies, while others fear job loss-related repercussions, especially where fraud involves a boss or a senior colleague.

Globally, there is a concerted focus on promoting and encouraging whistle-blowing in organisations through a system that can retain the anonymity of whistle-blowers, ensure fair treatment of their complaints, implement a reward mechanism and make the whistle-blowing process secure.

In India, the new Companies Act, 2013 makes it mandatory for enterprises to establish vigil mechanisms for their employees to report their genuine concerns. In the US, the Dodd-Frank Act of 2010 requires organisations to reward whistle-blowers by paying them between 10% and 30% of the fines levied for financial misconduct. In the UK, the Public Interest Disclosure Act of 1998 protects employees who 'blow the whistle'.

However, while whistle-blower systems are useful, they cannot be the primary or secondary detection tools in organisations, which should have in place internal organisational processes that identify and monitor key risk areas and address related issues at the outset.

CAN THERE BE RED FLAGS?

Red flags are warning signals, which alert companies of risk in their operations. These could be events or a set of circumstances. An organisation should be vigilant and attentive to red flags by immediately scrutinising issues, reacting to them and following up by taking appropriate action. By responding to red flags, fraud can be detected faster (and perhaps prevented) and quick action taken.

Unfortunately, globally organisations seem to be ignoring red flags. They fail to read the warning signs. Ignored red flags give license to perpetrators to continue their wrongdoing. It is also a missed opportunity to prevent fraud from taking place.

KPMG's Fraud Survey reported some good news—that in 56% of fraud cases, a red flag precedes their occurrence. However, the bad news is that only 6% of the red flags were acted upon.

CAN YOU IDENTIFY A FRAUDSTER?

According to the ACFE Survey report, one can. When employees are found to be living beyond their means or are involved in excessive control-related issues, this requires a red flag to be raised. The report stresses that most fraudsters have behavioural traits that can serve as warning signs.

SUSCEPTIBLE AND RISKY REGIONS

Economic crime is all pervasive and is geographically agnostic. The EIU 2013–14 Fraud Survey reveals that the highest rate of economic crime occurs in Africa, with 50% respondents of the survey reporting it. Not to be outdone, North America (at 41%), Western Europe and Latin America (at 35%). Surprisingly, the Asia Pacific reported a low 32% economic crime rate, perhaps due to the region's inherent propensity to not report such crimes.

Economic crime is a global threat. According to Ernst & Young's 12th Global Fraud Survey, such issues are more challenging in 'rapid-growth markets'. The survey revealed that in Brazil, 84% of the respondents reported that corruption was widespread; in the Far-East, 15% of respondents think that financial performance misstatements are justifiable acts; in Indonesia, 60% consider making cash payments to win new business is an acceptable practice and in Vietnam, 36% consider it acceptable to misstate a company's financial performance. This indicates that as companies expand their businesses in rapid-growth markets, they are confronted by a wide range of risks that need to be proactively managed—unfortunately, a significant 20% of organisations do not want to recognise the fact that 'new markets' bring new risks.

Non-acknowledgement of risk means lack of preventive steps. This encourages perpetrators of economic crime to look for more such opportunities.

GOVERNMENTS AND REGULATORS

Bribery, corruption and fraud are widespread. Some regulators have recognised this fact. During recent times, enforcement actions implemented under the US Foreign Corrupt Practices Act (FCPA) are active in rapid-growth markets. A total 31 of the 36 reported FCPA cases in 2011 related to illegal activities in Asia, Eastern Europe and Latin America. Many of these prosecutions were for payments made to employees or officials at state-run organisations.

Many countries are strengthening their enforcement regimes. For example, in the UK, the introduction of the Bribery Act, and in India, a range of proposed anti-bribery and anti-corruption legislation is in the offing.

With intensifying regulatory activity leading to the possibility of external investigation and enquiries, the senior management of companies should not be caught wanting in their preparedness should their companies be under scrutiny.

ARE THIRD PARTIES RISKY?

When entering new markets, the need for local contacts and procedural knowledge leads many companies to take the help of third-party agents or business partners. Such relationships can expose them to significant anti-bribery- and anti-corruption-related risks.

More than 90% of reported FCPA cases involve third-party intermediaries. Yet, despite the significant risks and specified demands of regulators, the corporate response to mitigate third-party risks is still inadequate. Many companies are failing to implement even the most basic controls to manage their third-party relationships.

According to Ernst & Young's survey, around 40% of companies do not even have simple mechanisms to put in place supplier databases—a worrying sign, since these are easy to install and help ensure that only bona fide third parties provide organisations with services. Companies' apparent lack of knowledge about the third parties they deal with is a serious risk for them.

PENALTIES NOT GOOD ENOUGH

Despite the risks they are exposed to, companies are not doing enough to prevent bribery and corruption in their operations. Mixed messages are emanating from their managements, with the overall tone often being diluted by their failure to penalise wrongdoing in their organisations.

According to a PriceWaterhouse Coopers study in 2011, more than half of global respondents would not agree to report illegal activities in their businesses to law enforcement agencies to enable the latter to take appropriate action against perpetrators of fraud. This is obviously not an encouraging development.

CORPORATE BOARDS NOT YET READY

Ernst & Young's survey indicates that not all boards of companies fully comprehend the way operations are conducted in their organisations.

According to the survey, more than half of the interviewees felt that their boards need to have more insight in their business operations to put in place effective safeguards against fraud or corrupt practices in their companies. In particular, respondents in rapid-growth markets felt that their boards' understanding of such issues need to be significantly enhanced. This is a worrying factor, since these growth markets face the highest fraud-, bribery- and corruption-related risks.

WHAT IS THE SIZE?

KPMG's 2011 study of loss due to fraud by geographies saw the Asia Pacific losing $1.5 million and the Americas, Europe, the Middle East and Africa around $1 million, on an average.

PriceWaterhouse Coopers's Global Economic Crime Survey in 2014 revealed that 18% of the respondents had lost between $1 million and $100 million due to fraud and corruption in their organisation and that around half of the respondents faced losses of less than $100,000.

The ACFE Survey in 2012 discovered that the median loss caused by fraud was $140,000, with average theft size being $120,000 and corruption size $250,000. However, the size of the median loss due to accounting fraud was high at $1 million, although only 8% of fraud arose from this cause. This clearly indicates that the average fraud size is fearfully high.

UNCOVERING FRAUD

According to KPMG's survey, it is taking organisations longer to detect fraud, compared to an average of around three years from inception to detection in 2007 and three-and-a-half years in the analysis the firm conducted in 2011.

It is interesting that detection of fraud in businesses takes an average of five years in Asia and around one-fifth remain undetected for 10 years or more, unlike in North America or Western Europe, where only about 3% of fraud goes undetected for over 10 years.

UNWILLING TO SHARE

Once fraud is detected in their operations, companies are generally not forthcoming in letting others know about this. They desist from making available details of fraud publicly unless required by law or if their losses need to be reported in their financial statements.

Worse is, according to KPMG's survey, almost three-fourth of investigations do not reach the public domain.

TAILPIECE

Fraudsters are usually good actors. It is possible to be fooled by their good looks, suave behaviour and impeccable conduct. The world would have been a safer place to live in if their minds could be read. As authors William R. Evans and Andrew Frothingham humorously said about a fraudster, 'No one has ever questioned his integrity—in fact, no one has ever mentioned it', and then went on to say 'You can tell he's lying: his lips are moving'.

1
Corporate Charlatans

Huge bribes are supposed to have been paid by the Italian defence group **Finmeccanica's** helicopter division, **AgustaWestland**, to middlemen to route illegal payments through Tunisia and Mauritius to two India-based companies in order to clinch helicopter supply contracts from the Indian Army. Arrests were made in Italy and in India in March 2013, and investigations are ongoing.

BAE Systems, the British weapon-maker, paid billions of dollars to Saudi Arabian officials for over 20 years to win contracts for supply of fighter planes and other military hardware in Saudi Arabia. Payments were made through a network of 'marketing advisors', who would set up offshore shell companies to hide the identities of officials to whom money was paid. This was a massive corruption racket that BAE ultimately owned up to in February 2010, and paid penalties of $450 million in the USA and the UK.

Cheats in the business world come in various shapes, forms and sizes. For instance, British businessman sold $78 million worth of fake bomb detectors for $40,000 each, without any working electronics components inside these, giving a false sense of security for their extensive use at Iraqi checkpoints. The man was convicted on fraud charges in April 2013. An illegal organ-trafficking network operating in Pristina, the capital of Kosovo, which involved doctors of a clinic called **Medicus**, lured poor people from Turkey, Russia and Moldova to sell their kidneys with a false promise that they would be paid $26,000 for this. The organs were then used for transplantation in wealthy clients from Israel, USA, Canada and Germany for $130,000 for each transplantation.

Five people were convicted on organ trafficking charges in Kosovo in April 2013.

However, detecting corrupt practices in corporate organisations is often difficult. For example, in April 2013, the German steel giant **Thyssen Krupp** announced a two-month amnesty for all its employees who would come forward with information on wrongdoing in the company. Such are the difficulties in unearthing corporate fraud and corruption that Thyssen had to eat humble pie in requesting its employees to identify rumoured widespread wrongdoing. Heinrich Hiesinger, the CEO, admitted that 'a great deal has gone wrong' in the company.

Global deceit and deceptions have become complicated and widespread. For example, an alliance of 22 law firms across the globe was formed in 2013 to protect the interests of individual and organisations that had been harmed by fraudsters. Headquartered in New York and operated from Madrid, this consists of law firms from the USA, the UK, Colombia, Israel, Italy, Turkey and India, among others. Its goal is to speed up coordination on between international litigation and reduce conflicts by punishing perpetrators of global fraud in cases where proactive action is hampered by national and local legislations.

Corporate frauds are often dependent on the corruption barometer and practices in particular geographies. Corruption seems to be a matter of societal ethos. For instance, while giving a 5% tip in a restaurant is considered adequate in Bangladesh, anything less than 10% of the bill in France or Germany is frowned upon, but in the USA, tipping less than 15% is hara-kiri! Tipping habits reflect how different countries vary in their habits, customs and rituals. It is not certain that an accepted practice in the USA will be honoured in China. What is considered a major fraud in the UK may be thought to be a trifling event in Nigeria, and what is considered acceptable payment in Thailand may be deemed to be bribery in Germany. Laws and regulations pertaining to corporate governance and ethics are not applicable universally. What may seem like corruption in one culture could tantamount to be a family allegiance in another.

Corruption, bribery and illegal gratification have been in existence from time immemorial. These are talked about, discussed, abhorred, loathed, but widely practised. In a corrupt society, one is as good as one's last bribe. Although such illegal activities are looked down upon in every society and preached against, and laws are formulated by the government to make it illegal, corruption continues to survive in some form or the other around the world.

The corporate world is not immune to economic crime. However, needless to say, corrupt practices are not prevalent in every corporation. Sound corporate governance and ethical practices are followed by many organisations, but it is the few bad apples in a basket that spoil the rest.

Instances of corporate fraud are many. To include them all is an impossible task. Only a few are highlighted in this chapter to provide a flavor of the recipes of fraud being served by enterprises across the globe to unsuspecting millions.

THE GREEDY CORPORATES

British Petroleum (BP), one of the largest companies in the world and an oil major, was held responsible for the oil blowout and spilling of millions of gallons of oil from the Deepwater Horizon drilling rig in the Gulf of Mexico in 2010, causing the deaths of 11 workers and fouling hundreds of miles of shoreline. The explosion was due to failure to interpret the results of pressure tests on the well, which gave a warning of possible explosions. Ultimately, in early 2013, the company pleaded guilty to 14 criminal charges and paid $4.5 billion as fine for its misdemeanour. It cost the company an additional $14 billion to clean up the coastline and $17 billion to make individual and business liability settlements. Apart from this, BP may still suffer a possible liability of up to $21 billion as civil penalty if it is found guilty of gross negligence under the Clean Water Act. Most importantly, this was not the first such incident involving BP, which has a history of oil spills and safety lapses. Its greed in extracting oil by circumventing basic safety precautions and its gross negligence and wilful misconduct is condemnable.

'We believe in taking responsibility for people' and '**IKEA** products must be produced under acceptable working conditions' are the *social responsibility* taglines of the Swedish cultural ambassador IKEA, the maker of inexpensive *Do-it-Yourself* (*DIY*) furniture. Yet it went against its core social values by flouting this rule for years. The company knowingly engaged political prisoners as forced labour to manufacture some of its products in former East Germany in the 1980s. In November 2012, the company finally admitted that it used bonded labour to keep its manufacturing costs low.

Corporate fraud perpetrated due to greed are of different kinds. **Tenet Healthcare Corporation**, abused patients' trust by conducting unnecessary heart procedures between 1997 and 2002 at its hospital, the Redding Medical Centre, in North California. Doctors conducted needless cardiac bypass surgery on hundreds of patients to increase the hospital's billings. When brought to book, Tenet agreed to pay $54 million as fraud settlement.

Let us take another example of corporate misconduct arising from the desire to save costs. **Trafigura**, a Netherlands-based company and one of the world's largest oil traders, dumped highly toxic petrochemical waste in the Ivory Coast in August 2006. A government report castigated the company for negligence and mismanagement. Sixteen people died and thousands fell ill when a tanker chartered by Trafigura dumped waste across the capital of the Ivory Coast, Abidjan. This waste was originally supposed to have been disposed of and treated in Amsterdam, but to save costs, the cargo was diverted to the Ivory Coast where it was irresponsibly dumped as landfill near poor neighbourhoods. In 2009, the company made an attempt to hush up the news by preventing *The Guardian* from reporting this dumping of toxic waste, but it failed in its attempt. In July 2010, a Dutch court imposed a fine of €1 million ($1.25 million) on the company for illegally exporting toxic sludge. It paid $200 million to the Government of the Ivory Coast to clean up polluted areas and $50 million to 30,000 victims and their families.

Tailpiece

It has been observed that when times are tough, corporate misdemeanours grow. It it is easier to hide such wrongdoing when financial conditions are favourable.

It is a fact of life that business enterprises exist to make profits. This sometimes overshadows good corporate behaviour and governance.

CONTRACT RIGGING, BRIBERY AND KICKBACKS: A WAY OF LIFE

Many banks, including **Barclays**, **UBS**, the **Royal Bank of Scotland** and **Rabobank**, rigged the London Interbank Offered Rate (Libor) interest rates set every day in 2007 and 2008. In 2004 and 2006, **Tyson Foods** in Mexico paid bribes as 'no-show jobs to wives' of food inspectors for their chicken product plants to allow exports with lax inspection. **Ralph Lauren**, the famous clothing retailer paid bribes, including perfumes, dresses and handbags, to government officials between 2006 and 2009 to avoid customs inspection of imports into Argentina. The CEO of **Société Générale** in Russia was arrested for taking kickbacks for sanctioning loans and fixing reduced interest rates in 2013. Doctors have been paid kickbacks by **Novartis**, **Amgen**, **Pfizer**, **Johnson & Johnson** and other pharmaceutical giants over the years for prescribing their medicines. And the saga continues. *Ipaidbribe.com*, a website in Pakistan, India and other countries features thousands of reports on petty bribes, highlighting this social menace. One wonders when these will end, if at all!

Corporate corruption is a malaise affecting big and small, the famous and the faceless. In spite of efforts to rein it in, its tentacles are pervasive and omnipresent. Some of the names in this gory game of corporate fraud include the esteemed and the respected.

Daimler

Even makers of the finest cars in the world could not escape this stigma. Mercedes Benz, the car manufacturer, bribed Russian officials, among others, to secure deals to sell cars for the country's police fleet and official motorcades. Daimler purportedly paid a bribe of $56 million in 200 transactions in 22 countries between 1998 and 2008. These payments included luxury holidays in Europe, armoured Mercedes vehicles for high-ranking government officials and birthday gifts to a senior Turkmenistan official (including 10,000 copies of the official's personal manifesto translated into German). These helped Daimler earn revenue of $1.9 billion and an illegal profit of $91 million.

> In March 2010, Daimler agreed to pay $185 million as fine to settle charges levied by the Justice Department and the US market watchdog, Securities & Exchange Commission (SEC). The company was also subject to a two-year deferred prosecution agreement and oversight by an independent monitor. Daimler's German and Russian units pleaded guilty to violation of US bribery laws.

Siemens

Siemens' executives were charged under the US FCPA, which prohibits American corporations from bribing overseas clients to promote their business, for paying $100 million to Argentine officials, including the country's former President, Carlos Menem, to secure a $1 billion contract. This is a classic case where multi-geographical connections featured in a bribery scandal. It was perpetrated in Argentina by a German company, and was committed by people who were not Americans and were living in Argentina, Germany and Switzerland. The reason why this case was taken up by the US FCPA is because the German company's shares were traded on US stock exchanges.

> Siemens settled the corruption charges by paying $800 million as fine to the USA and another $800 million to German authorities in 2008. However, the criminal case against eight of its former executives, all of whom live outside the USA, continues.

Walmart

'Wal-mart de Mexico was an aggressive and creative corruptor, offering large pay-offs to get what the law otherwise prohibited', *The New York Times* reported in December 2012. The newspaper revealed that Walmart paid bribes to obtain permits and set up its stores near Mexico's most famous landmark, the pyramids of Teotihuacan. There were apparently cover-up attempts made by the retailer to hide its corrupt practices.

> The US Justice Department and SEC, in cooperation with Walmart, are investigating possible violations of the US anti-bribery Law in Mexico, China, India, Brazil and some other countries.

Microsoft

The software giant is being investigated against allegations of bribery by its subsidiary companies in China, Italy and Romania. The company's practices are being looked into for potential violations of the FCPA. Claims that Microsoft had paid bribes in China were made by an unidentified whistle-blower who worked with the company in China and was apparently asked by his superior to pay bribes to government officials to promote its business.

> The US Justice Department and the SEC initiated preliminary investigations into bribery-related accusations against Microsoft in March 2013.

Coalgate Scandal

India is one of the few countries in the world that is endowed with ample quantities of 'black diamond', coal. Unfortunately, most of it is still under the ground. With the country's mounting energy needs, the Government of India decided to open up its power sector. However, it did not put in place a competitive bidding process. This resulted in rush of applicants for captive coalfields.

A murky coalfield allocation process was in practice between 2006 and 2009. The government appointed a screening committee to select entities to which the valuable assets should be allocated. It is contended that the decisions of the committee were subjective and often favoured applicants with close ties with political high-ups. The Comptroller and Auditor General of India (CAG) reviewed the process and castigated the government in August 2012. His report stated that the government's process of allocation was opaque, enabling the access of well-heeled and well-connected businessmen and politicians to undeveloped coalfields. It gave birth to the INR 1,860 billion ($31 billion) mining scandal, known as the Coalgate Scandal.

India's central investigating agency, the Central Bureau of Investigation (CBI), is probing the allocation of 64 coal blocks to 146 companies. The investigation probes into whether some companies that were awarded coalfield allocations falsified their information and documents to qualify for allocations for which they would not have otherwise been eligible. The companies being investigated include **TISCO, JSW Steels Ltd., Bhushan Steel Ltd., Hindustan Zinc Ltd., Ultratech Ltd., Tata Sponge Iron Ltd., Essar Power Ltd., Hindalco Industries, DB Power Ltd., Adani Power Ltd., GMR Energy, Arcelor Mittal India Ltd., GVK Power Ltd.** and **Lanco Group Ltd.**

> The CBI submitted its first report to the Supreme Court of India in March 2013, alleging that allocation of coal blocks was done without verifying the credentials of companies, which allegedly misrepresented facts about themselves. CBI is examinig the wrongdoings of several corporates. India's top court in September 2014 scrapped all but four of 218 coal blocks allocated by the government over the past two decades. Meanwhile, the Ministry of Coal is pursuing auction of deallocated captive coal blocks.

2G Telecom Scam

Businessmen with connections at the highest levels of the political corridor, ready funds to invest in licences, and changing and bending of rules at the last moment to suit the rich and the famous are some of the ingredients of one of the worst scandals in India.

The issue in question was the sale of second-generation or 2G airwaves by the Indian Government to cell phone operators in 2008. India is the world's second-largest market for cell phones with over 900 million subscribers, and it is growing rapidly.

On the day of allocation of spectrum, the Department of Telecommunications (DoT) changed the rules suddenly by making allocations based on a 'first come, first serve basis' at a predetermined price. Whoever reached the counter first with a fee of INR 17.5 billion ($290 million) secured the much sought after spectrum licence! 'This is bizarre', thundered the CAG, calculating a potential loss to the government exchequer of INR 1860 billion ($31 billion), compared to an auction process. The question is, were any of the companies tipped off earlier about the change in the rules? Andimuthu Raja, Minister of Telecommunications at that time, was jailed on charges of corruption.

The Supreme Court of India—the highest judiciary body in the country—was livid when it heard about the wrongdoing during the allocation process. In February 2012, it cancelled 122 telecom 2G spectrum licences on the grounds that the licences were allocated in an arbitrary and unconstitutional manner below the market price. The cancelled licences included foreign-held Indian joint ventures (JVs) with the **Telenor Group** of Norway and **Etisalat** of the UAE. The Supreme Court ordered new auctions to be held to allocate the wireless spectrum. Companies such as Bharti Telecom gained, as they had not been allocated licences during the allocation process in 2008.

The companies whose licences were cancelled feature among the Who's Who of the Indian corporate world. They include **Unitech Wireless Ltd (Uninor)**, **Loop Telecom**, **Sistema Shyam**, **Tata Telecom**, **Etisalat DB**, **S Tel**, **Videocon**, **Idea** and **Spice**.

The Indian investigating agency is examining possible wrongdoings by several individuals and corporates, and the matter is being argued in the CBI court.

Delhi Airport Scam

Those who come to India and those who live in the country can hardly avoid New Delhi, India's capital, or Mumbai, its commercial capital. Given enhanced business opportunities in India, it was necessary for the Indian government to have a modern airport in Delhi. It decided to get the old airport modernised through a public–private initiative in 2008. This led to setting up of Delhi International Airport Limited (DIAL). The **GMR Group**, a private sector company, which was to manage the airport, had a 54% shareholding in DIAL. The problem began therein. DIAL, for the primary benefit of GMR, decided to levy a development fee on all passengers using the airport. This was contrary to bidding conditions. Other bidders did not know that an extra revenue stream could be earned from the development fee. The revenue stream was estimated at INR 34.15 billion ($550 million).

The CAG complained that the government, had violated the provisions of the airport development agreement for the benefit of the concessionaire on several occasions. It is clear that there may have been a nexus between GMR and politicians, which enabled the former to secure favourable terms. The auditor pointed its fingers to this in its report in August 2012 and asked the government to locate the culprit.

Reliance Power

India is a power-deficit country. In order to boost its production of energy, the government has been encouraging setting up of various types of power projects, including thermal power ones. Utilisation of coal from allocated coal mines is controlled by the

Government to ensure optimal use of a scarce commodity. The CAG of India alleged in September 2011 that the power ministry had given 'undue benefits' to **Reliance Power Limited** in the Ultra Mega Power Projects, which have a capacity of more than 4,000 MW. This amounted to INR 1,200 billion ($20 billion) over the lifetime of the two projects at Sasan in Madhya Pradesh and Tilaiya in Jharkhand, calculated for 25 years.

What is the scam all about? The auditors complained that Reliance had been able to influence the government to change its coal-licensing norms to allow diversion of surplus coal from captive mines to its 'other' power projects. These concessions by the government were made in August 2008 well after its execution of contracts with Reliance in 2006 and 2007. This vitiated the bidding process for power projects, since the concessions were not known to the other bidders.

How was the benefit calculated? The difference was taken between the market price fixed by state-run Coal India Ltd. and the proportionate extraction cost of extra coal from captive mines. Furthermore, Reliance was able to use coal in projects with higher power tariffs. For instance, in Sasan, the rate is INR 1.19 ($0.20) per unit, but in the Chitrangi project, where Sasan's extra coal was allowed to be diverted, the tariff is INR 2.45 ($0.41) per unit.

There are several other examples of corruption and bribery in the corporate world, which include big and illustrious names such as **Rolls Royce**. The world's largest manufacturer of aircraft engines, which helps in flying the Airbus A380s, has been under investigation by the Serious Fraud Office of the UK regarding concerns about the company in certain Asian countries such as Indonesia and China in the 1980s and 1990s.

China's sixth-largest commercial bank, the **Postal Savings Bank of China**, has been facing corruption charges. Its CEO, Tao Liming, was under arrest for several months at the end of 2012. According to local Chinese newspapers, charges against Liming included issuance of illegal loans, taking of bribes and illegal fund-raising.

Oracle India sold software licences to the Indian government through local distributors between 2005 and 2007. Secret payments were made (not known to whom) by the distributors by their retaining a part of the sales proceeds for such illegal payments. Oracle agreed to settle the matter by paying $2 million.

Tailpiece

The anti-graft movement is making steady progress around the world. Global institutional investors from 50 countries have formed the International Corporate Governance Network, founded in March 1995 in Washington, DC, with $18 trillion under its management. Its aim is to scrutinise companies and vet their anti-corruption practices and principles.

'It's clear that corruption is a major threat facing humanity.... Corruption amounts to dirty tax, and the poor and most vulnerable are its primary victims', summarised Transparency International while issuing its world ranking on corruption in the public sector in 2013.

THEFT: ROUTE TO INSTANT GRATIFICATION

Theft takes place in all shapes and sizes. It is the quickest form of self-aggrandizement.

Siphoning off of shareholders' money is a form of theft. **Zenith Technologies**, the promoter of the Information Technology (IT) company, **Zenith InfoTech**, in India, took permission from its shareholders to sell some of its assets to meet its outstanding liabilities of Foreign Currency Convertible Bonds (FCCBs) in January 2011. After receiving permission, the company sold one of its divisions for $48 million to a related party, but siphoned off the sales proceeds. The bond liabilities, totalling $83 million, which fell due for payment in instalments in September 2011 and August 2012, devolved. Funds raised by selling the company's assets were diverted for the personal use of the promoters. This was theft of shareholders' money by stripping assets. The Indian market regulator, the Securities and Exchange Board of India (SEBI), banned Zenith Technologies and its promoters, the Saraf family, from dealing in securities.

Theft can be all-pervasive. Even new technology aggravates the matter. We all run the risk of becoming victims of theft of our smartphones. The New York State Attorney General took up the matter by writing to Apple, Google, Microsoft and Samsung, asking them about anti-theft measures to reduce theft of smartphones.

Even food aids are stolen, keeping thousands of children and others without food. For instance, the UN World Food Programme found thousands of sacks of grain and other supplies meant for famine victims stolen by unscrupulous businessmen and sold in open markets at a profit in Somalia. Stories of theft are unending.

Theft is the act of stealing. It involves taking other people's property without permission and depriving them of their rights. The term 'theft' is also sometimes used interchangeably with words such as stealing, filching, pinching, snatching, looting, embezzlement, robbery, fraud, burglary and larceny. All these are illegal acts and subject to punishment and penalties, depending on the law of jurisdiction where the acts have been committed and the nature of the crimes.

Let us look at a few instances of corporate thefts.

SAP

Oracle Corporation sued SAP—both business software companies—for 'corporate theft', claiming that SAP, its rival, had stolen copyrighted software and other confidential materials from it in March 2007. Oracle accused SAP of trying to gain repeated and unauthorised access to its password-protected customer support website. This apparently allowed SAP to copy Oracle software to its own servers to compile an illegal library of copyrighted software codes. Oracle claimed in its suit that this was theft on a grand scale.

> SAP agreed to pay Oracle $436 million as compensation in August 2012. This was to cover illegal access by SAP's US subsidiary TomorrowNow, to Oracle's computer systems by illegally using passwords it had obtained from the latter's customers.

Hilton Hotels

Hilton Worldwide, the world's largest hotel chain, was involved in stealing confidential documents from Starwood Hotels & Resorts Worldwide. These documents pertained to Starwood's successful W chain. In April 2009, Starwood sued Hilton and its two executives, Ross Klein and Amar Lalvani, accusing them of stealing more than 100,000 documents with competitively sensitive information belonging to Starwood. Klein and Lalvani were in fact former Starwood employees, who were poached by Hilton to develop its luxury hotel brand, Denizen, to compete with Starwood's W chain.

> Hilton agreed to pay Starwood a substantial amount to settle the theft suit in December 2010. It was also prohibited from starting any new 'lifestyle' hotels for two years.

MF Global

In October 2011, millions of dollars went suddenly missing from the coffers of MF Global, the brokerage firm. The fund was run by Jon Corzine, a former governor of New Jersey. The missing funds belonged to MF Global's customers. After these allegations, the firm filed for bankruptcy. A total of $1.6 billion was siphoned off from it. There was a complete breakdown of internal control systems. Money belonging to customers should have been kept separately from the firm's funds—the dictum 'never mingle customer's money with your own money' was not followed by MF Global. This is the basic duty of a financial firm—to keep a tab on customers' funds on an ongoing basis.

MF Global took enormous risks by betting on buying debts from Spain, Italy, Portugal, Belgium and Ireland at a large discount. It hoped that once Europe solved its fiscal problems, it could sell these bonds at a profit. But everything went wrong as Europe's financial position continued to be uncertain. MF Global ran out of cash when it was required to invest more money to support its trading position. It is not uncommon that when organisations fail, some money is unaccounted for. In the case of MF Global, the missing sum was rather too large.

After months of making efforts, most of the money was traced. It was discovered that JP Morgan played a vital role in lending money to MF Global and clearing its trades. JP Morgan was also the major recipient of MF Global's customers' money during the final chaotic days. What MF Global did was to use its customers' money and place extra collateral in the market to back its trades, especially in European bonds where it was losing money, thereby providing comfort to JP Morgan that its trade positions would be honoured.

When MF Global became bankrupt, JP Morgan seized these amounts.

> JP Morgan agreed to release funds belonging to MF Global, whose customers were ultimately paid back in full.

Tailpiece

Theft is among the oldest crimes in the world and is not going to be eliminated in the near or distant future.

'LIES, DAMN LIES AND STATISTICS' IN DISCLOSURES

Stiefel Laboratories, the world's largest privately held skincare company, was acquired by GlaxoSmithKline (GSK) for $2.9 billion at a price of $68,000 per share in 2009. Charles Stiefel, the owner of Stiefel Labs, bought back shares from its employees, which they owned under the company's stock plan, at an extremely low valuation of $16,469 per share, which he then sold at a four times higher price. The purchase was done by hiding vital information from its employees that the company was being sold to GSK just after buyback of the shares. Had he disclosed this information, he would have had to pay a much higher price. This is a classic example of cheating by an owner to enhance his personal wealth at the cost of his employees through incomplete and inaccurate disclosures. SEC accused the company and Stiefel of fraud in December 2011.

The usual mode of disseminating information about a company's performance is through annual reports, quarterly results, presentations to investors and press briefings. Apart from what is apparent from accounting-related information, potential investors also look at the management team, its confidence in the future of the business, its prognosis and body language.

Management is, therefore, expected to make statements that are true and fair, and which appropriately reflect the state of affairs in an organisation. Misstatements and painting a rosier picture of the company's health and business conditions than its actual state amount to fraudulent behaviour.

Let us look at some examples of poor disclosures.

Enron

Enron was a master in the art of deception. Apart from the numerous accounting jugglery in which it engaged during 2000, its top management fraudulently promoted one of its companies, Enron Broadband Services (EBS). In one of its corporate analyst conference in January 2000, the CEO and the others in in its top management knowingly made false and misleading statements regarding (i) the status of EBS's broadband network and (ii) its proprietary *network control software,* and (iii) misrepresented its business valuation at $30 billion, calling this a conservative estimate. In reality, EBS' position in all these matters was the reverse. It neither had the broadband network nor the critical proprietary network control software to run it. Furthermore, its valuation was grossly overstated by billions of dollars over what its internal and external valuation models had calculated. The management fraudulently promoted a non-performing business, knowing well that the real story was completely different.

Hewlett-Packard (HP)

One of the worst corporate deals in history was HP's acquisition of **Autonomy**—a British business analytics company, which it acquired for $11.1 billion in August 2011. Within a year, HP had to write down $8.8 billion from the acquisition value, revealing that Autonomy was worth 80% less.

What went wrong? HP attributed a $5 billion loss due to the 'wilful effort on behalf of certain former Autonomy employees to inflate the underlying financial metrics of the company in order to mislead HP' and 'the misrepresentations and lack of disclosure severely affected HP's ability to fairly value Autonomy.' Some critics, however, feel it was HP's foolishness in paying such a high price for the company. The matter is under investigation by various investigating bodies. This is a case of misplaced disclosure of the true business picture.

Ranbaxy—Daiichi Sankyo

Japan's Daiichi Sankyo acquired 64% of Ranbaxy Laboratories—India's largest pharmaceutical company—for $4 billion in June 2008. However, come September 2008, the US drug authorities banned Ranbaxy from exporting 30 generic drugs to the USA because of lapses in manufacturing practices at two of its plants. The acquisition formalities were finally completed in November that year. Ranbaxy pleaded guilty for its export of subpar drugs in

May 2013 and agreed to pay $500 million as penalty—the largest involving generic safety of a drug. Daiichi was furious with these developments and accused Ranbaxy's former shareholders of concealing and misrepresenting critical information about the investigation conducted by the US authorities.

The concern seems valid because a June sell-out by Ranbaxy was adversely affected by the US export ban a few months later. Surely Ranbaxy would have been discussing this for quite some time with the US drug authorities, since this was an eight-year-old dispute. Had a full disclosure been made, would Daiichi have bought Ranbaxy at such a high price? Or was it failure of Daiichi's due diligence process? This is another instance of a inaccurate high-profile disclosure.

Tailpiece

'There are three types of lies—'lies, damn lies and statistics', said Benjamin Disraeli. Some corporate organisations use this to justify deals mixed with falsification, falsehood and fiction.

BYPASS RULES—A SHORTCUT TO NEW BUSINESS

Such is the lure for new business that one of the most respected Indian companies, **Larsen & Toubro (L&T)**, the engineering and construction giant, was found forging documents to win a supply deal in 2008. The World Bank suspended L&T from bidding for new contracts from March 2013 through September 2013.

An employee of L&T was found to be falsifying documents to secure contracts to supply ultrasound scanners for a health project funded by the World Bank in Tamil Nadu, a state in India. The company acknowledged the fraud, revealing that the employee had falsified testimonials about L&T's scanners. It labelled the employee a *rogue* and he resigned.

This is not an isolated instance. Companies often bid or vie for new businesses when they need to either qualify to pitch for business or prove their credentials that they can deliver the desired output. Many times, the enterprises need to prove that their product quality is of the required standard. They may also be required to register with the appropriate authorities overseeing the type of business. And these are the areas where fraud takes place.

Taking another such example, **Ambit Capital**, **Edelweiss Financial**, **JM Financial** and **Motilal Oswal Securities**, four Indian brokerage firms, provided unauthorised broking services in the USA. These firms were not registered with the SEC as required under the Federal securities law, but were seeking new business and providing brokerage services to institutional investors in the USA without being registered. The firms were trading on behalf of and offering the securities of India-based companies to US-based clients. The four firms agreed to pay in aggregate a penalty of $1.8 million to settle charges of misdemeanour against them in November 2012.

Tailpiece

'Fraud in business is no different from infidelity in marriage or plagiarism in scholarly work. Even people committed to high moral standards succumb', said Miroslav Volf, Croatian theologian.

TAKING LABOUR FOR A RIDE

Rana Plaza, housing five garment factories located outside Dhaka, the capital of Bangladesh, collapsed in April 2013, killing more than 1,100 people and creating the worst tragedy in the industry's history. It was a catastrophe in waiting. Made of substandard materials with blatant disregard to safety norms, the building housed thousands of workers eking out a living by making cost-effective garments for European and American companies.

Abuse of labour is rampant elsewhere as well. Workers assembling iPhones and iPads in China often work in harsh conditions in lax safety conditions. Foxconn Technologies, one of the world's biggest electronics manufacturers, faced repeated labour protests including rioting in China, due to poor work conditions for labour.

Corporations are not made of bricks and mortar, but of human beings functioning together in an organised manner in accordance with set objectives. Through motivation, training, development and payment of appropriate compensation, human resources should work like a synchronised orchestra. But labour cannot be taken for granted and needs to be treated with fairness. There are many instances where employers treat their employees unfairly and in an unsavoury manner.

Tata Consultancy Services (TCS)

TCS, India's largest software company with a global presence, employs, among others, expats who are mainly Indians at various locations in the world. In the USA, the company required its non-US citizen employees to sign a 'power-of-attorney', delegating outside agencies to calculate and submit their tax returns to the US tax authorities. Up to this point, the steps taken by TCS were for the benefit of its employees.

However, strange as it may seem for a multi-billion-dollar global company, TCS required its employees to also sign an undertaking, which required them to *return* to the company any tax refunds obtained from filing their *own tax returns*. Personal income tax is the private liability of an employee. If there is any refund of excess personal income tax paid to the government, this should belong to the employee and not to the employer. But in this case, TCS wanted such refunds for itself.

TCS employees filed a suit against their employer, complaining about Tata's (TCS belongs to the Tata Group) unjust enrichment from employees' tax refunds. In February 2013, TCS agreed to settle the case after seven years of litigation by paying $30 million as fine. For a company of its stature, settlement of its employees' claim was a major embarrassment.

Samsung Electronics

The South Korean electronics giant Samsung suffered a serious blow to its global ambitions when a US-based non-profit organisation, China Labour Watch, accused it of breaching labour laws in six Chinese factories in September 2012. The accusations included workers working much more than the legally permitted 34 hours of overtime a month, not adhering to labour contract terms, and worst of all, some of them had to pay bribes equivalent to their half-month's salaries to secure employment.

According to Samsung, it found 'inadequate management and potentially unsafe practices'.

Furthermore, in 2011, Samsung was held responsible for not protecting its workers from carcinogenic substances at its semiconductor plants, which resulted in the death of two workers.

EXTORTION PROVIDES EASY MONEY

Zee News, a premier news TV channel broadcasting in Indian languages, a part of the **Essel Group**, was alleged to extort INR 1,000 million ($17 million) from sitting member of the Indian Parliament, Naveen Jindal's group company, Jindal Steel & Power Limited, in late 2012. The money was extorted for not airing news stories, which linked the company to the coal scam unearthed in India. It was not determined whether the threats were real.

Extortions often take creative forms, and **Standard Chartered Bank** proved particularly innovative. In late 2011, the bank raised undue credit card bills of INR 74,000 ($1,200) against a customer after finalising a settlement with him five years earlier. His name was then put by the bank on its *defaulter's list* due to which he could not avail services from other banks. The Delhi Consumer Disputes Redressal Forum held this as *extortion* by the bank.

Cases of extortion and blackmail abound in the corporate world. They come in various shapes, sizes and forms. Extortion involves an illegal act of demanding or extracting money, property or services through coercion, threat or force. Kidnappers use the ploy by making phone calls or sending letters to extort cash. But things are changing in the modern world. There are now pop-ups in computers or laptops that announce demands for payment of ransom.

In recent times, thousands of computer users saw a message from the Federal Bureau of Investigation (FBI) and some other law enforcement agencies, claiming ransom money in late 2012. These were the creations of hackers who now prowl the cyber world for money. The messages announced that computer users would no longer have access to their personal computers (PCs) or their files unless ransom was paid. These types of messages are known as *ransomware*. The methods employed involve infecting PCs with viruses that locked them. The attackers could then demand money before the computers could be unlocked. But there are numerous occasions where even after paying money, computers were not unlocked.

Hackers and extractors use different techniques and languages to scare users and extract money. In the USA, messages were said to be purportedly sent by the FBI; in the Netherlands from the local police and so on. Some computer users were gullible and paid the so-called fine only to find that it was a scam.

Demanding money for not leaking proprietary information of victims on the Internet is a new tactic to make a fast buck used by extortionist hackers. Hackers are also attacking websites for activist purposes. In 2011, they attacked PayPal in retaliation to its blocking donations to Wikileaks. They also attacked the websites of the FBI, the Motion Picture Association of America (MPAA) and others to protest against proposed anti-piracy legislation.

Extortion is an evil art, which cyber fraudsters seem to have mastered.

Symantec

In early 2012, hackers threatened Symantec that they would post the source code of its popular *pcAnywhere* antivirus software. They sent it an extortion notice which stated that they would not release the company's source code if they were given ransom money. The hackers called themselves 'Lords of Dharmaraja' and posted 1.3 gigabytes of Symantec's source code on a file-sharing site. It was distributed hundreds of times in a day after posting the extortion notice to the company. Symantec hd identified 16 *ransomware* gangs and tracked one such gang, which tried to infect more than 500,000 computers over a period just over a fortnight. Moreover, the hackers claimed that they had discovered Symantec's source code when they hacked India's military and intelligence servers in January 2012.

The hackers revealed that Symantec offered them money for not releasing further source codes. They however continued to ask for money, and when Symantec did not agree to this, they posted more codes. At one time, they gave 10 minutes time to Symantec to remit $50,000 to an offshore Liberty Reserve account, and when the company asked for more time, they posted some more source codes. Symantec reported that it has prepared itself for any eventuality relating to the rest of its source codes being posted for public consumption by the hackers.

> Symantec has announced that it had developed and issued a series of patches to clients by the end of January 2012 to protect its pcAnywhere software.

Journalists in Indonesia

Indonesia's Krakatau Steel was to make an initial public offer (IPO) of $300 million in November 2010. Allegations were made that reporters of four media companies demanded $71,000 worth of shares in the company as extortion money. The reporters were apparently given 'envelopes' to file positive reports. According to Indonesia's Alliance of Independent Journalists, they will be making enquiries into the matter, which came to light from a tip from a whistle-blower. The association's chairperson suggested that there may be some issues and that the articles would be checked. He said that in Indonesia not only journalists are to be blamed, but also government departments and companies take advantage of the situation by paying journalists to further their own interests.

In the Krakatau episode, the journalists apparently threatened the company with negative coverage if their demand for shares was not met. In Indonesia, many large media companies are run by big corporate organisations with a political agenda. Therefore, the independence of media may be a question mark in the country. However, the Krakatau episode went too far as far as ethics is concerned in Indonesian media.

Tailpiece

New technology has added firepower to prying eyes. Honey traps, stealth cameras, and worse, Photoshop or Google-glass—all can entrap the unwary. No one really cares if it is true or not when lewd pictures using modern technology are aired on the Internet. It is sometimes a game of no-return for the victims. Therefore, it is best to be clean and careful. Even walls have ears, they say, and the wired modern world has made it truer than ever before. 'There are reasons for flies to be around rotten eggs' goes the Chinese proverb, and extortionists take advantage of this!

WHO BOTHERS ABOUT CONFLICT OF INTEREST?

The corporate world is replete with conflicts of interest. Auditors' fees are paid by the companies' that are audited, the rating agency's fees by the organisations that are rated, the courts earn their fees by companies filing cases with them—such instances are legion.

A **Merrill Lynch** broker recommended that Infospace stock should be held on to in spite of its falling share price, without disclosing that the company would acquire Go2Net of which Merrill was the financial advisor. In another case, Airgas Inc., a large machinery company, sued the legal firm **Cravath, Swaine & Moore**, which was advising Airgas on finance-related issues, and a little later advised its rival company to make a hostile bid for Airgas. SEC found instances where key *credit rating agency analysts* were taking part in discussing the fees of clients, which they would ultimately rate. These are all *conflicts of interest* prevalent in our business world.

Conflict of interest is a term that is difficult to define but easier to explain. Let us attempt the difficult task first. How can one define it? Conflict of interest involves a situation when a person (or an organisation) acts in two or more separate capacities, and its objectives in these capacities are not identical when decisions are taken involving the entity and where there is its self-interest at stake. In such situations, it is expected that conflict of interest is disclosed and the concerned entity abstains from voting or sharing in the decision-making process involving these interests.

For example, Mr X is the chairman of ABC Co. and wants to appoint XYZ Consultants as the company's management consultants. Mr X is a partner in XYZ Consultants and has a conflict of interest in the proposed appointment of the consultancy firm, since he holds decision-making powers and office of profit in both the organisations. Therefore, when the board of ABC Co. decides on XYZ's appointment, Mr X should disclose his position in the consultancy firm, since he is likely to benefit financially from its revenues, and abstain from the decision-making process when ABC puts its vote to its board on its decision.

Conflict of interest is often difficult to surmise. What if the board member is not likely to benefit, but an action will benefit his business associate or a relative? How does one know the extent of the likely benefit?

Let us assume that a board member of a facility company asks it to repair the toilets at his home. This is a facility that is not normally provided by the company's charter to its board members or to its employees. While the cost involved could be small or the work carried out a part of the routine task of the facility company, should the board member disclose the conflict of interest.? What happens if he does not? These are challenging questions on corporate ethics and it is difficult to determine the nature of penalty levied on the board member concerned. The answer is, under good corporate governance, such situations need to be disclosed.

In real life, board members or top management often keep shareholders in the dark about developments that may involve themselves and makes it impossible for the latter to discover existence of conflict of interest.

Conflict of interest is not necessarily corruption, although in some cases it could be. However, it is impropriety. The difference is thin and often hazy. It amounts to poor governance and bad ethics in corporate management.

What constitutes conflict of interest and what does not is often left to the concerned individuals, and it is up to them to disclose the genesis of any possible conflict.

Sections of the legal community are sometimes of the opinion that if conflict of interest is disclosed, the interested person can even discuss or vote on the resolution concerned. However, more often than not, it is not good practice to participate in the decision-making process when one can directly or indirectly benefit from the decision taken.

Since conflict of interest necessitates judgement and self-disclosure, companies need to have codes of conduct that make matters easier to handle. A robust code of conduct should state upfront that the concerned board member should neither participate in the decision-making process nor vote, and should refrain from the decision-making procedure on the matter that could directly or indirectly benefit him or her. A code of conduct, however, does not supersede prevalent regulations or the law on the matter. It only helps to fulfil the law and prevent a potential problem from taking place.

The New York Times once summed up the challenge to determine conflict of interest very well—'in many cases potential conflicts can be identified by using the "sniff" test. If it smells bad, don't do it'.

Let us now look at a few examples of conflict of interest.

Freeport

Freeport-McMoRan Inc. is among the largest companies in the metals and mining sector. In December 2012, the company invested in the energy sector. It bought two oil exploration companies, McMoRan Exploration and Plains Exploration & Production. There was substantial conflict of interest in the deal.

Let us take these one by one. First, Freeport's Chairman, James Moffett, also partly owns and runs McMoRan. Therefore, Moffett's personal involvement in the investing and investee companies was the problem. James Moffett is the Chairman of Freeport and the Co-Chairman of McMoRan. How can the two boards objectively take investment decisions when Moffett is sitting in at the meetings and is involved in both the companies? Moffett is likely to influence the decision of Freeport's board in investing in another company, where he is again interested as a shareholder and the person who runs the company. Freeport's board cannot be impartial and unbiased in its decision-making process under such circumstances. This is a clear case of a conflict of interest.

Second, there is another conflict of interest. James Flores, Freeport's Head of Plains Exploration & Production, is also a board member of McMoRan Exploration, where James Moffett is a shareholder. There is therefore cross- conflict of interest.

Third, Freeport's investment in the energy sector apparently does not have a business logic. Why should a gold mining company invest in oil and gas exploration? What synergies can be expected from of the deal? Did the boards have adequate information to debate and discuss it?

Freeport may have been forced to invest its surplus funds to promote the interest of its chairperson in other businesses, especially in the energy sector, in this case.

Goldman Sachs

Sometimes companies such as Goldman Sachs face the conflict of serving their clients versus their proprietary trading operations. When investment advisors are supposed to provide advisory services to their clients on trading positions, it is their duty to protect their clients interests first and then those of their own or proprietary trading divisions. However, even companies such as Goldman Sachs have failed to fulfil norms relating to conflict of interest in certain cases.

In January 2010, Goldman Sachs admitted to its clients that investment ideas were often shared with its own trading arm without sharing these with the former first.

Reuters

A financial reporter of repute, reporting on companies in which he had a financial holding did not report it. This involved conflict of interest involving the journalist.

The well-known British columnist, Neil Collins, had been filing reports on companies in Reuters' Breakingviews columns, without disclosing his conflict of interest. For instance, Neil had owned shares in BP before and after writing about the company, and these shares were substantial. He wrote several articles on BP. Reuters removed the journalist from its service in October 2010.

When journalists write and comment on companies in which they have a substantial financial interest, the fact needs to be clearly disclosed after the article or comments from such journalists. This is ethical.

Japan Tobacco

Even governments holding shares in tobacco companies could constitute conflict of interest. With governments promoting healthy living and discouraging consumption of tobacco, their holding shares or owning cigarette companies is a serious conflict of interest. The Japanese Government planned to loosen its grip on one of the world's largest tobacco companies—Japan Tobacco—and sell a third of its 50% stake in February 2013. Many people in Japan blamed the government for not taking effective steps to pass legislation to protect non-smokers from cigarette smoke due to its large stake in cigarette companies.

According to the data compiled by the American Cancer Society in 2011, Japan has the highest number of smokers in the world, with a person puffing around 1,840 cigarettes a year, compared to around 1,000 cigarettes per person in a year in the USA.

Now, with conflict of interest in the tobacco industry on the decline, Japan will hopefully be more active in preventing cigarette smoke from affecting everyone.

Tailpiece

Buyers should be aware that *caveat emptor* is the rule for how conflict of interest needs to be dealt with. If you know that certain parties are interested or a person airing views has conflicting interests, take it with a pinch of salt and be wary of what the transaction bodes for you!

COLLUSION

Two of the most famous auctioneers of artefacts, **Christie's** and **Sotheby's**, supposedly bitter rivals, were alleged to match their fees, exchange confidential client lists and deal terms, and promise not to poach each other's employees. It was a collusion that boosted both their profits.

Toys "R" Us, a famous marketer of toys, forced manufacturers into selling them to competing discount stores at a higher price than it sold to it. It also worked on the manufacturers to keep the prices of Barbie, Mr Potato Head and other popular toys artificially high, so that competing discount stores could not store these. This was collusion.

Schering-Plough once paid $90 million to **American Home Products** and **Upsher-Smith Laboratories Inc.** to delay sale of a low-cost generic drug used by heart patients, so that the alternative to Schering's drug was not launched. Similarly, **Aventis Pharma Limited** paid **Andrx** $90 million to delay the release of a generic version of the former's popular heart drug. This was collusion at its worst, which worked against human interest.

What is collusion? It is an agreement or understanding between two or more parties for an improper or illegal purpose or to prejudice a third party. It is usually a secretive agreement with the purpose to deceive, mislead or defraud others. Collusion also includes agreements between organisations or individuals to allocate among themselves a market, set prices or limit production. It is usually illegal and such agreements are void.

Let us look at some more examples of collusion in the corporate world.

Hachette, Harper Collins, Simon & Schuster, Penguin, Macmillan and Apple

Five of the big publishing houses had been accused of conspiring and colluding over emails and dinners to set the prices of e-books. The publishers moved from a wholesale pricing model, letting retailers charge what the market could bear, to a system that allowed the former to price their e-books. This is known as the *agency pricing* model. The publishers revealed that they were trying to protect themselves from below-the-cost pricing of Amazon e-books, which for some models were priced at $9.99. The logic used by the publishers was that they had to collude among themselves to save their skins.

> Except for Apple, all the five publishing houses settled charges of collusion by agreeing to lift the restrictions they had imposed on discounting and promotion by e-book retailers by the end of 2012 and early 2013. Prices of e-books could therefore be reduced by retailers. The publishing houses were prohibited from entering new agreements with similar conditions or restrictions till the end of 2014.

Goldman Sachs, Bain, TPG, Blackstone, the Carlyle Group, KKR, Silver Lake

A group comprising 11 of the largest private equity (PE) firms was accused of colluding among themselves to bring down the price of corporate takeovers during the boom period of corporate buyouts. It was alleged that the PE firms had rigged the market for more than two dozen multi-billion-dollar takeovers of listed companies. This resulted in their depriving their shareholders, including the pension funds of companies taken over, of billions of dollars for their shareholding.

Civil anti-trust complaints were filed by the affected shareholders in 2007. These related to issues involving 'you scratch my back, I scratch yours' and 'if you did not bid on my deal, I will not bid on yours'.

During the period 2003–07, there was euphoria about leveraged buyouts, with PE funds pooling their money and buying companies out of these funds. The companies purchased during this period included the retailer Toys "R" Us, chip-maker Freescale, lodger Hilton Worldwide and Spanish broadcaster Univision.com.

> After a long period of uncertainty, the US Federal Court admitted the suit filed by the shareholders and agreed that the matter would be argued and heard. In June 2014, Goldman Sachs and Bain Capital agreed to pay a combined fine of $121 million to settle allegations of collusion without admitting their guilt. Silver Lake followed by paying $29.5 million to settle accusations against it.

Tailpiece

Collusion is an undercurrent in a usually placid stream. Its presence is not overt, but awareness can prevent probable sabotage and damage. For example, *auctions* are often held to create an illusion of transparency, but the ghost of collusion is most often present through bid-rigging.

PRICE FIXING, AN EASY WAY OUT

Corporate organisations love profit. One of the ways to fulfil this desire is to raise prices for customers. Would it not be wonderful if manufacturers could get together and agree to sell their products at a predetermined elevated price?

Secret meetings, offshore locations, golf courses and pseudonyms are used by some corporations around the world, sometimes to hoodwink customers and doctor prices.

We all watch television. Little do you realise that its key components have been subjected to price-fixing over the last few decades. When bulky cathode ray tubes were being substituted by liquid crystal displays (LCDs), seven companies held *greens meetings* on golf courses to fix the prices of picture tubes for television and computer screens from 1990s till 2006. **Philips**, a **Philips–LG JV**, **Panasonic**, **Samsung**, **Toshiba** and **Technicolor** were fined a total of $1.9 billion for this.

To add salt to the wound, when LCDs for flat-screen televisions were becoming popular during 2001–06, Taiwanese and South Korean manufacturers met around 60 times to fix prices. Fines totalling $860 million were imposed by the European Commission on Taiwanese companies such as **Innolux Corporation**, **AU Optronics Corp.**, **Chunghwa Picture Tubes Ltd** and **HannStar** in 2010. The South Korean company, **LG Display**, was also part of this group.

Consumers suffered either ways, while buying old or new TVs—picture tubes and LCDs—since the prices of both were rigged!

Fixing of prices among the sellers, so that consumers' choice is restricted on negotiation of price, is prohibited across the world.

Competition or *antitrust* laws comprise the legislative backing through which cartelisation or companies dominating a market are protected.

Chinese organisations are not immune to penalties. A group of Chinese companies, producing around 80% of the world's supply of ascorbic acid, or vitamin C, an ingredient in food and soft drinks including Coca-Cola, was fined $162 million by the US District Court in March 2013 when they were found guilty of price-fixing since 2001. There was an unusual twist to this tale, when the Chinese Government apparently supported price fixing amongst manufacturers. However, in spite of government backing, the Chinese companies were penalised by the US judiciary and treated at par with other companies.

The vitamin cartel is an old issue, with earlier penalties being levied in 1999. This was led by European companies such as **Roche**, the Swiss pharmaceutical giant, and **BASF**, the German chemicals company. A huge fine of $1.5 billion was imposed on them.

The car-part sector is a hotbed of cartel activity. Toyota, Honda, Nissan and Renault suffered for a decade due to price-fixing among manufacturers during 2000–09. Several car-part makers were fined €142 million ($177 million) by the European Union Competition Regulator. Of this amount, the highest fine of €125 million ($156 million) was imposed on **Yazaki**, the Japanese company, the world's number one maker of wire harnesses, which transmit electricity in vehicles. Other car-part makers which also had to pay fines included Japanese company **Furukawa Electric**, and the German company **Leoni**.

Throttling competition to enable increases in the price of products is a ploy employed by many companies. **Microsoft** was asked to offer users of its Windows software a wider choice of Internet browsers in 2009. However, although it promised that its new computers would allow easy downloading of other browsers from the Internet, failed to comply. In 2011, the company lied that it did what it was supposed to do. On complaints from rival companies in July 2012, it was found that Microsoft had failed to provide Internet users with a wide choice of web browsers and instead pushed its own browser. The company was fined $732 million in March 2013. It subsequently apologised for this.

Games companies playing in price-fixing arena are numerous. An European freight cartel, with big names including **United Parcel Services**, **Kuehne & Nagel**, **Panalpina World Transport Ltd.** and **Deutsche Bahn** fined a total of $225 million, were found engaged in original methods of concealing their discussions from 2002 to 2007. The participants innovatively used the names of vegetables such as *asparagus* and *baby courgettes* as code words for charging surcharges on trade routes between Europe and the USA.

If one of the cartel players, involved in fixing prices, 'squeaks' to the authorities, it would probably be excused from penalties. Such examples abound. DHL and Exel, subsidiaries of Deutsche Post, although involved in cartelisation, alerted anti-trust agencies on the European freight cartel. They went scot-free. Samsung of South Korea was not fined, since it was a whistle-blower in the flat-panel screen makers' pricing-fixing episode.

However, in spite of regulatory steps being taken, companies continue to walk on the thin line of price-fixing. They are often repeat offenders although they have been hauled up earlier. For example, **ThyssenKrupp AG**, the German steel-maker, was fined for price-fixing in the rail-steel market in July 2013. This was a repeat offence.

Tailpiece

The lure of profit honey-pot continuously beckons the corporate sector, in spite of high penalties for wrongdoings, although this may involve their victimising consumers and work to their detriment.

MAKING TOP MANAGEMENT RICH: BACKDATING OF STOCK OPTIONS

Jacob Alexander, the CEO of Comverse Technologies, a software communications company, after making millions of dollars for

15 years till 2006, fled the USA to relax in the beautiful climate of Namibia in southern Africa. Alexander made $138 million by backdating stock options, a scam for which he escaped being punished.

What Are Stock Options?

Employees' stock options (popularly known as ESOPs) are awarded to employees to reward their performance by companies giving them an ownership interest in them by giving their employees equity shares to supplement their earnings and encourage their participation in the growth of the organisations for which they work. It is meant to incentivise key employees and is used as a strategy to recruit, retain and motivate them.

How Does It Generally Work?

ESOPs are options given to employees to buy shares in the companies for which they work at a future date at a price that is predetermined. The predetermined price, also known as the *strike price* or the *exercise price,* is generally a discounted one over the prevalent market price of shares. The stock options could also be given free of cost. The price of the shares awarded to employees is decided at the time when the decision to allocate ESOPs was taken, which is usually at a board meeting date to discuss ESOPs.

Why It Is Called Options?

In this system, employees have the right to buy shares, but not necessarily the ones offered. They can therefore reserve their option to buy them and are not obligated to do so.

When Can Shares Be Bought?

Employees are given the option to buy shares at a future date, known as the vesting period. This could be after a year or more. It could also be spread over a few years. For instance, a company had offered 1,000 shares as ESOPs to every employee on 31 December 2012. This could be structured such that 20% or 200 shares could be bought after the first year or by the end of 2013, 30% or 300 shares after the second year or by the end of 2014, and the remaining 50% or 500 shares after the third year or by the end of 2015.

Why Are ESOPs Beneficial for Employees?

Stock options are generally issued at a discount compared to the market price. They can also be issued free of cost. Consequently, employees can buy them at a pre-determined low price and sell them at the prevalent market price, which is hopefully higher, and thereby make a profit. However, if the market price of the shares is below the exercise price, employees need not buy them.

In the Money and Out of Money

Employees' benefit if the prevalent market price is higher on the vesting date, compared to the stock option grant price. However, if the prevalent market price is lower than the stock option grant price, employees lose out and perhaps will not exercise the option to buy the shares. If the market price and share option price is the same, it is known as *at the money*.

Accounting Treatment

Whenever shares are *in the money*, it is beneficial for the employees of companies. However, companies need to take charge (show it as a cost) in their profit and loss (P&L) accounts as the difference between the market price and the grant price on the vesting date. This is known as 'deemed remuneration' given to employees, since it is likely to add to their benefits, as and when they decide to actually buy the shares and sell them in the market. Since the option to buy lies with the employees, the employer needs to take charge of the books of accounts upfront (when the shares are *in the money*), irrespective of whether the employees exercise the option. No such *charge* is required to be taken if the shares are *at the money* or *out of money* stage. The accounting treatment may vary between geographies, depending on local accounting guidelines or GAAP's requirements.

How Does Fraud Take Place in ESOPs?

There can be two types of fraud pertaining to ESOPs:

1. The first one is *backdating* stock options. Clearly, the option to buy equity shares in the employer company needs to be at a predetermined price, which is exercisable at a future date. The logic for this being the future price is unknown. It may be to encourage employees to work diligently to enhance shareholders' value, so that the future price of shares goes up. However, on the date the decision is taken, very clearly there is scope to play around with the price if the option date is decided on a backdated basis.

    For instance, assume the decision to provide stock options was taken on 31 December 2012 (vesting date) when the market price was $20 per share. However, in the books and papers of the company it was shown that the decision was taken on 30 June 2012 (grant date—falsified and backdated). In June 2012, no one knew what the price would be in December 2012. Therefore, if it was decided that the stock options would be priced at $16 per share, employees would be able to exercise their stock options and make $4 per share profit ($20 per share market price *less* $16 per share option price) in December 2012. *Backdating* of stock option-related transactions has the potential to be a fraudulent practice.
2. The second type of fraud relates to wrong accounting treatment and involves *non-recognition of the cost* in the income statement when the shares are *in the money* for employees.

Stock options are deemed remuneration for employees, although in theoretical terms, only till they encash it. As long as they are *in the money* on the vesting date, the differential amount needs to be shown as a cost in the company's books of accounts.

Backdating of Stock Options—Illegal?

Conceptually, stock options should be given to encourage employees to help a company perform better, enhance its shareholder value and enable its employees to participate in such enhanced value creation. If this is backdated, the basic premise is lost. Backdating stock options is like letting someone buy a lottery ticket after the date of the draw and the winning number is known. While backdating of stock options is not illegal, it is unethical. However, if illegality needs to be avoided, the full implication of backdated stock options granted must be disclosed in the company's financial reports, and the adverse cost implications (in the case of *in the money* options) fully indicated in its income statement. Moreover, tax implications, if any, should be taken care of by it. Non-disclosure of backdating is a fraudulent act.

Companies Involved in Backdating Stock Options without Disclosure

Many companies have at some point backdated stock options and incorrectly recorded the implications in their books of accounts.

Multinationals: **Research In Motion**, makers of Blackberry; **Apple**, personal computer-maker; **McAfee Inc.**, antivirus product-maker

Large quantum involved: **Broadcom Corporation**, $2.2 billion reduction in charges in accounts; **Symbol Technologies**, $530 million overstatement of profits; **Monster Worldwide**, $340 million understated costs

Practising backdating over a long period: **Trident Microsystems**, 1993–2006; **Black Box Corporation**, 1994–2006; **UnitedHealth Group**, 1995–2005

And the list continues.

FLEECING BY BUYING BACK SHARES

When a company makes profits and has surplus funds, even after paying Corporate Income Tax, it can either retain its surplus earnings to reinvest in its business or distribute the surplus in part or full to its shareholders. Distribution of cash to shareholders out of the company's profits is known as dividends.

There is another method of distributing cash to shareholders—the ultimate owners of any company. This is through *buyback* or *repurchase* of shares.

It is a programme by which a company can buy back its own shares, either from the open market or from existing shareholders, on a proportionate basis. This is usually carried out when shares are undervalued. It means that the market price of shares is lower than expected levels. When shares are bought back, this reduces the number of outstanding shares and helps a company to increase its *earnings per share* (i.e., at the same level of profits with a reduced number of outstanding shares after repurchase of the shares its earnings per share increase). This helps to enhance the market value of the remaining shares held by its shareholders.

From the objective of the share repurchase scheme, it is clear that this is aimed to enable an undertaking to use its surplus cash and increase the market price of its shares, and return some available cash to its shareholders so that they can make use it. It is but logical to expect that the programme should normally be implemented when a company has surplus funds and does not have immediate plans to use it. This obviously presupposes that it is doing well.

However, there are instances when a company is not doing well in reality, but yet returning cash to its shareholders through its share buyback scheme. This does not exactly constitute an accounting fraud, but is one perpetrated by its management by unnecessarily using the company's funds to meet employees' demands.

This usually happens when some employees hold shares under the company's employee stock option scheme, and this is a good way to benefit them by distributing cash, which should have been logically retained within the organisation for its further growth and operations. It involves a company paying remuneration to its employees through an indirect method by buying back shares without disclosing the employee cost as an expenditure in its books of accounts.

This type of fraudulent action was undertaken by **AutoZone**, a US-based auto-parts dealer. The company was in dire straits, with negative shareholders' equity of (-)$1.0 billion (negative shareholders' equity implying that its accumulated losses have wiped out its shareholders' contribution). It was declaring losses, but still retired its stocks through the share buyback scheme. This is a classic example where the hard-earned funds of a company were frittered away to repurchase stocks due to the existence of stock options in the form of compensation paid to employees. By doing this, AutoZone was able to avoid showing employee-related expenses or costs in its books of accounts, and yet use the cash to enrich their coffers. (Share buyback is not a cost in the income statement but constitutes allocation of distributable surplus funds).

What a scheme it was to take the company to the cleaners!

Tailpiece

What steroids are to athletes, stock options are to employees. Both are capable of providing instant kick and rejuvenation—although with possibilities of serious side effects if not handled appropriately.

TAXES TOO TAXING: LET'S GO TO TAX HAVENS

What is common between Aviva, Anglo American, Associated British Foods, AstraZeneca and Admiral Group? Apart from their names beginning with the first letter of the alphabet and belonging to FTSE 100 (top 100 listed shares on the London Stock Exchange), these are companies with a presence and linkages in tax havens.

Tax havens are geographical jurisdictions that offer low or zero taxation rates, secrecy and light regulatory frameworks to attract non-resident funds. There are around 50–60 tax havens in the world, and include jurisdictions such as Bermuda, the British Virgin Islands, the Cayman Islands, the Channel Islands, Dubai, Luxembourg, Liechtenstein, Mauritius, Monaco, Panama, Seychelles, Switzerland and Delaware (in the USA), among others.

In February 2013 *The Economist* estimated that around $20 trillion is stashed away in these locations, although it revealed that nobody knew how much money is really hidden in such offshore havens. The aim is to avoid paying higher taxes in the original jurisdiction of work and structure business transactions so that these can be shown to have been accrued in these tax havens.

The problem is, however, not low or no taxation, but the secrecy of offshore locations, which allows companies and individuals to engage in tax fraud and other nefarious activities. It is estimated that the USA alone loses around $40 billion of tax revenue every year due to the presence of tax havens.

The prevalence of financial secrecy in offshore jurisdictions creates and abets tax fraud, money laundering and funding of international terrorist organisations.

When corporations decide to use secret locations to perpetrate their fraudulent activities or avoid tax, there are very few opportunities to catch the wrongdoers and bring them to book. Various countries in the world should immediately pass legislation preventing their citizens and banks from entering any financial transaction with such jurisdictions that do not have transparency and encourage business to be conducted under secrecy.

Let us take the example of a country that advocates good corporate governance and where popular movement takes place, forcing corporations to pay taxes on profits earned in the country—the *USA*. Unfortunately, the country has a place that is at the forefront of financial secrecy—*Delaware*. It is just around 100 miles from the city that governs the USA—Washington DC. Delaware has the distinction of having the offices of global giants such as Apple, Berkshire Hathaway, Cargill, Coca-Cola, Ford, General Electric (GE) and Google, Walmart, and the list goes on. Around 50% of public corporations in the US are incorporated in this tiny city.

Why so? There reasons are plenty. It takes less than an hour to incorporate a company, against perhaps several days to even obtain a driving licence; profits can be moved from profitable corporations by transferring royalties and other revenues to the companies' holding branches in Delaware where very low taxes are levied, if at all—a drop box is all that is needed to register a company without employees, offices, and so on. And to top it all, it offers the highest level of secrecy, which encourages companies to flock to Delaware for obvious reasons, and gives the city the rare distinction of it being *the largest single hub of anonymous corporations in the world*.

[PS: If any reader is really interested in registering in Delaware, all you need to do is contact CT Corporation, a middleman with a one-third market share in the *drop-box company* game, which will do whatever it takes for you to remain anonymous, tax-free and hopefully stigma-free!].

There have been several cases where corporate organisations have been taken to task for offshore structuring. One such instance is one of Britain's oldest hedge funds, **Weavering Capital**, with more than $600 million under its management, which has been charged with having illegal offshore transactions with its sister firms. Magnus Peterson, founder of Weavering Capital, was charged by Britain's Serious Fraud Office with fraudulent accounting and trading in December 2012. This was a follow-up after the hedge fund collapsed in 2009 after being linked with inappropriate multimillion-pound offshore transactions.

Tailpiece

'A citizen can hardly distinguish between a tax and a fine, except that a fine is generally much lighter', said G.K. Chesterton. Not to be outdone, Erwin Griswold stated, 'We have long had death and taxes as the two standards of inevitability. But there are those who believe that death is the preferable of the two'.

TOO MUCH TAX? PLAN, AVOID OR CHEAT

Britain and France are targeting **Google** and **Amazon** and some other companies, and are complaining that the large local sales of these companies are not converting into adequate corporate tax payments. If these organisations can get away by paying low tax rates, why not you and me?

Most of us feel that we pay too much tax. And many of us would be happy if we could make do with less. Corporations are no different. Most of the time, they are on the lookout for opportunities to save tax. Or is it to avoid paying it?

There is an ongoing debate between *tax planning* and *tax avoidance*. Tax *planning* is legitimate. It is based on taking advantage of tax laws providing tax breaks (i.e., reduced tax liability), based on jurisdiction-specific strategies. For instance, a government may provide higher depreciation (reducing tax liability by increasing deductible cost) if a new factory is set up in a backward area. Similarly, tax impetus may be granted to encourage research and development (R&D) to enhance employment opportunities and support innovation. Taking a cudgel to these measures and reducing tax liability is legitimate and falls within the ambit of tax planning.

However, tax *avoidance* or evasion is where the problem arises. Many corporations may argue these are legitimate and should not be questioned, for instance, housing tax-gathering income in a tax haven jurisdiction, say, in the Cayman Islands, even when a company does not have any meaningful business operation there is a debatable issue and perhaps, borders on tax evasion if not tax fraud.

Apple

One of the most profitable companies in the world, Apple avoids paying billions in taxes through a complex web of subsidiaries spanning several continents, and perhaps going beyond what experts can even conjecture. US Congressional investigators stated in May 2013 that between 2009 and 2012, Apple moved income worth $74 billion out of the taxman's net. The company, which paid $6 billion in US taxes, would have had to pay a lot more had its entire income been transferred within the jurisdiction of the USA.

How did Apple do this? It set up subsidiaries in low-tax countries such as Ireland, the Netherlands and Luxembourg, which would receive the bulk of its profits on its European and Asian sales, although the company's operations were run from its headquarters in Cupertino, California, USA. Essentially, its *intellectual properties*, including copyrights on iTunes or downloading of songs and so on, were in Ireland, helping Apple accumulate its taxable profits for sales outside the USA in the country.

Being a manufacturer of digital product, it is easier for Apple to shift its profits to low-tax countries, unlike a furniture or toy shop, whose physical activities are concentrated. Buy an iPhone in India and Ireland books most of the profits, paying a mere 2% negotiated tax. Only if the profits are brought to the USA will these be subject to 35% tax, less tax already paid abroad.

Is it superb planning or tax evasion?

Pfizer, Microsoft, Intel, J&J, Citi, Facebook, Linkedin, HP–Corporates Love Ireland

The low corporate tax rate of 12.5% in Ireland has attracted many multinational corporations that have set up shop in the country. For decades, its low tax rates have been leveraged by *Ireland* to attract investments and for companies such as Pfizer, Microsoft, Intel, Citi and others to set up operations in it. In order to reduce tax rates, companies have entered numerous arrangements, including moving income in and out of the country. **Google**'s primary source of revenue includes receipts for advertisements from customers. The company enters advertising contracts through its Irish office, rather than the local European ones. Similarly, books bought from **Amazon** are always shown as sales from a Luxembourg-based entity, another low-tax country. The whole objective of these companies is to transfer their accrued income to low-tax jurisdictions.

General Electric (GE)

'Imagination at Work'—the GE tag line—suits its elephantine tax department, consisting of around 1,000 employees, well. The company pays a trivial amount of tax in the USA, where it is headquartered. With global profits of $17 billion for 2012, its tax liability was shown as only 15% ($2.5 billion) against the US rate of 35%.

How do these companies do this? Their managements' focus on saving taxes is the key to their success. Innovative accounting, accrual of profits offshore and fierce lobbying for tax breaks (resulting in high depreciation allowances and *green energy* credits on wind turbines) are some of GE's practices. However, its most significant tax-planning methods have been to operate its profitable financial business of leasing and lending—GE Capital—in offshore locations.

Starbucks

The famous coffee retailer Starbucks faced public ire in Britain for not paying Income Tax during 2010–12, although it generates healthy sales of £400 million ($600 million) at its 700 British stores. The company saved taxes in Britain by channelling sales through its subsidiaries in low-tax countries and paying royalty (a cost shown in the UK, which helps to reduce companies' profits) to countries such as the Netherlands, where the tax rate is very low. To quell public anger, Starbucks agreed in December 2012 to pay £10 million ($15 million) as annual Corporate Tax in Britain, revealing that they would not pay royalty outside Britain for a couple of years to improve its taxable profits.

Tailpiece

Large companies are now being targeted by governments that are looking for ways and means to tax them for profits earned in their respective jurisdictions. The EU is thinking of making it compulsory for the big businesses to reveal their profits and taxes on a country-by-country basis. Under the aegis of the Organisation for Economic Cooperation and Development (OECD), 45 countries have taken the initiative to tackle transnational tax fraud, tax evasion and aggressive tax planning.

The furore over avoidance of taxes by large companies has become too loud for political leadership to ignore.

As British economist J.M. Keynes said, 'Avoidance of taxes is the only intellectual pursuit that carries any reward'.

PRIVACY CAN BECOME AN OPEN BOOK

It was a special day for John—he wished to propose to his heart-throb, Patsy. He took her out to an exclusive restaurant, and found a cosy and quiet corner to celebrate the special moments, not realising that a bespectacled person at a distant table was hearing their very private conversation and was also taking pictures. This was made possible by Google's wearable computer, *Google Glass*—a pair of lens-less frames with a tiny computer attached to the right earpiece. A wink snaps a picture. Such will be the future, with probable invasion of our privacy, perhaps when it is least expected.

Privacy of data or information involves protection of personal identifiable data, which should normally not be disclosed without prior permission. This personal information may include biological mapping and genetic material, health care and financial records as well as ethnicity.

Data is being increasingly used by various data companies to track consumers' habits and preferences. MasterCard, for instance, analyses transaction data to help companies target advertisements at consumers who are more likely to buy a particular type or class of product. For instance, it can track the likely consumers who will buy electronic items.

The legal rights for data privacy protection vary from country to country. Protection of privacy is stricter in Europe than in the USA and Asian countries. In the EU, personal data may only be transferred to another country, which will provide an adequate level of data protection. However, there is a move to soften tough data protection rules in EU countries, which should provide relief to tech groups and data-related companies such as Google and Facebook, which collect large amounts of personal data.

A few examples are cited where data privacy rights have been compromised by corporations:

Google

Cars, fitted with sophisticated cameras and computers, drove past people's homes, collecting secret personal information about residents in their homes and offices, who were unsuspecting users of computers. Information on emails, medical and financial records, and passwords was collected as the vehicles went by. You feel this is a scene from a James Bond movie! In reality, Google, the Internet company, has for over several years been prying into people's lives, while photographing houses and offices lining the world's avenues, boulevards and lanes.

This was essentially data espionage on millions of unencrypted wireless networks. a worldwide uproar ensued and investigations took place in at least a dozen countries, including in Australia, Germany and the USA. Google acknowledged to US state officials in March 2013 that it had violated people's privacy during its *street view* mapping project. It agreed to pay a fine of $7 million and set up a privacy programme within six months.

Unfortunately, Google had been violating the privacy policy for years and does not seem to be learning from its past mistakes. For instance, in 2012, the Federal Trade Commission of the USA fined the company $22 million for bypassing privacy settings in its Safari Browser. In 2011, the company agreed to be audited for 20 years by the commission after admitting to having used deceptive tactics when initiating its Buzz Social Network.

Strangely, in the past, Google had given an assurance that it would build a strong privacy-monitoring policy, with layers of oversight and controls over employees who could breach the privacy provisions. Clearly, a company of this stature and goodwill did not honour its commitments year after year.

Facebook

Most of us are on Facebook. How would you feel if your habits, likes and dislikes were being shared with others? That is precisely what the social networking company has done.

Facebook was charged for deceiving customers by repeatedly making information public that users believed would be kept private. The company was accused of breaching the US Fair Trade Act repeatedly, allowing private information to be shared with users or to be made public. Mark Zuckerberg, CEO of Facebook, agreed by saying, 'I'm the first to admit that we have made a bunch of mistakes'.

> The Federal Trade Commission entered a settlement agreement with Facebook in November 2011, where the company was required to take several steps to ensure that it abides by its commitments on privacy. This included Facebook taking prior permission from users before sharing information beyond their privacy settings, maintaining detailed privacy programmes and undergoing privacy audits once in two years conducted by independent auditors.

WhatsApp

We are all so happy that we can text our friends and relatives free of cost, using the popular WhatsApp application on our mobiles. But beware! Your address book is perhaps being accessed!

WhatsApp, the popular mobile phone text-messaging application, has been accused of breaking privacy laws by data-protection authorities in Canada and the Netherlands. It has been accused of downloading address books from users of smartphones, even of those who have not granted permission to WhatsApp. This application uses phone numbers from its users' devices to identify other people who are using this service. Moreover, the data-protection authorities feel that WhatsApp also has the phone numbers of non-users—although it may be storing this data in an anatomised format.

> While Canadian authorities seem satisfied with the steps taken by WhatsApp to protect the privacy of its users, Dutch authorities are not.

Tailpiece

The price of progress has resulted in our compromising our privacy in this wired world. 'Relying on the government to protect your privacy is like asking a peeping tom to install your window blinds', said John Perry Barlow, an American poet, commenting on the dichotomy of the modern world.

WHY BOTHER ABOUT POLITICAL OR ECONOMIC SANCTIONS?

Thousands of tankers illegally carry oil from Iraqi Kurdistan every day to Iran, skirting the economic sanctions imposed on Iran due to its nuclear ambitions. The **Elaf Islamic Bank** in Iraq and a network of other financial institutions happily help to channel the export proceeds of millions of dollars. Export of oil therefore continues unabated to Iran, which in turn sells power to Iraq. This is a happy coexistence in the face of ongoing sanctions. Machinations are often employed to circumvent embargoes.

Several banks have been caught trying to evade US sanctions against certain countries. **Standard Chartered**, the British bank, hid the key details of at least $250 billion in transactions with Iran, lied to the regulators and falsified records—very serious charges, given the goodwill the bank commands among its customers. Similarly, the French bank **BNP Paribas** admitted to having hidden billions of dollars in transferring funds from 2002 and 2012 to New York banks from entities in Sudan, Cuba and Iran. It was fined $8.9 billion in June 2014. **ING Bank** has also moved billions of dollars to countries under US sanctions, including Cuba, Sudan and Libya, and paid a fine of $619 million in mid-2012 to settle compliance-related investigations.

Due to exigencies in world politics, sanctions are sometimes imposed, controlling relations with certain countries in the world. For instance, in view of Iran's nuclear programmes, which are considered to be anti-humanitarian, the USA, under the aegis of the United Nations, has issued sanctions against the country. Then there are embargoes on countries such as Sudan, Syria and North Korea. Such lists change and are 'chopped', depending on developments in world politics.

Let us look at an example where there has been mass violation of sanctions.

The New York Times undertook a study in March 2010 and reported that during 2000–09, when there were sanctions on Iran, 74 companies did business within or with the country. The list of violators included **Daelim** (South Korea), **ENI** (Italy), **Petrobras** (Brazil), **Repsol** (Spain), **Royal Dutch Shell** (Netherlands), **Statoil** (Norway) and **Total** (France). These companies are engaged in Iran's energy sector. Their investments have been deemed by the US Congress and the US State Department as possible violations of the Iran Sanctions Act, which requires the President of the

USA to sanction companies that make investments of more than $20 million in one year to develop the country's oil and natural gas reserves.

Tailpiece

Sanctions are political impositions. As water always finds its own level, so do certain businesses. They find their way through the labyrinth of controls to service-sanctioned regimes for profit. Some are caught; others escape detection. It was reported that during mid-2013, **Dell** computers reached the Syrian Government, the Bashar al-Assad regime, through the company's distributor **BDL Gulf** in Dubai, in spite of US sanctions. There must be many other such instances.

PRESS CAN IMPRESS FRAUDULENTLY

One of the most promising and respected young staff writers for *The New Yorker*, Jonah Lehrer, conjured up an imaginary dialogue with Bob Dylan, one of the most famous musicians alive. Dylan's made-up quote was—'It's hard this to describe. It's just this sense that you got something to say'. Lehrer lost his job for this journalistic fraud.

Jayson Blair, a journalist with the more than a century old newspaper, *The New York Times,* committed years of journalistic fraud and deception. He would habitually mislead readers by making them believe that he was reporting from *on the spot* when he was hundreds of miles away in New York, fabricating and conjuring up comments and developments. Jayson eventually resigned from the newspaper. Even NYT was not infallible!

Media can sometime go overboard in reporting events. While Nelson Mandela was lying in a critical condition in a hospital at the end of June 2013, unable to handle the media frenzy, his eldest daughter Makaziwe Mandela cried foul. She described the media as 'vultures, waiting when a lion has devoured the buffalo, waiting there...for the last carcasses.... They can violate everything in the book.... It's in bad taste. It's crass'.

Reports in the media, including newspapers, magazines and TV, need to be objective and unbiased. Trust is the cornerstone of journalistic success. When we switch on the television or pick up a newspaper, the basic assumption is that news reporting is impartial, dependable and truthful. There are several instances where this trust has been betrayed.

News Corporation: *News of the World's* Phone Hacking Scandal

In the cut-throat competitive world of news tabloids, Andy Coulson, the chief editor of the *News of the World*, the weekly paper, had set up a hyper-competitive environment within the organisation, to report gossip, scoops and revelations. One reporter calls it the *do whatever it takes* culture. The tabloid was illegally eavesdropping and intercepting calls on the mobile phones of royals, celebrities and politicians in Britain in the mid-2000s.

News of the World's chief reporter on the royals, Clive Goodman, and an investigator, Glenn Mulcaire, hacked into the voicemail of Britain's royal household. Scotland Yard tracked this eavesdropping and discovered that the tabloid eavesdropped on the private telephone calls of the members of the royal family, including Princes Harry and William, in 2005. This helped it report confidential information the next day with alarming promptness and accuracy. Goodman and Mulcaire apologised for *gross invasion of privacy* in early 2007. Both the men were sentenced to several months of imprisonment and dismissed by the *News of the World*.

But that was not the end. It was discovered in 2011 that the *News of the World* had repeatedly hacked the voicemail account of a British schoolgirl who was reported missing in 2002 and later murdered. This phone-tapping by the tabloid took place when no one knew what had happened to her. Its actions were reprehensible, since it not only intercepted messages left on the girl's phone, but also deleted some of these when her voice mailbox became full, so that new messages could be tapped. This gave hope to the girl's family and confused the investigators that she was still alive, since she seemed to be deleting her messages, although she was long dead. Many other people are suing the tabloid because their phones have been hacked by it.

The New York Times reported that the *News of the World* was hardly alone in phone tapping and that it was an industry-wide practice to garner spicy gossip. Quoting a witness, a spokesperson of the newspaper said, 'Talk to any tabloid journalist in the UK, and they can tell you each phone company's four digit code' (referring to hacked phone codes) and that 'Every hack on every newspaper knew this was done'.

> *The News of the World*, owned by Rupert Murdoch's News Corporation, was shut down in July 2011 when it became clear that its reporters and editors had routinely eavesdropped on the private phone conversations of celebrities, as well as of a teenager who was abducted and murdered. Several investigations on phone hacking scandals are now under way. Andy Coulson, former editor at *the News of the World*, was convicted in June 2014.

BBC: Sex, Lies and Videos

The advent of the Internet has been eroding the moral values of traditional media, including TV, in more ways than one. Even the BBC has become involved in various scandals over the years. It wrongly implicated a senior Conservative Party politician, Alistair McAlpine, for sexual abuse at a children's home in North Wales in the 1970s and 1980s. Then a sexual abuse broke out in October 2012 when it was found that Jimmy Savile, one of the BBC's best known presenters for three decades, had abused around 300 young people for over four decades, some on the broadcaster's premises. Even after Savile's death at the age of 84 in October 2011, the BBC continued to cover up his heinous wrongdoings and killed the investigative report in its *Newsnight* programme, despite at least one lady reporting on tape that she had been molested by Savile. As the *Daily Mail's* headline aptly put it, 'BBC shelved Jimmy Savile's sex abuse investigation to protect its own reputation'.

By mid-2013, the BBC had received more than 150 complaints pertaining to sexual abuse and harassment from 81 of its current and former employees. What was more significant was that these horrendous episodes came to light when *The Daily Telegraph* unearthed them by filing a 'Freedom of Information' request. The revelations question the BBC's workplace culture, and what it may have condoned and overlooked (and continues to) over the years.

On disclosure of the horrendous Savile episode, the British Police started *Operation Yewtree* in 2013. A dozen of yesteryear celebrities, male predators who would help themselves to girls who came their way, were arrested—with many an instance when BBC looked the other way.

Tailpiece

'What the media offers is not just news, but entertainment that is intended to be consumed like food, forgotten, and the replaced by a new dish', said W.H. Auden. Talking about media, Samuel Butler once said, 'The most important service rendered by the press is of educating people to approach printed matter with distrust.' Such is the role of media, which we devour, but hate to admit, we do not trust.

FOOD NOT EXCLUDED FROM FRAUD

Delicious chicken legs served by **KFC** restaurants in China were found to contain chemical residue in 2012. KFC's parent **Yum Brands** sourced some of its chickens from farmers using excessive antibiotics in their chicken feed. Then, the world's leading producer of ketchup, **Kraft Foods**, bought tomato paste and puree with a high percentage of mould from **SK Foods** in 2009 and jeopardised the safety of the product. SK Foods had apparently bribed Kraft's buyers.

It was discovered that baby food products of the Nanshan Bywise brand, manufactured by **Hunan AVA Dairy Industry Co. Ltd.**, had excessive quantities of aflatoxin, a carcinogenic substance, in early 2013. **Cadbury** chocolates were recalled in the UK having found to be contaminated by *salmonella* bacteria, and food authorities in India found insects in the Cadbury chocolates some time ago. Not to be outdone, **Kellogg's** has been recalling its products over the last few years, first its popular cereals Apple Jacks, Corn Pops, Froot Loops and Honey Smacks in 2011 for a strange odour and taste, with consumers suffering from nausea and diarrhoea, and then in 2012, Mini-Wheats due to contamination by metal fragments.

Global companies with world renowned brands have on occasion sold unhealthy food products. So how do we know what we eat and drink are safe? Which kind of food is good for us? We move to herbal products to remain at safe distance from chemicals, but are we sure that we are protected?

Chinese herbal medicine, the supposed elixir of health, was found to contain residues of pesticide in a Greenpeace study. The story of pesticides being found in Chinese herbal medicine became gorier when it was found that 48 of the 65 samples from nine pharmacies in nine cities were tested positive for adulteration, with some samples containing banned substances and one a level that was 500 times higher than the EU maximum. Should you not think twice before you sip the next cup of Chinese herbal tea?

Food-related horror stories keep coming out of the closet. In India, 68% of the milk, loose or packed, sold in the country has been found to be contaminated, and it was the Central Government that informed the Supreme Court of this horrendous statistic in July 2013.

Counterfeit products abound in the food industry. In mid-2013, an almost invisible factory in English countryside was caught producing millions of bottles of counterfeit spirits filled in genuine vodka bottles and sold as Glen's Vodka. On analysis, it was found to contain methanol, which causes blindness.

The New York Times, quoting the US Manufacturer's Association, reported that adulteration and counterfeiting of global food and consumer products cost around $10–$15 billion every year. If this is true, it is frightening to imagine what is entering our stomachs every day.

Worldwide, food fraud is almost an epidemic. Fraudulent activities have been discovered in every country where food is produced. Be it turmeric or oil, chocolate or sugar, honey or vinegar, every food item with an economic value is vulnerable to adulteration and can be tainted. While fraudsters generally do not mean to harm humans, but their desire to make profits makes them callous that their actions can lead to fatalities. How do we sift the bad from the good?

Tailpiece

Most of us live to eat and not eat to live! 'There is no more sincere love than the love of food', said the legendary Irish playwright George Bernard Shaw. If food and liquor—basic human needs—are tampered with by their producers and providers, there are few crimes that can be more heinous than that.

What if I now tell you that **McDonald**'s so-called vegetarian delight, its mouth-watering French fries, were sometimes as fried in beef-flavoured oil to pep up their taste? **Burger King** served horse meat whopper-sandwiches; **Beech-Nut**, the famous Swiss baby food company, sold fake apple juice for babies without apple in it, but with corn syrup so that babies would lap it up. All these companies were found guilty of serious wrongdoing.

Isn't it time we stood up to be counted to concertedly initiate action against such acts?

2
Can We Trust Our Banks?

Bruno Koch, a lonely 83-year-old man, with no one to talk to usually, was delighted to receive a phone call from a person with a pleasant voice one afternoon, who said she was from National Health Net Online. She asked whether Bruno would like to update his health insurance card. 'Of course', said Bruno. He gave his bank account number—a mistake. A fraud followed. Money was withdrawn from his bank, but no new health insurance card ever arrived. The bank involved was the 140-year-old **Zions Bank** of Salt Lake City in the USA, which despite being aware of the suspicious activity of the telemarketer allowed money to flow out of Bruno's account. The bank was perhaps a conduit to the fraud.

Saquib Khan, a multi-millionaire with a wholesale cigarette and grocery business, wrote $82 million of worthless cheques to himself over a two-week period, deposited them in his bank and transferred the money to other bank accounts under his control. The bank, considering Khan's background, believing the money would be transferred in, allowed the funds transmissions, only to realise later that it was a fraud. Saquib took advantage of the trust the bank had on him, and the bank was negligent in not verifying deposit of funds before money was allowed to be transferred from it.

The nature and variety of banking fraud are many. There are (i) banks committing fraud, where self-aggrandisement is the prime motive; (ii) there is fraud committed *in* banks, where fraudsters are working within the banking system and (iii) fraud committed *on* banks where scamsters from outside defraud them.

EVEN BANKS COMMIT FRAUD

Do people trust banks? Quite a few do not. This is bad news, to say the least.

A survey conducted in 26 countries by Edelman in 2013 clearly indicated that 20 countries do not trust banks. Countries whose financial sectors were not affected by the worldwide recession place their trust in banks. In India, Singapore, Canada, Malaysia, Indonesia and the UAE, the majority of the people feel that banks provide good service. However, the overwhelming majority of people in the world do not think so. In Spain, Ireland and Italy, over two-thirds of the respondents are distrustful of the banking sector. In fact, globally, half of the respondents no longer trust banks.

Even in India where banks are trusted, it is surprising to know that over a three-year period up to March 2013, public sector banks lost almost INR 230 billion ($3.7 billion) due to cheating and forgery—a statistic revealed by none other than the Director of the investigating police agency—CBI, Ranjit Sinha.

You and I deposit our lifetime earnings and savings in banks. We expect our money to remain safe forever and that whenever we want to, we can withdraw our money. We also expect to receive a fair return from our savings in banks.

Dealing with a bank is a matter of trust. We take it for granted that banks are keeping our money safely, investing it carefully and collecting dues diligently. However, if banks do any mischief, this trust is lost and our faith in the banking system is battered. Any wrongdoing on the part of banks leads to the wheels of trade, commerce and industry getting clogged, which the banking system helps to run with your and my money.

Unfortunately, all over the world, sometime or the other, the banking system has failed to deliver on the confidence reposed on it. Numerous instances of mistrust, fraud, scams and cheating committed by banks have occurred across the world.

The biggest cause of banking-scandals is primarily due to internal factors in banks, for example, corruption, greed for enhanced compensation and conflict of interest' according to Edelman's 2013 Global Trust Survey.

Let us discuss a few instances of fraud and scandals in banks in recent times.

THE LIBOR SCANDAL: BANKS CAN FIX ANYTHING

'Can we reduce our fixings today please?' requested a trader. 'Yes no problem', replied the primary submitter of rates. 'I am like a whore's drawers', retorted the trader. These are some exchanges between a trader and a submitter, while manipulating Libor's benchmark, based on which millions of people pay or receive interest across the world.

London Interbank Offered Rates (Libor) is the most influential interest rate and the most controversial of late. It is a benchmark interest rate that affects how consumers and companies borrow money across the world. It reflects the cost at which a number of big banks can borrow unsecured funds from other big banks for a certain period and in a certain currency. This rate is used to price hundreds of trillions of dollars worth of loans, bonds and derivatives around the world. Libor is a reference rate for benchmarking interest rates charged by the financial community. It is set by the British Banker's Association (BBA), an industry group in London.

How is Libor fixed? Let us see how the Libor rates are fixed, since this will help us understand what went wrong and how the famous Libor Scandal took place. To fix the benchmark rate, every weekday, leading banks across the world submit figures to the BBA. These are the rates at which banks can borrow from other banks. On receipt of these daily rates, the association ignores the highest and lowest 25% of submissions. What remains is then averaged to calculate the Libor rate, which is calculated for 10 different currencies and 15 borrowing periods. Eighteen banks submit their respective rates to calculate the US dollar Libor.

What affects Libor? If Libor rates are set inaccurately or incorrectly, it could cause financial instability, mispricing of financial risks and asset bubbles. Unscrupulous insiders can cause havoc in financial systems and gain an unfair advantage by setting fraudulent benchmarks.

Which areas does Libor affect? Let us look at the two most important areas that are affected by Libor—*derivatives* and *debts*. In the case of derivatives, Libor is used as the benchmark to price financial instruments such as *swaps* and *futures* transactions. It is estimated that around $350 trillion in derivatives are tied to Libor. As regards debts or loans are concerned, Libor is often used as the base for fixing the interest to be charged on loans. It is understood that in the USA around half of mortgage and student loans are dependent on Libor.

How interest rates are fixed? Libor is used as the minimum base, and then an additional margin is charged, based on the risk profile of the debt.

What was the Libor scandal? The benchmark rates fixed were manipulated. The banks that feed information changed the rates while submitting them for consolidation. The final rates announced were either lower or higher, depending on a bank's targets and not on its true interest costs.

Did it affect customers? Yes, it did—both ways. Some customers, who borrowed based on Libor rates, need to thank Barclays for playing around with the rates, since the rates were mostly reduced rather than the other way round. Their housing and car loans were reduced, although artificially. However, investors in consumer loan-based products suffered. They earned lower income on their investments, since the rates were low balled.

Who played tricks? The list of banks involved in the Libor scandal includes the who's who of the banking community. Fines amounting to $5 billion have been imposed. **Barclays**, **UBS**, **Rabobank**, the **Royal Bank of Scotland** and **ICAP**, a London-based interdealer broker, have all been individually penalised for the wrongdoings of their employees. The EU fined a group of the world's largest banks in December 2013. **Citigroup**, **JP Morgan Chase**, **Deutsche Bank** and **Société Générale** were found to be among the recalcitrant lot.

Was it local or global? If the Western world was adversely affected, why leave the eastern hemisphere—has been the motto of the banks. Singapore authorities censured 20 of the world's largest banks over their attempt to manipulate the Singapore interbank rate (Sibor). The banks included the **Bank of America**, **JP Morgan**, **Credit Suisse**, **Citigroup** and **ING**. Around 133 traders at these firms have tried to influence the Sibor for their financial gain since 2007.

Now let us look at some of the banks and how they played the Libor game for their own benefit.

Barclays Bank

Barclays, the British multinational bank, played a major role in manipulating Libor rates. Between 2005 and 2007, the bank's employees working on its trading desks convinced other employees to accumulate and submit daily interest rates to fix Libor and alter the bank's rates. These alterations were suggested and done, based on the trading desk's derivative trading positions, to bolster the bank's profits. If the rates were reduced or shown to be higher, the benchmark rates would be correspondingly altered, and in turn, reduce or enhance the rates at which the bank traded on swaps or loan markets. Based on the request from the trading desks, some employees of Barclays coordinated with other banks to alter their rates as well. By influencing other banks, Barclays made sure that benchmark rates were altered.

Barclays did not stop here. During September 2008–March 2009, when the financial crisis was at its peak, it submitted artificially low rates to give the impression that it could borrow cheaply and that it was healthier than it actually was.

When manipulations in rates were taking place during 2005–07, interesting conversations took place among Barclays' employees to instigate one another to play the market.

On 13 September 2006, a senior trader from the bank's trading desk in New York wrote to a rate submitter, 'Hi guys, we got a big position in 3m Libor for the next three days. Can we please keep the Libor fixed at 5.39 for the next few days? It would really help. We do not want it to fix *any higher* than that', clearly suggesting that a rate should be fixed. On 14 December, 2006, another trader wrote to a rate submitter, 'For Monday, we are very long 3m cash here in NY and would like the setting to be set as *low* as possible', thereby suggesting a low rate. Yet another trader instructed a fellow rate submitter to set rates as high as possible, 'Please go for 5.36 Libor again, very important that the setting comes as *high* as possible.'

To summarise, Barclays engaged in two kinds of manipulations to help itself. First, it submitted false rates to help traders, mostly in-house, but sometimes to help other firms as well, to enable them to make money on bets taken. Secondly, it reduced its borrowing costs to make itself seem financially better off than it was.

> Barclays paid $450 million to authorities in the UK and the USA, admitting that it had manipulated the Libor.

UBS

The Swiss Bank engaged in deceptions between 2001 and 2010, where it reported forged rates to squeeze out extra profits for itself and side-track enquiries on its financial health. There were more than 2,000 instances of illegal acts involving dozens of employees.

In UBS, the wrongdoing mainly occurred in its Japanese unit, where traders colluded with other banks and brokerage firms to 'play' with yen-denominated Libor rates and fill its coffers. Its regulatory filings point out that the bank made more than 1,900 requests to brokers and other banks to alter the rate. UBS' employees also paid $24,000 per quarter to outside brokers, who helped in the rigging process, for 18 months. Moreover, numerous, colourful emails are on record, which reveal the 'game' UBS' employees were playing to pep up its balance sheets.

In September 2008, one of its employees, wanting to keep submitted interest rates low, wrote, 'I need you to keep it as *low* as possible. If you do that, will pay whatever you want, I'm a man of my word.' To retain rates unchanged, a UBS trader wrote to a broker, 'I will pay you, you know, 50,000 dollars, 100,000 dollars, whatever you want.'

At a time when borrowing costs were high, the bank's employees were artificially working to compress rates and project a healthy image. In July 2007, its employees were directed to err on the lower side of rate submissions. One employee thought there was something wrong and warned the others that things looked a bit 'dicey', saying, 'I'd be very careful how you play it ... might get people questioning you.'

In order to make things real while communicating false rates, the employees even altered the rates on computer screens. They celebrated when comments were made by employees on a fellow colleague to describe him as *superman* and encouraged others by saying, 'Be a hero today'.

UBS not only manipulated Libor, but was also involved in falsifying the Euro Interbank Offered Rate or Euribor and the Tokyo Interbank Offered Rate or Tibor.

> UBS agreed to a combined $1.5 billion in fines to settle with British and American authorities the multi-year interest rate manipulation charge against it—the largest fine on rigging. The bank's Japanese subsidiary pleaded guilty to the fraud.

RBS

The Royal Bank of Scotland (RBS) manipulated Libor rates rather casually. One trader joked that he 'shifted rates like a prostitute shifting her undergarments down and up'. RBS admitted that it manipulated Libor rates in Japanese yen and Swiss francs between 2006 and 2010. According to the UK Financial Service regulator, 21 RBS employees were involved in these manipulations, with 96 written requests from traders to submitters to alter rates.

> On February 2013, RBS agreed to pay a fine of £390 million ($600 million) to UK and US regulators, and admitted to criminal Libor price-fixing charges.

Tailpiece

A dozen banks, inter-dealer brokers and Libor-related scandal tarnished the name of the City of London, which was the conduit for tampering with Libor benchmark rates. In order to save the skins of millions of borrowers and lenders, NYSE Euronext, the transatlantic exchange operator, has taken over the much hallowed process of fixing Libor rates from 2014. Some banks have therefore lost the opportunity to profit at the cost of the public.

The Libor rate fixing scandal is not the only one where greedy bankers manipulated rates. Doubts have been cast on at least 15 banks on their rigging *spot foreign exchange* rates in the $5 trillion-a-day forex spot market.

MONEY LAUNDERING

Deep in the savannahs is an airstrip in Venezuela that is an important transit point for cocaine sent to the USA—usually sourced from Colombia. Cocaine consignments are sold to retailers in the USA, and payments are made to wholesale consignors in cash in small denominations of $10 or $20. The money then moves to border towns such as El Paso and is changed to larger denominations of $100 bills for ease of handling. It then moves to Mexico, where it filters to the business community, especially cash-based retailers such as restaurants and salons. It is then bought by several willing banks such as **HSBC** or **Wachovia**. The money can now be remitted from these banks to anywhere in the world. Thereafter, *money laundering* commences. The chain goes on, with the money again perhaps ending up in the hands of cocaine dealers and traffickers to start another cycle of drug dealing.

Money laundering is prohibited by almost the entire developed world, primarily because funds from the banking system may end up financing drug dealers or terrorism. The International Monetary Fund (IMF) and the World Bank have estimated that globally, a colossal sum of between $2 and $3 trillion is laundered every year.

Regulators have now become active and unafraid to penalise *entities* failing to comply with the principles of anti-money-laundering provisions.

Who do these provisions cover? Normally, anti-money laundering and anti-financing of terrorism regulations cover a wide range of business entities including banks, insurance companies, futures traders and dealers, trustee and finance companies, credit unions, certain financial advisors, casinos and finance leasing companies.

What do these entities need to do? The entities exposed to potential money laundering need to engage in written risk assessment, and set up programmes to detect, deter, manage and mitigate money-laundering risks. They should also appoint compliance officers. Customers generally need to provide more information, including on the source of funds.

Governments insist that *dirty money* created by money laundering and funding of terror, lying in the branch of a foreign bank, is 'frozen' and handed over to the jurisdictional government in which the bank is located. This is usually done through international law enforcement treaties requesting a country to act proactively by seizing and helping to stop funding of nefarious activities. However, these efforts usually work when the two countries are bound by treaties, but this is generally a dead end route.

Vatican Bank: Even God's Bank Launders Money

Italian initials IOR, formally known as the Institute for the Works of Religion, the Vatican Bank, set up by Pope Pius XII in 1942 to manage the Vatican's finances, has seen several investigations into its money laundering activities.

The bank has been struggling for a long time to dispute its reputation for lack of financial transparency. It does not generally give loans, but manages deposits and patrimony for certain religious institutions, clerics and accredited diplomats.

In 2010, Italian prosecutors had seized €23 million ($29 million) from a bank account in Rome, which was registered to IOR amid allegations of money-laundering violations. The Chairman of the bank, Ettore Gotti Tedeschi, was fired in May 2012 and is under investigation for money laundering.

The EU is pressuring the Vatican to clean up its operations and apply European banking regulations in their totality. The Vatican has been reluctant to disclose the identities of its account holders to external monetary authorities and subject itself to any sort of scrutiny for its past transactions. This has led some believe that it may be housing Italian political 'slush' funds or that some of its accounts are tied up to organised crime. The Italian authorities are scrutinising whether accounts held by clerics are in fact fronts for other interests. In fact, in 2012 July, a priest was arrested on charges for allowing a lawyer to use his Vatican Bank account for insurance frauds.

A high-ranking cleric was arrested in July 2013 after being accused of plotting to smuggle $26 million into Italy from Switzerland. Two top-ranking managers of the scandal-ridden bank resigned soon after.

Vatican, the modern abode of God, may not be bestowing its blessings in handling the Vatican Bank's financial affairs in a heavenly manner!

> Pope Francis has begun making sweeping changes to shake up the scandal-tainted Vatican's financial image. Plans are in place for the management of billions of euros being handed over to external banking specialists, subject to reviews by an auditor general.

HSBC: The Multinational Money Launderer

A multi-agency investigating agency, investigating over several years, discovered that HSBC has been involved in money-laundering activities involving transfer of billions of dollars to Mexican drug cartels through the American financial system in order to launder tainted money.

The bank has also apparently worked hand in hand with the Saudi Arabian banking system to link itself with terrorist organisations.

It failed to maintain an effective anti-money-laundering programme, conduct adequate due diligence on its foreign affiliates and violated UN-sponsored sanctions. Narcotic traffickers used accounts held with HSBC's subsidiaries to launder funds. Funds also landed in sanctioned countries with which the bank should not have conducted any business.

> HSBC paid $1.9 billion in December 2012 to settle charges of money laundering, and funding of Mexican drug cartels and Saudi Arabian terrorist outfits. The bank managed a *settlement* rather than an indictment. It entered a deferred prosecution agreement, admitting that it had violated New York State Law. According to its Group CEO, Stuart Gulliver, 'we accept responsibility for our past mistakes'.

ICICI, HDFC and Axis Bank

These India-based private sector banks were accused of money laundering in an undercover sting investigation carried out across the country in March 2013. Startling videos were exposed, which purportedly showed executives of these banks helping an undercover reporter posing as a minister's aide launder black money. Their attempt was to convert the ill-gotten money into 'white' money by using the banking system (in contravention of banking norms). Some of the schemes allegedly offered under the scheme included investing cash in insurance products and gold, in the bank's own investment schemes by opening fake accounts, using others' bank accounts to channel black money for a fee and demand drafts to make investments so that these did not show up in customers' bank accounts, allotting large lockers to customers to store cash, although banks' lockers should not be used for this purpose and many others.

It is alleged that one popular method of money laundering in the case of Indian banks is by their investing in insurance products.

People with lot of cash deposit it in insurance agents' bank accounts in tranches. Thereafter, the agents, through friendly contacts in amenable banks, help these people invest in insurance products after making demand drafts from the cash deposited. Any deposit in India, which is more than INR 50,000 ($800) needs to be made by cheque, and therefore people with unaccounted cash can follow the insurance route to convert black money into white money. Huge commissions from insurance companies entice the agents and banks to engage in these nefarious acts, and money launderers are able to legitimise their ill-gotten wealth.

> The Reserve Bank of India (RBI) imposed fines on all the three banks for violating guidelines on customers' identity 'Know Your Customer' (KYC) regulations in June 2013. Continuing its probe, the RBI fined 22 other banks INR 500 million ($8 million) when it found evidence of their violating money-laundering norms. These included the State Bank of India, the Bank of Baroda and the Punjab National Bank.

Money laundering involves withdrawal of funds from the banking system or routing it through the system and using it for illicit purposes. Banks need to conduct due diligence to prevent money being used for illicit purposes such as drug trafficking or terrorism. This is what many banks fail to do, either due to the lure of profits or their inadequate internal controls.

Tailpiece

New methods of money laundering are invented with monotonous regularity. Fraudsters have found art ideal for hiding their money laundering activities; in the art world deals are shrouded in secrecy and anonymity. For instance, a painting landed in the USA from Brazil with an air bill of $100 in 2007. It was discovered by US federal investigators in early 2013 that this was worth $8 million—a painting by the American artist Jean-Michel Basquiat. The objective was to remit the sum in the USA in kind (the painting) instead of cash.

MISS-SELLING BY BANKS

Banks are institutions in which we have always trusts. However, of late, this trust has got eroded in some cases, with several banks resorting to shortcuts to fill their coffers at the cost of the common man. Some banks have also been miss-selling risky products to unsuspecting investors.

Mortgaged-backed Securities

The well-known Hard Rock Hotel in downtown Chicago was looking for a loan in early 2007. Just when the boom period was ending, it took a risky mortgaged loan from **JP Morgan** like many home owners. It had to only pay interest, with no principal repayment obligation during the life of the loan. It was a good deal for Hard Rock at that time with minimum outgoing in loan servicing. JP Morgan merged this loan with other loans into a bond or commercial mortgaged-backed security. The resultant loan pool was what is commercially known as a Collateralised Debt Obligation (CDO). Credit rating agencies gave a triple AAA rating to it—notifying highest safety of loan repayment. JP Morgan sold the CDOs to investors. The recession began in 2008. Hard Rock failed to fulfil its interest payment obligations. Foreclosure was the only option. Investors faced losses on the CDO as its value suffered, but JP Morgan earned its commission.

During 2000 and 2006, numerous US bankers gave housing loans, based on the security of the financed properties. Many of the borrowers did not have loan repayment capabilities, yet loans were disbursed at a time when the housing market was red hot. Such loans were known as *sub-prime mortgage loans*. Bankers bundled hundreds of such loans together into bundled instruments, known as CDOs. The CDOs were either guaranteed by government-sponsored agencies such as **Fannie Mae** and **Freddie Mac** or they were insured with companies such as **AIG**. Most of these CDOs were then rated by rating agencies such as AAAs. With the highest ratings in hand, the banks comfortably off-loaded these instruments, together with their attendant risks, to global investors. This is where the trouble started.

What was the problem? Banks packaged sub-prime, sub-standard loans together with some prime mortgages, arranged credit insurance, got these loans rated and then sold them to investors. The sub-standard loans were thereafter hived off by banks to investors.

Why call it fraud? Investors thought they were buying risk-free investments, whereas these were poor-quality debts backed by borrowers with little ability to repay the loans they had taken. Moreover, the quality of mortgaged properties was sub-standard. Over $2.5 trillion CDOs were issued with AAA ratings around the world. Unfortunately, 90% of the AAAs was downgraded to junk status when the financial crisis began in 2007. Many investors lost money and the financial crisis set in.

Claims against banks? US banks are facing numerous lawsuits asserting that they sold shoddy mortgage securities that collapsed during the financial crisis. Claims have been filed for more than a $1 trillion worth of securities (backed by residential mortgages) against **Bank of America**, **JP Morgan**, **Wells Fargo**, **Citigroup** and others by investors, insurers, prosecutors and regulators.

What are the suits against? Banks are fighting on several fronts, including investors seeking to force them to buy back bad loans, prosecutors alleging fraud and regulators claiming that they have duped investors into buying bad mortgage securities.

What liabilities can banks have? If banks lose all the law suits, their estimated loss could go up to $300 billion. It is difficult to gauge how much banks have paid so far since the financial crisis, and how much they will need to pay to put the mortgage crisis behind them. However, there are expectations that future settlements may dwarf settlements paid till date, since only a small fraction of lawsuits against the banks have been settled so far.

Fallout of mortgage loan: Even after several years of the mortgage crisis, there are still millions of home-owners who owe more than their home is worth. These people are therefore still under the water. Consequently, many of them have given up their houses and settle their loans to whatever extent they could or have simply walked away from them, which tantamounts to *foreclosure*. Banks and investors both sit on the side-lines without doing very much, since any action taken by them would entail a loss for them. As the housing market improves, the scenario should improve and the values of homes exceed outstanding loan amounts.

Let us look at some instances of miss-selling. **Abacus Federal Savings Bank**, a New York-based small bank, mainly catering to the needs of the local Chinese community, were found to have inflated the qualifications of mortgage applicants to meet the standards for federal loans.

What the bank did was simple manipulation of mortgage loan seekers. On hundreds of loan applications, prospective borrowers were instructed to show higher than their actual earnings and asset value, and falsify their job titles. Abacus also created fake papers, which indicated that borrowers had enough money to make down-payments and this money had been gifted to them. This was done so that loans (typical mortgage-backed ones) given to borrowers were backed by the security of borrowers' property to meet Fannie Mae's requirements. (Fannie Mae is a government-sponsored mortgage bank, the Federal National Mortgage Association, which guarantees mortgage-backed loans of a minimum threshold quality issued by smaller banks, so mortgaged-backed loan papers can be resold to onward investors at a pre-decided discount.)

This fraud is similar to the stream of events that led to the financial crisis in 2008 when the risk of mortgages to borrowers was hidden and passed on to gullible investors by indicating that the loan papers were rock-solid in their quality. Abacus followed this fraudulent practice from May 2005 to February 2010. Manhattan prosecutors charged 19 of Abacus' employees for falsifying and cooking up loan papers to obtain government-backed guarantees.

In another instance where the investors were taken for a jolly good ride, **JP Morgan** was fined an unprecedented $13 billion by the US Justice Department in November 2013. The bank put together residential mortgage into complex securities between 2005 and 2008, and sold these with the false assertion that they were reasonably safe. It promised to alert investors about any likely risks in the securities, and gave the impression that JP Morgan had provided an additional layer of assurance. None of these were however honoured by the bank—a blatant example of miss-selling of mortgage-backed securities.

Tailpiece

Banks are showing a keen interest in settling their shoddy mortgage practice with regulatory bodies. **Citigroup** settled suspected mortgage misdeeds by paying a huge cash penalty of $7 billion in July 2014 and **Morgan Stanley** in February 2015 by agreeing to pay $2.6 billion. Many other banks are facing material threats from pending lawsuits.

Will penalising banks help in their ending their slapdash practices?

Tax Evasion Schemes

Worldwide, more than $3 trillion worth of annual tax revenue is lost by around 145 governments due to tax evasion. Banks sometimes help their clients to structure transactions to save or avoid paying tax.

One popular method is to deposit unaccounted or undeclared money in Swiss banks to take advantage of their tradition of maintaining banking secrecy. Many Swiss banks solicit deposits, promise secrecy on bank account details and enable their clients to avoid paying taxes on money deposited and interest accruing. Their view has been that since they do not have offices in foreign countries, depositors from these countries cannot be held liable for tax avoidance, since it is permissible under Swiss law to promote banking secrecy.

Certain countries, especially the USA, Germany, the UK and France, have been fighting hard for some time to rein in tax evasion through Swiss bank accounts—the world capital of offshore accounts prodded by the veil of secrecy.

Wegelin Bank, the oldest Swiss bank, has helped several US taxpayers hide more than $1 billion from its tax authorities. It seems that certain taxpayers first approached UBS, but only to discover that US tax guys were after them on disclosure-related issues since 2008. Smaller banks such as Wegelin then tapped clients fleeing from larger banks, and assured them secrecy. Between 2002 and 2010, it helped its clients set up secret accounts at the bank and helped them hide from the tax men the existence of their Swiss bank accounts and the income these generated.

> In January 2013, Wegelin Bank admitted that it had helped American citizens evade US taxes and had to pay $74 million in penalties. This is the first time any foreign financial institution pleaded guilty to tax violations.
>
> UBS, the largest Swiss bank, was also found guilty of helping its clients avoid tax, paid a fine of $780 million and turned over 4,500 clandestine accounts to save prosecution. The USA won its case against Swiss banks' tax evasion schemes.

Will the veil of secrecy ever be lifted from Swiss banks? There seems to be some possibility of this. Sixty countries, together with Switzerland, have signed a treaty to unmask the wealthy clients of these banks. Some banks have begun sharing their confidential data. However, the difficulty is that Switzerland has had a law since 1934, which makes violation of client confidentiality a crime for bank managers. The demand for more disclosures by several affected countries is jeopardising Swiss banks' tradition of secrecy. The secrecy of Swiss Bank accounts to protect the ill-begotten wealth of a few is likely to continue for some time.

Tailpiece

The desire to save tax is insatiable. When banks help their customers save tax, prudence often overtakes greed. Mitigation of risks should be the strategy to follow.

Wealth Management

Banks are usually allowed to offer wealth management services (including discretionary or advisory services), but not non-discretionary or investment management to its retail customers. However, whatever they do, it needs to be for the benefit of their customers.

A wealth manager in the Gurgaon branch of **Citibank** in India duped around three dozen high-net-worth individuals of INR 4,600 million ($74 million) by selling wealth management products promising returns of 20% in 2010. The bank's employee used its letterheads to offer a fictitious product and asked its customers to transfer funds into a Citibank account for further investment. The account was allegedly in the names of the employee's relatives. The money was siphoned off. How did Citi's internal system allow opening of such a bank account, given its KYC norms?

Some relationship managers sold a debt product, Debentures, from the Indian branches of **Standard Chartered Bank** to its private banking clients. It is alleged that the bank promised to buy these back at a higher price in 2010–11. The amount involved INR 1,500–2,000 million ($24–$32 million). It was illegal under banking regulations.

> Wealth management product sales regulations pertaining to banks are under examination by the RBI after Citibank and Standard Chartered Banks' fraudulent selling scams.

In order to beat yield ceilings in China, the **China Construction Bank** (CCB), the **Citic** and the **Huaxia Bank** began selling wealth management products in 2012. These typically offer higher returns than bank deposit rates of 4%–5%. The banks were selling loan products to onward investors by promising them higher returns, but this led to a wealth product scandal. The CCB's products comprised a mixture of equity, debt and money market instruments, Citic gave loans to steel companies and Huaxia's investments were in pawn shops and health care providers. Many of the borrowers defaulted, resulting in the banks failing to deliver the promised returns. The products backfired.

Tailpiece

Wealth management is all about the future—the past being only a guide. In bad times, scepticism overtakes desire. In good times, while optimism enthrals, it is often easier to lose money. Care and caution therefore need to drive ambition and aspirations in wealth management.

Derivatives

Derivative contracts are either used to protect risks or allow companies to speculate. Banks had structured derivatives, apparently for risk mitigation, in the past, but were in fact selling speculative instruments. They also overcharged corporate bodies and posed risks to the economy. **AIG** is one such organisation whose bets on derivatives went incredibly wrong and led this insurance company to the verge of collapse till it was extricated by the government.

In several cases, banks have sold derivatives as tools to engage in fraudulent acts. Some such incidences are discussed below.

Banks in India sold around INR 25 trillion ($400 billion) in foreign currency derivatives to an Indian corporate organisation at a time when the Indian currency was fluctuating wildly. From a level of INR 44 per US dollar in January 2007, it appreciated to INR 39 in January 2008, and then weakened to INR 49 in January 2009. It is during this volatile period that banks forecasted rates that frightened corporate organisations and led them to enter derivative structures to protect their inflows. For instance, in early 2007, banks forecasted further appreciation of the dollar from INR 39 to around INR 35. However, the reverse happened and the rupee swung the other way. Derivative products sold to the corporate world presumably to protect them left holders of derivatives with huge losses arising from the difference between the earlier spot price and the contracted price of foreign currencies.

The CBI reported in 2009 that these transactions violated the Indian Foreign Exchange Management Act, although it did not amount to criminal conspiracy. In 2011, the RBI levied token penalties on 19 Indian banks. These ranged from INR 0.5 million ($8,000) to INR 1.5 million ($25,000) and proved that the banks had miss-sold derivatives and should desist from such misdeeds in the future.

In the UK, the Financial Services Authority believes that *interest rate swaps* or *derivates* are being mis-sold to small businesses since 2002. **Barclays**, **HSBC**, **Lloyds** and the **Royal Bank of Scotland**, the four largest banks in the UK, have agreed to review individual sales and provide compensation to customers, if required.

Tailpiece

Regulations governing derivatives are weak and although the world is trying to rein in this 'instrument of mass destruction' (as aptly described by Warren Buffet), banks are trying to protect their profits. It is a war of wits, it remains to be seen who will win.

DANGEROUS BANKS: UNINSURED OR UNLICENSED

Banks are the veins of an economy through which the blood of its financial system flows. They are therefore regulated by the national governments of every country. They are licensed, required to follow laid-down rules and regulations, insured when required and subjected to supervision and audit by countries' regulatory bodies.

The Poles were happy to invest in **Amber Gold**, a para-bank, which purportedly invested in onions and potatoes and promised a 100% annual return in five years to unsuspecting depositors. Its website advertised 500 zloty ($160) deposits becoming 13,000 zloty when cashed in five years. The police arrested the head of the organisation on the suspicion of it offering illegal banking services. Investors are claiming that it has fleeced over 300 million zlotys and does not have even one-third of this amount as its assets. How can a bank ever give a 100% return unless it is illegal?

Fraud and scams take place when sham banks crop up in an economy.

Loan sharking, the coldly efficient marauders of loan markets, unorganised and unauthorised, also known as the black-loan market, is a problem in most countries. Perpetrators hide from the eyes of the regulators by running their operations underground. Incredibly efficient with quick disbursement of funds, making a minimum of fuss is the hallmark of their popularity. However, the downside are their very high interest rates, matched by their often inhuman recovery methods by using violence or threats, makes this mode of financing anti-social, undesirable and illegal.

Tailpiece

The tentacles of unlicensed banks have extended to the realms of anonymity—the cyberspace domain. **Liberty Reserve**, a digital global currency exchange outfit, helped money laundering of $6 billion and 55 million transactions being conducted around the world by bypassing banking regulations. By flouting banking regulations, cyber criminals and fraudsters can move money unhindered between Malaysia, Nigeria, Vietnam and Russia among other countries.

While Liberty Reserve's main conspirators were arrested in May 2013, but there are many more unlicensed financial outfits duping the unsuspecting even as you are reading this.

SHAM DEALS

While some banks can be shams, there can also be sham banking deals. Normally, banking transactions are assumed to be genuine, and it is this positive perception that banks sometimes take advantage of to make extra profits.

Enron, which lied to investors, regulators and employees to conceal its crumbling fortunes structured several sham deals to hide its high indebtedness and losses.

So, what did banks do? Between 1992 and 2001, some very credible banks engaged in con 'games'. Certain sham transactions were structured to help Enron project a robust balance sheet.

Barclays Bank structured several sham transactions by creating a Special Purpose Entity (SPE) in which Enron's debts were hidden. The SPE was named *Colonnade* after the street in London where Barclays was headquartered. Under the laws at that time, if the SPE had an external shareholding of more than 3%, its balance sheets were not to be consolidated with the parent company's balance sheet. Some portions of Enron's high debts were accounted for under the sham SPEs, hiding its huge debts. Barclays paid a fine of $144 million to settle fraud claims against it.

Enron roped in **Merrill Lynch** to help it to improve its finances. What did Merrill Lynch do? It structured two types of transactions—(i) a sham *sale* to boost year-end profits and (ii) a sham *option sale* to improve Enron's financial results. How was the sham sale structured? Merrill Lynch entered a sham *asset parking* arrangement with Enron on 29 December 1999 to boost the latter's sales and profits. It agreed to buy certain Nigerian barges from Enron with the express understanding that Enron would arrange to sell the barges to it within six months at a pre-determined rate of return.

This was a sham transaction, since the risks and rewards remained with Enron and did not pass on to Merrill Lynch. No sales or profits could be booked in the books of the seller unless a property or the accompanying risk in the assets sold was transferred to the buyer. However, in this case, this did not happen. Not only that, Merrill Lynch knew that Enron would be booking $28 million as revenue and $12 million as profits in this transaction. In 2000, Enron arranged to take Merrill Lynch out of the barge deal and gave it the pre-agreed rate of return.

How did the sham *option sale* take place? During the last days of 1999, Merrill Lynch and Enron entered two energy option transactions for a nominal term of four years. But the intent was clear that no option trade would take place for at least the next nine months, within which the transactions would be unwound (reversed). The option deal was unwound in June 2000 before the expiry of nine months and any transaction commenced under it. This added $50 million to Enron's income. Merrill Lynch charged it a fee of $8.5 million to structure this, was caught by the SEC for the fraudulent act and paid a fine of $80 million.

FRAUDULENT LOANS

Banks take deposits for short- or long-term periods from members of the public. However, funds deposited in banks do not lie idle. They are lent to others who use it in business, trade and commerce.

Before this money is lent, banks however need to make sure that the loaned amounts will be duly returned and the agreed interest paid. But, loans that are given without the requisite precautions may not be paid back.

Fraudulent loans are sometimes given by banks, breaking people's trust in them.

Afghan Bank—Bank of Kabul

Kabul Bank, one of the largest private banks in Afghanistan, came into existence after the Taliban era as part of the broad plan to implement a healthy financial system to get the country back on track.

However, in August 2010, panic-stricken depositors began withdrawing their savings, and the nascent financial system faced a collapse. In January 2011, it transpired that as much as $900 million has been siphoned off by well-connected bank officers, politicians and the high and mighty, including the brother of the then President of Afghanistan, Hamid Karzai, and a brother of the first Vice President, Mohammad Qasim Fahim.

The way the bank functioned was simple. It solicited deposits from members of the public through attractive advertisements and lucky draw schemes (with the lucky draw winners always being bank employees!). The loans were only disbursed to a few known persons, with an unwritten understanding that they were *gifts*. Fictitious companies were created with rubber stamps and other phony documentation to prove that the loans were being disbursed to genuine business concerns. It was almost a *Ponzi scheme*. Loans given to recipients were generally not returned, and the bank's coffers were filled by fresh deposits from the gullible public. These were again 'loaned' with a not-to-be returned understanding.

> In order to improve the banking sector, the Afghan Government split Kabul Bank into two parts in April 2011. One was the *good* bank with deposits and genuine loans, the other handled millions of dollars of bad loans. In April 2012, a special prosecutor was appointed to try all those involved in the near collapse of the bank and trials began in November 2012. In March 2013, an Afghan court convicted the founder and former CEO of the bank and sentenced him to five years imprisonment and a fine of $500 million. In total, 21 defendants were found guilty for their role in the bank's failure. This rescue mission cost the country 5% of its GDP and was one of the largest single bailouts relative to its size.

Citi, BankAm, Amex, Stan C, HSBC, Grindlays, Deutsche Bank, Federal Bank, Banque Indo-Suez and the British Bank of Middle East

India faced a huge stock market scandal in 1991 and several banks participated in the party.

In 1994, the RBI levied fines of $42 million on 10 foreign banks for their involvement in the securities scam. The list included **Citibank** and several others. Fines were also levied on 20 Indian commercial banks, including the **State Bank of India**.

The banks were indicted on account of illicitly diverting government bonds to a select few stock brokers to help them speculate in the stock market and misreport fund balances during the 1991 Indian stock market scam. The banks manipulated share prices to reach unreasonable heights for no real reason.

Fines were imposed on the banks for failing to fulfil the *cash reserve maintenance* requirement—their failure to maintain a minimum cash balance as required by the RBI's guidelines. There are several other examples where banks were found to have given loans fraudulently around the world.

The Greek financial institution, **Proton Bank**, controlled by a high-profile Greek oligarch, Lavrentis Lavrentiadis and his associates, gave hundreds of million of euros in bad loans to dormant companies. The Greek authorities arrested him in December 2012 and seized his assets on charges of embezzling from the bank to help his struggling businesses.

In another instance, several smaller **Brazil banks** have failed over the last two years, and there has been a move for stronger oversight. In October 2012, something strange happened in Brazil. The authorities arrested the well-connected father and son duo, Luis Felippe Indio da Costa and Luis Octavio Indio da Costa, the CEOs of a small bank that was purportedly involved in an accounting and loan scandal. The country has a history of banking scandals, but very few bankers have ever been arrested or imprisoned. People are upbeat about the fact that at last a banking oversight system is being thought of in Brazil.

Tailpiece

Many of us have taken loans. Fraud can take place while granting or taking of loans, since big money may be involved. Therefore, before signing on the dotted line, the giver or the taker should pause, think and then sign, lest there is fraud lurking around the corner!

CAMOUFLAGE AND CONCEALMENT: DISGUISING DEBTS

Banks provide loans that need to be repaid by borrowers in accordance with the terms of loans. Debts are loans taken by borrowers. However, if loan transactions are structured in the borrower's books as infusion of equity (instead of a debt), the quality of the borrower's balance sheet immediately improves (since *equity* is always looked at favourably as opposed to *debts*). Banks are often well placed to suggest to their clients (i.e., borrowers) ways and means to structure their loan transactions, so that these can be hidden from their books.

A complex financing deal was set up by **Citigroup** in 1999 through a Delaware company called Buconero (the Italian word for *black hole*). Citigroup loaned Buconero $137 million and the latter loaned the money to a Swiss subsidiary of *Parmalat,* which thereafter transferred this as *equity* (not debt) to several other subsidiaries of Parmalat. Citigroup received a fat fee of $7 million at a high rate of interest of 6%. It was alleged that Citigroup had structured the debt in a way that amounts loaned to a Parmalat group company (through Buconero) would eventually be shown as equity infusion by Parmalat, although it had all the trappings of debt.

Tailpiece

One hundred and fifty eight-year-old **Lehman Brothers** collapsed in September 2008, not only due to its unwise investments, but also because it had been concealing its borrowings of billions of dollars. An accounting sleight of hand could not save the company from collapsing.

ENDLESS POSSIBILITIES: MISCELLANEOUS BANKING FRAUD

Four employees in the UK branch of **UBS**, the Swiss Bank (in its International Wealth Division), engaged in unauthorised trading 39 times. There were systems and control failures in the bank, which allowed unauthorised transactions to take place in trading of currency and precious metals from January 2006 to December 2007. This fraudulent practice was discovered by a whistle-blower, who complained that a fund transfer was likely to take place from a customer's account to the personal account of a bank employee. UBS paid £8 million ($13 million) as a fine in November 2009 and $42 million as compensation to its clients.

Instances abound in the area of banking misfeasance. Moreover, it is often difficult to identify the exact cause of fraud in the banking sector. Frequently, it is a mixture of managements' greed and poor governance.

Italian Bank—Monte dei Paschi di Siena: Doctored Accounting

Founded in 1472, the oldest surviving bank in the world, Monte dei Paschi di Siena, popularly known as MPS, has stood the test for centuries during good and bad times. However, it ultimately succumbed to greed. Secret transactions were entered to hide and conceal huge problems faced by the bank for some time.

Ultimately, in February 2013, members of the public came to know that a loss of €730 million (around $1 billion) had been incurred by the bank due to several questionable transactions. While sketchy details were made available about the nature of the fraud perpetrated and the reasons for these issues, it seemed that the bank's shady practices included false accounting and its entering poorly structured derivative transactions.

MPS's problems mounted after it acquired the **Antonveneta Bank** for €9 billion ($11 billion) in 2008. This was an astronomical sum, which still defies logic. And what was strange was that MPS acquired Antonveneta just months after the Spanish bank Santander had bought it for €6.6 billion ($8 billion). There were charges of bribery on this transaction.

Spain—Bankia: Accounting Skulduggery

Bankia, a Spanish mortgage lender, has been accused of engaging in accounting irregularities in 2010, which led it to restate its financial results in 2011—with its profit figures of €300 million getting restated into a loss of €3 billion! Bankia was seized by the Spanish Government in May 2012.

The bank was at the centre of the financial storm, which led Spain to seek a European bailout of €100 billion ($125 billion) in 2012. The case has been highly politicised and one wonders whether the charges against the bank are genuine or arose from political vendetta. It is believed that the bank had longstanding ties with the then governing political party, the Popular Party. However, the main opposition political parties jumped into the bandwagon by casting aspersions on it, rightly or wrongly. Rodrigo Rato, the former Chairman of Bankia, has since vehemently opposed the Popular Party's questions in July 2012, saying he left a better bank than what he took over at the start of his two-year tenure at its helm.

Apart from lending, banks also conduct several other activities, including trading. They not only trade in foreign currencies, but also in energy-related products. Trading in electricity is one such business.

In January 2013, US officials found that **Deutsche Bank AG** was involved in *market manipulations* to make additional money while trading in electricity. The bank was slapped with a fine of $1.7 million, since it was found that its energy trading arm had made illicit profits from the California electricity marketplace in 2010. It was shocking that a bank of the stature of Deutsche Bank was found to have engaged in a fraudulent scheme by providing false and deceptive information in the deregulated electricity marketplace by inflating the value of its trade in order to make extra profits.

Deutsche Bank was not the only one. Other banks involved in manipulations in the energy market were **Barclays** and **JP Morgan**.

Tailpiece

Placing one's trust in banks is good, but placing blind faith in them may be foolhardy! Pretence and ruse cannot be ruled out. Display care and caution in bank dealings. It will be constructive.

BANKS ARE VICTIMS (FRAUD IN BANKS)

Is it not a scary thought that banks, in which we deposit our life's savings, are casualties of fraud themselves? Unfortunately this is sometimes true. Banks are often vulnerable to fraud perpetuated by their employees, contractors, customers or others who are involved with them. The reasons could be many, and may include failure of internal control systems, greedy management taking risks to maximise banks' returns or simply by fraudsters prying on financial service businesses.

Rogue Traders

Rogue Trader, a 1999 film where the lead actor risks everything to beat the system, depicts the story of a real-life rogue trader—Nick Leeson. He not only stole millions, but also led his employer, **Barings Bank**, to bankruptcy through gambling.

Banks are run by smart people. But some are smarter than the others, with sharp minds that are creative in engaging in more than ordinary business. Disaster strikes often when these so-called super-bankers are in important positions in banks, often resulting in huge losses to them, instead of turning banks into a money-making proposition. Very often, personal interests are linked to these acts, especially when bonuses are paid, based on the business size and profit volumes of banks.

There are several instances when employees, known to be super performers in banks, ended up engaging in activities that resulted in their employers incurring huge losses.

Société Générale

Such was the state of affairs in one of the France's largest and most respected banks, Société Générale, with a low-level employee creating havoc on the bank's balance sheet by incurring losses of €4.9 billion ($6 billion) through bad bets on stocks. An unassuming bank employee, Jerome Kerviel, managed to evade the multiple layers of computer controls and audits for over a year while committing this fraud. It was uncovered in January 2008, when the bank's risk-management team found that Kerviel was hiding his loss-making trading by offsetting it with fake orders to balance each of the genuine orders he had placed.

Kerviel had apparently learnt to hide losses during his earlier days in the bank's risk-management office, and he knew its back-office systems and controls very well. He created a fake client and named him Matt to cover unauthorised bets with brokers. When a broker raised questions about Matt, Kerviel explained that his rugby-loving client worked for a hedge fund and wanted to make a billion-dollar profit, and he was consequently pushing for more trade.

Kerviel was sentenced by a French court to three years in prison.

UBS

Kweku Adoboli was a director on exchange-traded funds and UBS' much vaunted Delta One derivative desk. This was a similar desk for which Kerviel worked at Société Générale. Adoboli carried out a series of unauthorised trading that resulted in a whopping loss of $2.3 billion to the bank between 2008 and 2011. The British regulator imposed one of its largest fines of $48 million on UBS, and sent Adoboli to jail for seven years. UBS was found to have serious weaknesses in the internal controls in its investment banking division. Lack of supervision from the bank's top management and seriously defective internal systems and controls enabled Adoboli to engage in unauthorised trading over such an extended period.

This was not the only time UBS suffered due to rogue traders. In 2009, the British regulator fined UBS £8 million ($12 million) when an employee in the bank's London Wealth Management unit conducted unauthorised trade with money belonging to its customers. A director of the British regulator—Financial Services Authority—commented, 'Failures of this kind in firms of the size and standing of UBS not only damage the firms concerned but also wider confidence in the integrity of markets and the financial system'.

Barings Bank

The venerable British merchant bank, Barings, collapsed in 1995 due to a rogue trader, Nick Leeson. After moving to Singapore, he became a star performer in the bank within a very short time. He took bets on ill-fated Japanese stock prices and bond markets, and incurred a loss of $1 billion within a two-week period. Leeson pleaded guilty of fraud and forgery, and was jailed for four years in Singapore.

How can a single individual, no matter how corrupt or misguided, bring down a bank within weeks? It seems that cost-cutting led to lack of supervision, and Leeson was asked to verify his own trade, since he was the chief trader and overseer. He took full advantage of this and *toppled* his employer.

Thereafter, Nick Leeson became rich and famous. His ghost-written memoir, *Rogue Trader* (1997), earned him a reported advance of $700,000. The memoire was later made into a film that was released a few days before his release from the prison. The *rogue* became renowned. Not stopping at this, Nick shared his experience by writing another book, *Back from the Brink: Coping with Stress* in 2005!

Citigroup

Citigroup's trader Gail Edmonds engaged in unauthorised trading in buying and selling gold and silver in 2002 and 2003. This resulted in a loss of $20 million to the bank. The rogue trader hid contracts and reported bogus prices, and exceeded her trading limits more than 75 times in the month prior to being dismissed in January 2003 when the hidden positions were discovered.

Citigroup was fined $0.5 million by the New York Stock Exchange (NYSE).

It was also reported that an internal audit conducted in 2000 had found that there was inadequate control in Citigroup's Precious Metals desk, but its management did not do anything about it. It is clear that laxity of controls led to this fiasco.

MF Global

The giant commodity broker MF Global fell victim to a trader, Evan Dooley, operating far away from the madding crowds of Wall Street, when he made unauthorised bets on wheat futures with money he did not possess. Dooley had bought 15,000 wheat future contracts, the equivalent of 10% of the monthly market size of such contracts. When MF Global found out, the trader had already run up losses of $141 million for the firm. Although it had an electronic system designed to prevent brokers from trading beyond a limit, MF Global had deactivated these controls for Dooley, since they slowed execution of the transactions. Dooley took advantage of the weakness of the controls.

There have been many other instances of rogue traders taking banks to the 'cleaners'.

A New York-based rogue bond trader, Toshihide Iguchi, caused the **Daiwa Bank** to lose more than $1 billion in the mid-1990s. He apparently told the *World Street Journal* that his days in jail were less painful than those when he was trying to hide his rogue trades. He also wrote a book, *The Confession*, which was widely read in Japan.

Malfunctioning of computers creates God-sent opportunities for fraudsters. Taking advantage of computer glitches, Joseph Jett, a former trader and head of the Government Bond desk of **Kidder, Peabody & Co.**, converted his loss-making trades into profits. He generated fake profits by entering non-existent trades into the company's computer system. Although Jett was never criminally charged, his firm fired him for a loss of $350 million in 1994.

Rogue traders can be so powerful that there are often nicknames given to them to depict their market prowess. The chief of copper trading operations in **Sumitomo Corporation** of Japan, Yasuo Hamanaka, a copper-market superstar prior to discovery of his misdeeds, was known as *Mr 5 per-cent*, referring to the share of world copper trade he was supposed to control. Through his rogue trades, Hamanaka brought about a loss of $2.6 billion to the bank. He pleaded guilty and was jailed till 2005.

EVEN BANKS ARE FALLIBLE: FAILURES IN INTERNAL CONTROLS

Internal control failures and ill-judged bets on derivatives caused JP Morgan Chase to lose a massive $6.2 billion. US bank regulators charged the bank for its failure in risk management that led to this enormous loss by a trader, nicknamed *Voldemort* and *London whale,* with his outsized trading positions going terribly wrong around April 2012. The bank would typically hedge positions and invest excess deposits available with it, but this is where it accrued losses due to internal systemic failures, its deficient governance, the failure of its internal audit process, inadequate management of its financial models and its failure to keep its board adequately informed.

Why did the large exposure on derivatives escape JP Morgan's internal control measures? The bank had unwisely kept very high limits of Value at Risk (VaR), an indicator of the maximum potential loss in trading. Therefore, the limits were not triggered due to high thresholds. This enabled the trader to breach risk limits. However, since he was keeping his exposure positions within the limits set and incurring losses, the bank's internal systems did not highlight this, nor did it take steps to stop it.

JP Morgan was engaged in breach of trust by taking huge risks by using depositors' money. The US and UK authorities fined the bank $920 million in September 2013 for the fiasco.

Banks ought to have proper internal controls, risk assessment and board oversight. Failures in any of these systems could lead to a hot-bed of fraud. Large bank losses have taken place, precisely due to this systemic shortcoming.

In another example of failure of controls in banks, a relationship manager of **Yes Bank**, an India-based bank, was accused of forgery amounting to INR 6.6 million ($110,000). The employee, who was working in the bank's wealth management division, forged the signature of one of its clients, made a duplicate client-company seal, changed the bank's original mandates with forged signatures and seal, and withdrew money from a maturing mutual fund investment.

Bribery among banking officials is an indication of the failure of banks' internal control systems. It has been alleged that the top officials of the **Bank of India**, **Central Bank of India**, **Punjab National Bank** and **LIC Housing Finance** have taken bribes of thousands of dollars from a Mumbai-based financial services firm, **Money Matters Group**, headed by Rajesh Sharma. The bribes were in exchange for loans to be sanctioned to corporate organisations that had applied for loans, but were hampered by the banking system. The names of 21 companies (including **DB Realty** and **Hindustan Construction**) were linked with Money Matters for giving bribes to obtain loans between 2009 and 2010. Eight senior officials of the financial institutions and three officers of the Money Matters Group were arrested and jailed for a period.

Tailpiece

William Feather, an American author, once said, 'Business and life are like a bank account—you cannot take out more than you put in'. But fraudsters try to do precisely that!

BANKS CAN BE VULNERABLE (FRAUD PERPETUATED *ON* BANKS)

Just imagine that you wake up one morning, open the newspaper and find written in bold—'Bank fraud wipes out millions'! When you delve deeper into the news report, you find that the concerned bank is where your lifetime savings are! The sinking feeling in your heart will be confounded with the immediate thought—'Is my money safe?' Such is the importance of safety and security in banks.

Banks need to be completely safe and secure as regards their depositors' money is concerned. They should not have any doubts about being able to take out their money when they need it. Otherwise, no one would ever deposit money in banks. However, it is common knowledge that banks are often defrauded and money is withdrawn by fraudulent means.

The security system of banks should be so robust that stealing money is impossible.

Let us look at some examples where fraud have been committed on banks.

Scamsters Love Our Credit–Debit Cards

Can you imagine $40 million stolen from prepaid debit cards issued by the Bank of Muscat in Oman in 36,000 transactions in 24 countries in 10 hours? This happened on 19 February 2013. It was one of the most sophisticated card fraud perpetrated in the cyberspace, where the hackers infiltrated credit card-processing companies, **ElectraCardSystems** in Pune and **EnStage** in Bangalore, handling Master and Visa cards in India. The fraudsters secured 12 account numbers of cards already issued and raised their withdrawal limits by hacking into the processing firms' systems. Eight men were indicted, of which one was found dead in the Dominican Republic.

In another example, around two dozen decent-looking young men were habitually stealing credit card data and using it to make counterfeit credit cards. The forged cards were used by them to buy electronic goods and then re-sold at a profit throughout the USA in 2009–11. They stole over a million dollars, and used their own yahoo email accounts to buy, store and sell the goods. It took the US Secret Service to unearth the scam, since the original credit card holders were blissfully ignorant of the fact that they were piling up liabilities with their banks till the settlement bills came to them a month later.

Debit–credit card thefts may affect anyone, since we all use them and they are frequently the vehicle through which we make payments at retail outlets. However, when a credit card is swiped in the market place, can there be the possibility of someone stealing the card number for unauthorised use later on? What if the card is swiped more than once and money taken out multiple times?

Credit card fraud can be of various types and take many forms. The objective of a fraudster may be to purchase goods without paying for them or to obtain unauthorised funds from a bank account.

Credit card fraud is also an adjunct to *identity theft or theft of identity fraud*. In this case, imposters steal the credit card identities of the holders, including their names, dates of birth and social security numbers (wherever applicable) and uses this to plant their own details on these. Thereby, the imposters assume the identities of customers with sound credit profiles, and thereafter obtain fresh credit cards to make purchases at the cost of the victims of identity theft.

In order to catch credit card thieves, the FBI laid a trap to outsmart them in June 2012. Hackers are usually in search of information such as credit card numbers. The FBI created a site called Carder Profit, which looked enough like eBay for thieves to be attracted to steal card details. Once the hackers were lured by the website and tried to obtain card details from it they were caught by the FBI. After a two-year undercover exercise, authorities in 13 countries arrested 26 people who were engaging in cybercrimes. The arrests took in place in countries including Britain, Bosnia, Bulgaria, Norway and Germany. This type of operation warns hackers that their ability to prowl on the Internet with impunity is being hampered by multinational joint enforcement action being undertaken against them. However, they still continue to enter secure websites, often on overseas servers, to obtain personal data and card details.

Fishing for *Phishing*

The insidious act of *phishing* involves online scammers looking for crucial personal information in numerous fraudulent ways, including by sending emails and building websites that look too authentic to be ignored.

When an email comes to your mailbox from a Nigerian Minister asking for your personal details so that his heirlooms can be transferred to you as his trusted chosen one, you immediately know that the email needs to be ignored or deleted. But, when it comes from your father asking for your bank details so that he can complete his will, you would probably provide the details. The only difference is that even the second email is fake. This is known as *spear phishing*, which is proliferating rapidly, and comes from a trusted face with an authentic looking message. Google, Symantec and RSA Security have all been under attack from such pernicious attacks.

In January 2013, *The New York Times* suffered due to cyber-attacks and suspected spear phishing through emails to its employees. Spear phishing is an *art*—a message could seem to come from a colleague down the corridor, complete with the appropriate jargon, official language or acronyms usually used. It is very difficult to sift the chaff from the grain!

A huge financial fraud (based on phishing) was unearthed through Operation Phish Phry, which was carried out by the FBI in the USA in 2009. The victims had accounts in the Bank of America and Wells Fargo. The fraudsters tricked people into providing their personal banking information and stole around $2 million during 2007–09. The fraud was planned in Egypt, from where mass emails were sent that looked like authentic communication from banks. Whoever clicked on these email messages was directed to fake identical looking bank sites, where they were asked to enter personal information details pertaining to their bank accounts as well as their social security numbers and driving licences. Based on this information, fraudsters in the USA transferred funds to their own accounts and remitted some to their accomplices in Egypt.

In early 2011, a massive security breach took place where names and email addresses were stolen from a marketing firm, **Epsilon**, a unit of **Alliance Data**. The victims were customers of big names such as JP Morgan, Citibank, Target, Barclays, US Bancorp, Walt Disney, Ritz-Carlton and Best Buy. These sorts of fraudulent activities lead to phishing attacks, wherein emails are made to look as though they are from authentic business partners, but the main purpose of the fraudsters is only to acquire account numbers and other personal details of their victims.

The danger increases if the scammers can link names with banks. They can then devise highly customised means to phish for personal information—akin to spear phishing. Therefore, even the most mundane outsourcing of email marketing could be a security breach and make people targets of phishing.

Phishing attacks are on the rise. In 2013, $6 billion was lost around the world due to phishing attacks, compared to $1.5 billion in 2012. And according to the RSA Fraud Report published in January 2014, India incurred the highest loss of $225 million among the APAC countries.

Fraudster Haven: Internet Banking

A young scammer devised a plan to make money by using his laptop. He hacked into an unsuspecting local furnishing shop's Internet database and obtained a list of its debtors (i.e., customers who owed money to the shop). Thereafter, he sent *bad* cheques to the shopkeeper and also *over-paid* them. He then made an immediate request for refund of the excess payment, which the furnishing shop did readily by issuing *good* cheques. The man made money by just sitting at home! This is a typical Internet fraud.

Crimes pertaining to e-Commerce, online auctions, credit cards and Internet-bank overpayments are all under the ambit of Internet fraud, which has become rampant across the world with the introduction and advancement of the new technology gadgets.

Citibank: Even Citi Can Be Fooled!

Individuals' bank accounts are susceptible to fraud. However, when it strikes a bank such as Citi, it is a *shocker*.

Paul Amos, a Nigerian living in Singapore, as well as some of his accomplices, worked out an elaborate scheme to defraud Citibank. In September 2008, the bank received official-looking documents from officials of the Ethiopian Bank to honour its fax payment instructions. There was a list of officials who could be called to confirm such requests. The signature appeared to match that in Citibank's records. In October the same year, the bank received several faxes for money transfer. Citi transferred $27 million to accounts controlled by the fraudsters in Japan, South Korea, Cyprus and other countries.

It was a huge fraud that was perpetrated on the bank. The Ethiopian Bank's instructions came from Nigeria and not from National Bank of Ethiopia in Addis Ababa. The persons to be called for verification were fraudsters. The conspirators posed as bank officials and approved the money transfers. And Citi did not discover this before the money was transferred.

Bank of New York Mellon: Scamster Makes a Fool of Charity Funds

A young computer contract technician, Adeniyi Adeyemi, working with the Bank of New York Mellon, used his skills to steal more than $1 million from several charities and the identities of more than 150 bank employees. This continued from 2001 to 2009 without anyone noticing discrepancies in the bank. Money stolen from charities and employees were transferred to dummy accounts, and later withdrawn or credited to a second layer of dummy accounts.

Tailpiece

The tentacles of Internet fraud have extended to disguised Internet gambling. In most countries, gambling over the Internet is illegal. The owners of the three largest Internet poker companies, **Absolute Poker**, **Full Tilt Poker** and **PokerStars**, have been charged for conducting Internet betting operations through the banking channel between 2006 and 2011. They deceived US banks about their processing the proceeds from gambling by disguising the purpose of the payments. The companies accepted credit cards from players for a particular purpose, but the money was used to enable betting over the net.

TRICKING BANKS TO OBTAIN DEBTS

The US-based **Republic Bank**'s former president arranged to sanction $5 million in unsecured loans to himself while he was in office over a four-year period ending in 1990. He was sentenced to 155 years of imprisonment for obtaining these huge loans fraudulently.

The now defunct **Bank of Credit and Commerce International**, originally headquartered in Karachi and London, had unwritten rules and kept certain loan documents secret, even from its auditors. The bank took deposits from around a million customers across the world, only to provide millions of dollars as advance to its Arab and Pakistani owners and favoured customers. The loans were given without documentation in violation of banking lending limits. Thereby, bank loans were obtained by fraud committed by its shareholders.

These are examples of bank loans granted by fraudulent means. The methods are many, but the objective is the same—to take money out of banks illegally.

Around 1995, **Parmalat**, the Italian dairy giant, decided to obtain loans outside its books through fraudulent means, since the company was ineligible for fresh loans (because it was incurring losses in its operations, which was hidden from the outside world). The transaction was conducted through three overseas shell companies based in the Caribbean islands. They pretended to sell Parmalat's products and produced fake invoices, which were produced before banks for working-capital debt funding. Two objectives were met through this fraudulent act. First, funding was obtained on fake invoices, which did not exist. Second, this funding was for off-shore locations and protected the parent company's (Parmalat in Italy) balance sheet from reflecting its additional debts.

Then there was **Biotor Industries**, an Indian company manufacturing castor oil, duped several Indian banks including the Bank of Maharashtra, the Oriental Bank of Commerce, IDBI Bank and Central Bank of India of INR 15 billion ($240 million). The company received the sanction of banks for post-harvest loans to procure seeds from farmers directly for conversion into oil. In order to show their genuineness, the loans were supposed to have been given directly to the farmers by the banks. But instead, 8,000–9,000 bank accounts were opened in fictitious names and the amount was siphoned off through them. The matter came to light in January 2011, when the CBI undertook a probe. How did the banks allow opening of so many fictitious accounts? What happened to KYC norms? How did Biotor convince the banks about its business model?

WHY PAY BACK LOANS?

Whatever we borrow must be returned. Borrowings from banks are no different.

However, instances abound where loans are taken with fraudulent intent. Diversion of funds borrowed to other businesses or for personal use is common in the business world. Loans not being repaid could also be due to the adverse business conditions faced by the borrower.

Even newspapers, which are supposed to be the hallmark of objectivity, sometimes shun fairness when it comes to loans. **Deccan Chronicle Holdings**, an India-based media company publishing the *Deccan Chronicle* newspapers, has been charged by the public sector lender, Canara Bank, for siphoning off funds loaned to it. Deccan Chronicle seems to have engaged in fraudulent activities over the past several years. First, it entered multiple banking arrangements, which allows it to borrow from banks on a one-is-to-one basis without having in place a consortium system.

It is alleged that when the company borrowed these funds, it did not let all the banks know its true indebtedness. This was suppression of factual information. Then, its balance sheet of March 2011 reflected a cash balance of around INR 4 billion ($65 million), only to report a net debt of INR 43 billion ($690 million) at the end of 2012—perhaps by doctoring its accounts earlier. Third, doubting its corporate governance, Canara Bank appointed Deloitte to undertake a forensic audit on the company in September 2012. Deloitte could not trace the money lent to it, which led to the belief that the borrowed money may have been siphoned off.

> Several recovery proceedings have been initiated by the 28 banks duped, and some banks have begun to secure outstanding loans by selling pledged shares and properties.

MAKING A FOOL OF BANKS THROUGH FAULTY SECURITY

When any loan is taken, it is but natural that the borrower is asked to provide security, which could be an asset such as a property or fixed deposit receipts. Should the loan not be repaid on time, the lender has the right to recover the loan amount by encashing the security given. Therefore, the security provided must be genuine and its ownership should vest with the borrower.

However, loans are sometimes taken by companies by providing collaterals, which have already been previously offered as security to another institution.

Mideast Integrated Steel Ltd., a part of the **Mesco Group**, an Indian business conglomerate, offered shares for a loan taken from Industrial Promotion and Investment Corporation. These shares were already pledged with another lender, the Industrial Development Bank of India. The loan amount was INR 170 million ($3 million). This was naturally a fraudulent act, since the security for the loan was pledged twice.

> The promoters of the Mesco Group, Rita Singh and her husband J.K. Singh, were accused of cheating, fraud, forgery, diversion of funds and tax evasion. They were imprisoned for some time in mid-2000. The group was involved in several businesses including shoes, pharmaceuticals, shipping, airlines and steel.

ITSY-BITSY BANK FRAUD: MISCELLANEOUS CAUSES

Even the top brass of organisations may be involved in duping a bank. In August 2014, S.K. Jain, the Chairman of **Syndicate Bank**, was arrested for allegedly taking a bribe of INR 5 million ($80,000) for irregular enhancement of the credit limit of some companies, thereby bypassing the bank's rules. His arrest is the first of its kind in India's recent banking history.

The largest ever fraud in Iran's history, amounting to Dh 9.5 billion ($2.5 billion), took place between June 2009 and August 2011 when several **Iranian banks** were the victims of a massive fraud. It has been alleged that it was perpetrated by one man, referred to as 'Mr X' in the local media. The man apparently developed a network, used forged letters of credit to purchase assets and bought the largest steel producing company in Iran, Khuzestan Steel Company, through fraudulent means. He also unsuccessfully attempted to form a new bank. This was a good ploy—to steal money from normal banking channels to open an illegal bank in order to continue with personal aggrandisement schemes. The **Bank of Saderat** and seven other banks were hard hit by the fraud.

In another instance, some *intelligent* fraudsters recruited 94 people to perpetrate a money transfer fraud at **TD Bank NA**, a part of the Toronto-Dominion Bank group, by taking advantage of its lax internal control systems. This occurred in 2010–11. What the fraudsters perpetrated was a mix of economic crime, identity theft and cybercrime.

The methodology was that the new recruits deposited fraudulent cheques into TD Bank savings accounts from closed or non-existent TD Bank accounts with insufficient funds. The weak TD bank system allowed new account holders, who were using their real names, to transfer the money from their new savings bank accounts into their checking accounts, by-passing the waiting period to ensure that money was available in the savings bank accounts before the transfer. The transaction involved transfer of non-existent money into checking accounts. These funds were immediately withdrawn through ATM cards issued by TD Bank, which allowed withdrawal of sums as large as $5,000 and did not have any maximum withdrawal limit. Strangely enough, the perpetrators of the fraud were given a pittance (often only around a few hundred dollars and a meal at McDonalds) as reward for such a successful crime. While the entire amount involved did not exceed $1 million, it was the act of a small group of people with imaginative minds and criminal ideas to make profits.

The woes of TD Bank did not end there. In January 2012, it was found that it had played a role in a $1.2 billion Ponzi scheme, when an account in a TD Bank branch was used extensively and even a mock TD Bank website was set up, where the false account balances of investors were shown.

Tailpiece

'When money talks, the truth keeps silent', says a Russian proverb. Banking fraud is no different.

BANKS' FRAUD STORIES

Super brands with a global presence and too big to fail—banks are an integral part of our economy. But sometimes their conduct is not above board. There are horrendous stories of misuse of trust, management greed and lack of internal control in banks, when they need to be honest, efficient, transparent, worthy of their customers' confidence, ethical and have good governance. However, time and again, several have faltered.

UBS

When it comes to banking scandals, UBS beats all. The Swiss banking giant had a series of missteps in the recent past. At last, its Chief Executive, Oswald Grubel, resigned in November 2011 over a rogue trading scandal that raised fresh questions on the adequacy of financial control and supervision at the bank. Grubel decided to resign when the bank faced a loss of $2.3 billion due to a low-level rogue trader conducting unauthorised trade by sidestepping the bank's internal control mechanism. A series of crises, together with the loss caused by the rogue trader, made it impossible for Grubel to run the bank. Its reputation needed to be repaired. In November 2011, UBS had to pay £30 million ($45 million) in fines for having inadequate internal control systems, which enabled the rogue trader to cheat.

The name UBS means nothing. It is an amalgam of the former Union Bank of Switzerland, the Swiss Bank Corporation and the American investment bank, PaineWebber. It is reported that the bank's effort to grow at all costs had resulted in compromising its ethics and standards of banking behaviour. This led it to repeatedly falter in its path of growth and prosperity.

UBS was involved in rate manipulation of Libor and Euribor. The bank allowed a large group of its traders to collude with brokers to manipulate the benchmark rates. This led to its having to pay a huge fine of $1.5 billion in December 2011. UBS CEO, Sergio Ermotti, admitted, 'We discovered that the behaviour of certain employees was unacceptable. We deeply regret their inappropriate and unethical behaviour'.

UBS's employees conspired to rig bids in the municipal bond derivative market during 2001–06. Several of its former employees repeatedly manipulated the bidding process of municipal bond offerings, when local governmental entities and non-profit organisations wanted to invest in these bonds. In May 2011, UBS agreed to pay $160 million as fine for its misdeeds.

Between 2007 and 2009, UBS played an active role in structuring tax evasion products for wealthy Americans. The Justice Department of the USA publicly threatened it with criminal prosecution, since it was the most aggressive of all the banks to sell these *shady* products. The bank's executives would fan out to places where rich people usually congregated, for example, at golf courses and celebrity events—wherever there was whiff of the presence of the super-rich! In 2009, the Justice Department declared that UBS had conspired to enable 17,000 rich persons to engage in tax evasion. The bank agreed to pay a fine of $780 million and also to divulge the names of 4,500 of such account holders.

UBS sold its products by misleading customers. In 2008, the bank agreed to pay a fine of $150 million and repay its customers $19 billion, when it became clear that it had defrauded its customers by selling what it described as 'nearly risk-free auction-rate securities'. It knew fully well that the market was on the verge of collapsing and the products it was selling were risky. The markets shrank, and investors were stuck with products dumped by UBS executives.

UBS's asset management arm failed to put in place adequate procedures to prevent a former broker from defrauding its customers between June 1994 and March 1998. The trader invested customers' money in highly speculative gold mining companies, from which he received secret payments of $1 million. UBS' systems were too weak to *catch* these illegitimate acts. It was fined $0.5 million in August 2003.

One of the worst contravention of banking principles was UBS' involvement in the mortgage-backed securities market before it collapsed during the financial crisis in 2008. The bank incurred a loss of $38 billion, only to be bailed out by the Swiss Government. Suits have been filed against it, alleging that it knowingly sold sub-prime products to investors.

Time and again, UBS has involved itself in murky transactions. Moreover, despite its promises of rectifying it operations and its apologies, it continues to get into trouble.

JP Morgan Chase Bank

According to *The New York Times* report, US regulator accused JP Morgan of engaging in manipulative schemes, converting 'money-losing power plants into powerful profit centres' and making 'false and misleading statements'. These schemes were adopted by the bank to make an illegal profit of $83 million between September 2010 and June 2011, by selling energy to state energy bodies through false calculations, which made these appear attractive. This had a harmful effect on the US energy market.

After bailing out the nation's banks, Americans were of the opinion that they would rectify their ways and act responsibly, and that a repetition of the recklessness and fiascos, which led to the financial crisis, was unlikely to recur. However, such hopes and wishes were short-lived.

Almost immediately after emerging from the financial crisis, JP Morgan faced trading losses, arising from its bungled trade practices—which has come to be known as *London whale*—of around $6.2 billion in 2012. Jamie Dimon, the bank's CEO, blamed 'errors, sloppiness and bad judgement' for the losses, and said that they had occurred due to a hedging strategy that went wrong. Apparently this was a complicated hedging strategy that involved derivatives, which were set up to offset potential losses in the bank's holdings of bonds and loans. However, the hedge backfired and caused losses. Rather than offsetting its other potential losses through gains in derivatives, the product behaved the other way to counter losses. It seems ridiculous (and even its top management thinks so) that a bank of JP Morgan's size committed such basic errors.

JP Morgan did everything possible to hide these losses from the public. The Senate report, which investigated the mess, found out that it had hidden its money-losing derivative positions, that risk limits created to prevent losses were exceeded by the bank routinely and its risk models were modified to report lower than its actual losses. How could a bank with such a good reputation lie blatantly? How could its internal system fail to such an extent that it incurred such huge losses so that its underlying derivative trades exceeded $200 billion to record such losses?

In another instance, JP Morgan agreed to pay $227 million to settle complaints that it (together with 13 other banks) had abused housing loan foreclosure norms in January 2013. The banks wrongfully foreclosed on homeowners who should have been allowed to stay in their homes, which they had bought by taking housing loans from them. Such abuses included flawed paperwork, excessive fees, botched loan applications and wrongful evictions.

In July 2011, JP Morgan agreed to a $211 million settlement to resolve allegations that it had cheated the state governments in the USA by rigging the bidding process for reinvesting the proceeds of municipal bond transactions. Apparently, the bank won the investment business because it extracted information from bidding agents about its competitors' bids.

In recent times, JP Morgan, America's strongest bank, has been increasingly finding itself at the centre of unethical practices. In January 2014, it was fined $2.6 billion for non-disclosure of the dubious transactions of Bernard Madoff in the famous Ponzi scheme he was running. The Madoff Ponzi scheme was almost run exclusively through its various accounts with JP Morgan, but it failed to raise an alarm in spite of internal alerts being sounded.

To top it all, the bank paid an all-time record corporate fine of $13 billion in November 2013 for its dealings with soured mortgage securities and for failing to fully disclose the risks to investors buying mortgage securities between 2005 and 2008. More so, this was just after it struck a whopping $4.5 billion settlement with a group of investors over its sale of questionable mortgage-backed securities, which collapsed later.

During 2013, the bank paid penalty of $20 billion to settle some of its wrongdoings.

JP Morgan's spokesman summarised the state of affairs at the bank in March 2013 by saying, 'We are wholly to blame for our errors', and the US attorney in Manhattan, Preet Bharara, commented in January 2014, 'JP Morgan failed—and failed miserably', while imposing the Ponzi-related fine on it.

Goldman Sachs

The once untouchable money-making machine, an epitome of Wall Street's prowess, Goldman Sachs, had for decades been the embodiment of the best stock underwriting deals and attracted the best talents. The bank contributed the best brains to the American Government. These included its former CEO, Henry Paulson Jr, who was the former Treasury Secretary, and another CEO, Jon Corzine, who was a former New Jersey Governor.

Such was the halo around Goldman Sachs that several best sellers were written about the bank, and perhaps the highest number that used a particular bank's name. These included *Money and Power: How Goldman Sachs Came to Rule the World* by William Cohan, which states that while Goldman Sachs claims to be the perfect company, but behind its closed doors, it straddles the line between conflict of interest and legitimate deal-making, and upholds a culture of power struggles and toxic paranoia.

In 2010, the SEC accused Goldman Sachs of securities fraud, stating that the bank had created and sold a mortgage investment that was secretly intended to collapse. Goldman Sachs created an investment vehicle, Abacus 2007-AC1, in February 2007, so the bank and some of its clients could bet against the housing market and make money. A prominent hedge fund wagered that the housing bubble would burst. It did. The hedge fund earned money, but investors who bought the bonds lost $1 billion.

These included pension funds, insurance companies, European banks IKB and ABN Amro, which would have only profited if the bonds had gained value. They did not, since the housing market collapsed. The SEC imposed a penalty on Goldman Sachs, which agreed to pay $550 million (among the largest penalties levied on a Wall Street firm to settle charges of fraud).

Goldman Sachs was one of the many banks that created the now infamous CDOs—complex mortgage securities—when the housing market was booming between 2004 and 2007. The former Goldman Sachs trader, Fabrice Tourre, was found guilty of making misleading statements and compromising ethical standards, and the bank was fined $50 million for this in August 2013.

Neil Morrison, a vice president in Goldman Sachs, helped a politician, Timothy Cahill, campaign between 2008 and 2010. They gave the bank lucrative banking business in Massachusetts. A $12 million penalty was levied on Goldman Sachs to resolve such *pay to play* accusations. Morrison was apparently a fund-raiser and speechwriter during the working hours when he used Goldman Sachs' office infrastructure.

The bank failed to monitor a rogue trader, Matthew Taylor, who was trading equity derivatives in 2007. It fabricated huge positions to conceal its losses on $8.3 billion exposures and to protect his bonus. The trader pleaded guilty of falsification; Goldman Sachs paid $1.5 million to settle the case and lost $118 million when alleged deals unwound. The bank's control mechanism could not check and find out that the trader had exceeded the risk limits it had set.

A bestseller written by an ex-executive director perhaps summarises Goldman Sachs's activities aptly. *Why I Left Goldman Sachs* by Greg Smith describes Goldman Sachs as a mean-banker existing only for profits and often referring to its clients as *muppets* (puppets).

HSBC

HSBC has a presence in more than 80 countries and has more than 50 million customers. It advertises itself as 'a global bank with local thinking'. However, it is mired with controversies involving a long list of corporate governance-related issues. It will take a long time for this 'world's local bank' to emerge from the mess in which it has entangled itself.

Let us look at some of the issues the bank is battling with.

It has been charged and fined $1.9 billion for violations of money-laundering regulations and movement of tainted money through the banking system, involving transfer of funds to Mexican drug cartels and Saudi terrorist outfits.

The bank has been facing several lawsuits for having helped the multi-billion-dollar Ponzi scheme run by Bernard Madoff. Along with JP Morgan, it was alleged that it had turned a blind eye, even when internally it knew that Madoff's returns were too good to be true. In 2009, Madoff pleaded guilty of wrongdoing. Of the several class actions against HSBC, the bank settled one of them, filed by the Thema International Fund in Ireland, by paying $62.5 million (without admission of wrongdoing) in 2011.

Among the various banks that are being investigated on the Libor benchmark rate rigging and for colluding in fixing gold prices, HSBC is also under the scanner.

The bank has had its fingers in some of the major recent scandalous pies, including wealthy customers having accounts in its Swiss arm to evade tax. It is undergoing severe government and regulatory scrutiny—perhaps the most stringent ever undertaken in banking history.

'I very much regret HSBC's past failures and I apologise for them. Our controls should have been stronger and more effective', said the bank's CEO, Stuart Gulliver, in July 2012. This summarises the bank's ongoing woes.

Tailpiece

Robert Frost once said, 'A bank is a place where they lend you an umbrella in fair weather and ask for it back again when begins to rain'. Sometimes, it sounds so very familiar.

3

Quick-rich Financing Schemes

> Avarice, or the desire for gain, is a universal passion, which operates at all times, at all places, and on all persons.
> **David Hume**, Scottish philosopher.

It is this desire to get rich quickly that drives both fraudsters and their victims. Phantom schemes and fictitious stories are often conjured up by schemers to light the fire of desire in the greedy and propel them to fabricate fraudulent financing schemes.

Erich Fromm, a German social psychologist, once said, 'Greed is a bottomless pit, which exhausts the person in an endless effort to satisfy the need without ever reaching satisfaction.'

KING OF THE MONEYMAKING RACKET: THE PONZI SCHEME

Robin Hood, the hero in British folklore, would rob the rich to provide succour to the poor. Robin Hood's success was dependent on his ability to rob more and more rich persons. If his ability to rob the rich had been stopped, his providing relief to the poor would also have ceased. It was robbing Peter to pay Paul. This is the principle of the Ponzi Scheme at its basic level.

In a Ponzi Scheme, investors are wooed to join a plan where they receive more than market returns under the garb that the investment manager is savvy and has a secret recipe to obtain above-average returns from the money invested. Repayment of interest on time is made at the early stages. Investments from fresh investors are used to pay money payable to earlier investors. Once cash flow from new investors stops, the chain is broken and the scheme collapses.

Charles Ponzi is perhaps the most famous scamster in the history of financial fraud. The Ponzi Scheme is named after him. He started it, driven by the genuine intention of opening a Securities Exchange Company in December 1919. His plan was to buy international exchange coupons or postal reply coupons in European currencies at fixed and mostly outdated exchange rates, and sell them at a higher price in the USA, always generating a profit (commercially known as an *arbitrage gain*). But as time went by, he could not match the promised returns through the exchange scheme and began paying earlier investors by taking money from the new ones. The Ponzi Scheme was born. Charles was arrested in August 1920 when he was caught duping investors by luring them to buy foreign postage coupons, promising returns of 50% in 45 days.

The Ponzi Scheme works on fresh funds coming in to pay for the old money received. This is because such schemes have no legitimate sources of earning. At times of economic difficulties, people have little or no money to spare. Ponzi Schemes usually come to light during tough times when their continuously fooling people through intoxicating hopes of high returns dries up. All Ponzi Schemes, by definition, collapse. The question always is—when will they end?

Another aspect of a Ponzi Scheme is that it attracts gullible investors who fail to do their basic homework. It is the insatiable human desire for quick gains that lures people into such con schemes. The moment a smart perpetrator of such a scheme begins paying high returns in the beginning, the heady feeling of making a fast buck peps up investors. Now let us look at some famous Ponzi Schemes that are fairly similar.

- **Bernard Madoff**
  The biggest and widest Ponzi Scheme ever was perpetrated by Bernard Madoff who was sentenced to 150 years in prison at the age of 71. The fraud entrapped hundreds of

small investors, millionaires, celebrities, hedge funds, private foundations and even a charity run by Elie Wiesel, a Nobel Prize laureate.

A whopping $65 billion were invested by gullible customers in Madoff's scheme, and was all lost. Madoff, when he pleaded guilty in March 2009, said that his fraudulent scheme had begun in the early 1990s and not in the 1980s as the government contended.

His exact modus operandi was not clear, since he refused to explain it. All that he said was, 'I am responsible for a great deal of suffering and pain. I understand that'.

- **Allen Stanford—Stanford International Bank**

A bank in the Caribbean island of Antigua, with a credible name like the Stanford International Bank, defrauded 30,000 investors in 113 countries of $7 billion by issuing them fraudulent high-interest deposit certificates.

The scheme operated for over two decades, and no one suspected that anything was amiss. Such was the name and fame of Allen Stanford, a Texas-based investment banker fraudster. He received a knighthood, and owned a cricket team, yachts, jets and mansions.

Stanford siphoned off $2 billion for his personal expenses by issuing false financial statements, which indicated that investors' certificates of deposits were safe and arranged for auditor's certificates from Antiguan auditors whom he bribed.

Stanford was convicted in March 2012, and sentenced to 110 years of imprisonment.

- **Saradha Realty Ltd**

Tens of thousands of people fell into the charm trap of Sudipto Sen, a scamster, when he floated Saradha Realty Ltd. in West Bengal, India. Under the guise of a real estate business, his company collected deposits with a promised annual return of 12%–24%. The money was collected under the premise of booking new flats or land. Sen hoodwinked

SEBI, the market regulator, for over three years, and provided 60 boxes of bogus documents, promising another 170. The funds collected between April 2008 and April 2013 is estimated at INR 21 billion ($340 million). The company went bust in April 2013. Sen was arrested while fleeing in a car, having crossed over 2,000 kilometre to seek refuge in the dream valleys of Kashmir.

Ponzi Schemes in India

There is a long history of Ponzi or pyramid schemes in India. Financial products are sometimes also known as chit funds, which are essentially Ponzis. In the 1980s, **Sanchayita Investments** robbed people of INR 1.2 billion ($20 million). In the early 1990s, **Sanchayani Savings & Investments** defrauded investors of INR 2.1 billion ($35 million); in 1997, **Golden Forests** swindled depositors of INR 30 billion ($480 million); in 2012 **Stockguru** stole INR 10 billion ($160 million) from investors, and the list goes on.

The Indian market watchdog SEBI was not able to stop fly-by-night collective investment schemes earlier, since these were outside its official ambit. However, the Government's jaws have been getting strengthened since 2013 to empower SEBI, the regulator to crack down on Ponzi and other investment fraud.

Increasing awareness in the market and judicial activism is helping to reign in rogues and racketeers. The **Sahara Group**, purportedly India's largest private financial institution, has been under the scanner of the country's Supreme Court and market regulator SEBI. The group has been asked to return INR 200 billion ($3 billion), which it had apparently collected from millions of depositors. Whether this is a Ponzi Scheme or a money-laundering gateway for India's super-rich, or a hybrid of both, is yet not known. However, broader awareness in the market is likely to put a brake to the machinations of this 35-year-old company promoted by its founder Subrata Roy, and perhaps discourage many other fraudsters.

Ponzi Schemes in Russia

Russia continues to surprise when it comes to illegitimate means of making money. Even the former Chairman of the stock market regulator, Igor Kostikov, commented in August 2011, 'There are hundreds of foreign exchange (FX) clubs that are little more than pyramid (read, Ponzi) schemes. Nothing can be done to stop them, as they are completely legal at the moment'.

Ponzi Schemes masquerade as investment funds. Flashy large ads of FX clubs lure small investors with the hope of earning handsome returns. They then sign contracts at offices in Russia before investing their savings. When they want to withdraw their money, they are told, 'Sorry, the investment club made some mistakes and has lost all your money'. However, the clubs do not defraud everyone. Some investors get their money back, but most do not, since the balance is appropriated by the promoters. And there is no law to stop this falsehood!

Tailpiece

Greed and gullibility leads to proliferation of Ponzi Schemes. As you are reading this, somewhere in the world, a Ponzi Scheme is in operation and is eating away the savings of the naive and the innocent. The scheme is already hundred years old and will perhaps continue for another century until we become more prudent and less avaricious.

Ponzi Red Flags

Even a bull gets enraged on seeing a red flag. Why should it not be the same with people?

- *Beware of Goats, Birds, Wood Providing High Returns*
  Fraudulent schemes are launched with tall promises with monotonous regularity. In the last few years, investment in

goats, birds, pigs, teakwood, and of late, potatoes, are finding favour with fraudsters. All such schemes promise unusually high returns. In West Bengal, SEBI stopped a potato-bond scheme launched by **Sumangal Industries** in April 2013. The scheme fraudulently envisaged purchase of potatoes on behalf of investors during the cultivation season, storing them in cold storage and selling when prices increased. It promised 20%–100% return in 15 months—a typical Ponzi Scheme aimed at gullible investors.

- *Beware of Friends and Relatives*
  The success of Ponzi Schemes is due to a large number of so-called amateur selling agents, who normally sell these schemes among their circle of friends and relatives. Their trustworthiness pre-empts their being questioned on the authenticity of the schemes. In Kerala, an Emu bird (an Australian bird) scheme was launched by the **Susi Emu Farm**, promising that an investment of INR 150,000 ($2,500) would become INR 330,000 ($5,500) in two years. The scheme was marketed among friends, colleagues and relatives and the investors' money was lost.

- *Do Your Own Due Diligence*
  The value of conducting research in a scheme before investing is critical. A simple Google search of the company, the persons involved and the manager's name could reveal a lot. Easy, but not many do it! The lure of easy money is a temptation hard to resist. For example, **Beetal Livestock & Farm (P) Ltd.** solicited investments under their *Own your own goat scheme* in 2011–12, promising 2% monthly returns. According to its business model, Beetal would rear goats on behalf of investors. Since each goat gives birth to four kids every year, the kids would be sold to other investors, giving a four-fold return in the first year. The multiplying scheme was to continue giving multi-fold returns to investors. Proper due diligence could have easily revealed the hollowness of the scheme, since there was no surety that there were any goats at all and even if there were, their multiplying four-fold every year was unfeasible. This was a Ponzi Scheme.

- *Beware of High Returns*

  Any scheme promising high risk-free returns must be viewed with immense caution, if not ignored. A Mumbai-based company, **City Limousine (India)**, promised investors INR 4,000 ($65) every month for five years if each of them invested INR 97,000 ($1,550) in the scheme. The project was launched in 2002, supposedly to invest in buying cars that would run as taxis. A good idea, but the flaw was that the returns promised were not deliverable. The company had also issued post-dated cheques to gain credibility. The scheme went bust in 2007.

- *Consistent Earnings Are Worrying*

  Returns on investment fluctuate. Be suspicious of returns that are continuously generating a regular and high income, regardless of the general market scenario. **James Risher** and **Daniel Sebastian**, based in Florida, posed as a PE fund and lured over 100 investors with promises of annual returns of 124%. The duo feigned to be successful equity traders and publicized that their sophisticated trading strategies would generate substantial returns. They ran the $22 million scheme as long as the Ponzi chain was in vogue.

- *Difficulty in Receiving Dues*

  Suspicion should be immediately raised if payments are not received on time or any difficulty is faced in encashing an investment. Very often, a Ponzi schemer will want to roll over entitlements at higher promised returns. This is a sure sign of impending danger. The celebrated former University of Georgia football coach, a hall of fame inductee, **Jim Donnan**, offered a 50%–200% return on a so-called low-risk investment in **GLC Ltd**. He claimed to be a wholesale distributor who made profits by sourcing and distributing extra merchandise to discount stores. Most investors were college coaches and former athletes. In late 2009 and early 2010, Donnan could no longer pay the rates and the company began missing interest payments due to investors. It was a

Ponzi Scheme of $80 million, built on the trust reposed on an ex-coach of high repute.

- *Unregistered or Unlicensed Investment and Sellers*
  Ponzi Schemes are typically not registered and neither are the people selling them. To sell a financial product, registration of the investment scheme, as well as of the marketers, is mandatory in most jurisdictions. The absence of this procedure needs a big red flag to be raised. During 2005–08, **Agape World Inc.** falsely promised investors returns as high as 12%–14% in a few weeks. The scheme spread like wildfire in Long Island's middle-class communities as they promoted the offerings as being safe and profitable. None of the sales agents were registered with the appropriate registration authorities—SEC in this case, nor were they associated with a registered broker or dealer. Agape peddled non-existent investments and lured investors into a Ponzi Scheme.

- *Beware of Recruiting Further Distributors*
  There are savings schemes where payment of commission depends on the number of distributors recruited, and sells these to them rather than to other people. **SpeakAsia** was launched in India with great fanfare, splashing ads on TV and print media, as a market research company. People were to fill survey forms, and each person was also to get more people to join the scheme for handsome rewards. This was also a Ponzi Scheme.

- *Beware of Chit Funds*
  These savings schemes where each person from a group deposits a certain sum of money as an instalment. There is a periodical draw of lots and the winner gets a prize. Usually, these are Ponzi Schemes where payment to subscribers is dependent on payment being obtained from new members. **Fine Indisales Pvt. Ltd.**, an Orissa-based online chit fund, took deposits from taxi drivers, shopkeepers, rickshaw-pullers, etc. The Ponzi Scheme collapsed in two years. There are, however, genuine chit funds that invest money collected in legitimate programmes and give fair returns to their members.

- *Beware of the Lure of Internet-profit*
  Cyber-space, the face-less device, has the power to convince gullible people, through well-documented schemes and attractive websites, to sell non-existent dreams. Without due diligence, such schemes are potential fraud traps. A scheme generated on the website **ZeekRewards.com**, floated by the **Rex Venture Group**, was one of them. Investors were promised a 50% share in the company's daily profits for purchasing securities in the form of investment contracts. However, these were unregistered securities. It was a $600 million Ponzi Scheme.

Be wary of get-rich-quick schemes, since there are no easy ways of making money!

SELLING DREAMS THROUGH FALSEHOOD: THE PYRAMID SCHEME

Six *smart* individuals get together to launch a get-rich-quickly scheme and each of them contributes $10 to market a consumer product and share the profits equally. They go looking for six members each. In round two, 36 members (six multiplied by six) get together with $360 as their total contribution. In round three, each of the 36 members get another six new members and the total membership becomes 216. The total amount collected is $2,160 before distribution or use of the money collected. In round four, the membership number is to become 1,296, in round five 7,776, in round six 46,656, and if one goes on to rounds seven, eight, nine and ten, membership numbers would rise to 279,936, 1,679,616, 10,077,696 and ultimately 60,466,176, with the number at each stage being multiplied by six and assuming each new entrant is bringing in another six new members. The collection at this stage would be $600 million. If you proceed further to round 11, the membership number would increase to 362 million (membership of 60,466,176 at round 10 multiplied by six), higher than the population in the Euro zone, with the total amount collected being $3.6 billion! However, as you must realise, this sort of expansion is never possible.

Therefore, this scheme of multiplying numbers through a chain of new members being brought in by old members is bound to fail. This is a pyramid scheme and is always heading for a collapse.

A pyramid scheme is somewhat similar to a Ponzi Scheme. Both make promises about non-existent business or investment schemes. The returns are paid out of subsequent inflow of fresh funds. In Ponzi Schemes, returns are paid for some time out of new investors' contributions. This continues as long as investors are enrolled and pump in fresh cash, and old investors do not try to withdraw too much of their money.

In the case of pyramid schemes, there needs to be an ever-growing layer of new recruits to provide gains to earlier investors. Normally, fraudsters go to great lengths to make their programmes look like a legitimate multi-level marketing ones, but use the money coming in from new recruits to pay off early-stage investors. Eventually, the pyramid must collapse.

Multi-level Marketing: Most of us have heard of *Tupperware* parties, where high-end kitchenware is sold. It is an iconic marketing strategy to sell *one-on-one*—a typical multi-level marketing or direct selling initiative. It is a home-based business and not a pyramid scheme. There is no upfront *head hunting* or large investment fee from new recruits. It does not promote *inventory loading* by requiring distributors to buy large volumes of non-returnable inventory. Unfortunately, this multi-level marketing has been twisted by some intelligent folks to make illegitimate money—sans the product with genuine intent to sell. A similar example is *Amway Corporation*, a multi-level global seller of the famous *Nutrilite* and *Artistry* range of products.

Warning Signs: A pyramid scheme purports to sell a product, but often hides its pyramid structure. Such a structure usually has two flaws—loading of inventory and lack of retail sales.

Loading of inventory occurs when a company forces recruits to buy more products than they can ever sell, often at inflated prices.

If this happens, the people at the top, the ones who started the scheme, sit happily at the helm, reaping the benefits of contributions made by the chain of people below them. The bottom of the pyramid suffers, since they are unable to sell the inventory and are simply *stuck,* may be due to the high prices of the products.

Lack of retail sales is another red flag for pyramid schemes. Fraudsters frequently claim that their products are selling like hot cakes. In reality, such sales only take place between people inside the pyramid structure or to new recruits and not to consumers.

In a large pyramid scheme, the pyramid eventually becomes too big. The promoter cannot raise enough funds from new investors to pay earlier ones, and people lose money.

It is well known that a mammoth pyramid scheme, which was in existence in Albania, virtually made the country bankrupt, immediately after the fall of communism. More than 15% of Albania's three million people were duped by pyramid schemes.

Koscot

In the early 1970s, the US market regulator SEC examined a pyramid scheme, posting it against a legitimate multi-level marketing venture. Koscot Interplanetary Inc. made an offer to members of the public to become beauty advisors and sell its cosmetics. The company's incentive structure did not really encourage retail sales. Instead, it motivated members to pay $2,000 for the title of *supervisor* and purchase Koscot cosmetics worth $5,400. Bonuses were paid for recruiting others to make similar investments. This was an illegal entrepreneurial chain—a pyramid scheme.

A Philipino Scheme

The families of overseas workers were targeted with a pyramid scheme in the Philippines in the early 2000s. Investors were enticed to join an annual income scheme that promised returns of 60%. Investors were to recruit others, promising the same sort of returns.

Additionally, they were paid a commission for bringing in new members. The plot lasted as long as new customers were enrolled. The scheme and along with two others, collapsed at the same time, with two million victims who lost $2 billion—the largest ever fraud in the Philippines history.

Credit Development Corporation (CDI)

Operating a pyramid scheme in the financial sector, CDI lured customers by asking for an initial payment of $130 and subsequently monthly payments of $30. They could then become a part of its *Platinum Infinity Reward Program*, and thereafter of its *3*7 Forced Matrix*, which promised commissions going down seven layers. This required each participant to recruit just three members. CDI promised them a return of $18,000 a month. Apart from this, it also offered them an *unsecured* Visa or MasterCard, with a $5,000 credit limit, at a low interest rate of 6.9%. This offer was especially attractive to consumers with poor credit histories. *Guaranteed approval, no credit check, no verification* was an offer that was too hard for them to resist. This was a pyramid scheme, which duped hundreds of gullible consumers.

Steps to Avoid the Allure of a Pyramid Scheme

No one can help us if we do not help ourselves before investing in schemes. The following simple dos and don'ts will protect us from the greedy eyes of schemers and fraudsters:

1. Beware of exaggerated earning-related promises.
2. Beware of schemes that offer a commission for recruiting new members.
3. If there is the sale of a product involved, verify whether its inventory price is inflated and if members need to buy such costly inventory.

4. Find out whether members make most of their sales *within the pyramid scheme* or outside it.
5. Beware of any scheme that claims to have a secret plan, unique strategy, overseas connection or special relationships that are difficult to verify.
6. Beware of any scheme that delays in meeting commitments, while asking members to *retain faith* in them.
7. Since a pyramid scheme can only survive by getting new recruits, beware of promoters trying to appeal to a sense of community or solidarity while denigrating outsiders or sceptics.
8. Beware of modern, hi-tech or newly deregulated market-related schemes.

Tailpiece

Think twice! We all want to become rich overnight. Many a time, we fantasise about this. But there are no shortcuts to accumulating wealth. It needs patience, shedding of sweat, display of intellect and a bit of luck.

Be cautious, don't be imprudent; display discretion—instantaneous enriching schemes should neither enslave nor enshroud you. Beware of anyone selling you dreams by trying to entice you into schemes relating to goats, birds, potatoes and teakwood—these are likely to be pyramids of dreams!

4
Stock Market Swindles

Phone calls are often received from credible sounding financing firms, announcing that a stock with as bright a future as that of Infosys or Unilever is going cheap. News that a particular company is declaring a dividend, which should be picked up before the share price moves up is often circulated amongst friends and companions; false announcements of a company's financial performance is often placed on the Internet; fake companies are floated with multimillion-dollar ads announcing how brilliant its future plans are. All these enticing gullible investors to put in money in its equity capital, and instances abound in the stock marketplace of such bamboozles and bluffs.

Stock market fraud comes in all shades and sizes.

THE INSIDIOUS INSIDERS: INSIDER TRADING

Rajat Gupta, the former Chairman of *McKinsey & Company* and a director in *Goldman Sachs*, had a good friend, Raj Rajaratnam, the former head of **Galleon Group** hedge fund. The two started a Private Equity firm, Galleon, with Gupta contributing the proceeds of his gold-plated Rolodex watch to raise money for the fund. He was accused of leaking Goldman Sachs and Proctor & Gamble's boardroom secrets to Rajaratnam on several occasions from 2007 to 2009. In one such instance in 2008, Gupta, who had participated in a Goldman Sachs' board call during the financial crisis, learnt that the billionaire Warren Buffet would make a $5 billion investment in the firm. The call ended at 3.53 p.m. Seconds later, Gupta called Rajaratnam to give him the news. A minute later, Rajaratnam gave instructions to buy $35 million worth of shares in Goldman. The market closed at 4 p.m. This was insider trading. In October 2012, Gupta was sentenced to two years' imprisonment.

Insider trading now attracts stringent punishments.

In May 2013, the Federal Court of Manhattan sentenced Anthony Chiasson, the founder of hedge fund **Level Global Investors**, to six-and-a-half years of imprisonment and imposed a $7 million in fines for illegal profits made by trading shares in *Dell* and *Nvidia*. This was based on secret information obtained from inside sources in the companies. Chiasson used expert network firms, which were research outlets connecting money managers to the employees of public companies, to obtain inside classified information.

Historically, the Indian market-regulator SEBI has a poor record of fighting insider trading. However, it seems it is getting its act together. In 2007, **Reliance Petroleum Ltd. (RPL)** was merging into **Reliance Industries Ltd. (RIL)**. To keep up RPL's share price, RIL short-sold 4% of the former's shares—worth INR 40 billion ($650 million)—in the futures market, knowing very well that RPL's shares would need to be sold later due to the merger plans. RIL sold the shares in the spot-market later and made a good profit. It was taken to task for insider trading and was levied a penalty of INR 110 million ($2 million) in June 2014.

Investors in equity shares take a view on buying or selling shares based on information available in the public domain. This is the proper method, since every potential investor needs to have access to such information about a company and none of them are unequally placed with respect to any information that could affect their decision-making on the shares.

However, when an individual has access to non-public information, such a person is in a better position than others to take a decision on the price of the shares. This is *insider trading*. For example, the finance director of a corporation knows that it could fail to repay its debt. He can sell the shares he holds in anticipation of the downward swing on the market price of the company's shares due to the bad news. He may sell them in advance in anticipation of the fall in the share price and thereby prevent a possible loss to himself. He could also sell forward certain shares at the current price (technically known as *short selling*) and then purchase them when the price falls. He would thereby make a profit due to his being in possession of non-public information. This is insider trading.

Let us convert the example given above into numbers. As the finance director knows, there is going to be a default in his company repaying its loan, he would normally expect the share price to fall once this news hits the market. He could sell 1,000 shares at $10 per share (at the current market price) for delivery after 15 days. In 10 days, the loan default occurs. The price of the company's shares falls to $8 per share. He then buys the shares from the market at $8 and fulfils the original delivery obligation of $10 per share. He, thereby pockets $2 per share on 1,000 shares (or $2,000) just because he had access to non-public information of a probable loan default. Such acts of insider trading are treated as improper and illegal.

We can now look at a few notable instances of insider trading.

SAC Capital Advisors (SAC)

Since 1992, this $14 billion Stamford-based hedge fund founded by Steven Cohen had defied gravity by regularly returning 30% annual returns to investors. Naturally, the finger of suspicion pointed to its probable ruse and scheming.

The company was involved in illegal share trading, tied to a new Alzheimer's drug. SEC alleged that SAC Capital portfolio managers helped the company to sell nearly $1 billion worth of shares of the two drug companies, Elan and Wyeth, in July 2008 because they had obtained secret information from a doctor about the problems faced on clinical trials for a drug being developed by the organisations.

SAC agreed to plead guilty for insider trading violation in November 2013 and paid a record penalty of $1.8 billion, the highest ever by a Wall Street firm. In addition, it agreed to discontinue its business of managing money for outside investors.

The SAC settlement dwarfed other all others—including that of Raj Rajaratnam, who was convicted in 2011 ($156 million), and that of Ivan Boesky, who was involved in trading scandals (worth $100 million) in the 1980s.

Galleon Group

Raj Rajaratnam, the founder of the Galleon Group, was sentenced to the longest ever prison sentence for insider trading for 11 years in October 2011. He had used a corrupt network of well-placed informers, including former executives of IBM, Intel and McKinsey. This helped him make illicit stock trading gains of $72 million for his hedge fund.

In order to trap Rajaratnam, government agencies secretly recorded his telephone conversations over a nine-month period in 2008. They found him blatantly but secretly exchanging stock tips with corporate insiders and Galleon traders. 'Yesterday they agreed on, at least they've shaken hands', a tipster was recorded as reporting to Rajaratnam about an upcoming deal; 'I heard yesterday from somebody who's on the board of Goldman Sachs that they are going to lose $2 per share', Rajaratnam was heard telling one of his traders in advance of an announcement on earnings. This was ample evidence for nailing him on insider trading charges.

KPMG

Scot London, a Senior Partner in KPMG, routinely received envelopes with $100 bills wrapped in $10,000 bundles, expensive tickets to concerts and an expensive Rolex Cosmo-graph Daytona watch from Bryan Shaw, a jeweller. These gifts were given to him for sharing secret information about KPMG's clients. Based on these tips Shaw traded on shares, earning more than $1 million of illicit profits.

The clandestine information passed on by the KPMG partner included information on Herbalife, the nutritional supplement company; Skechers, the footwear manufacturers, and several others. Reports on quarterly earnings announcements of upcoming mergers and acquisitions were also passed on.

Both London and Shaw confessed to their wrongdoings in April 2013.

Martha Stewart Living Omnimedia

Innumerable ladies across the world savour and read Martha Stewart's lifestyle tips, try out her finger-licking recipes, decorate their homes with her ever-changing original ideas and spend hours watching her TV shows. She is a modern-era lifestyle icon. However, even such a rich and famous lady succumbed to the lure of making money in stocks by obtaining insider information about a company in which she held shares.

Found guilty, she was jailed for a year, paid a fine of $195,000 and was barred from serving as a director of any public company for five years.

In 2001 SEC complained that Ms Stewart received illicit tips from her broker, which helped her make illegal profits by selling around 4,000 of ImClone Systems' shares when she came to know that her friend Samuel Waksal, the company's founder, and his daughter were selling their own stock due to the failure of a cancer drug test. During the course of investigations Martha Stewart lied and tried to cover up her actions by altering phone messages from her broker.

Such is the ethical standard of certain iconic figures of our society!

Polaris Software Labs

All stock price-sensitive information needs to be provided to the stock market for all to know.

However, Arun Jain, the Chairman of Polaris, an Indian IT company, did not disclose that he had called off its proposed acquisition of Data Inc., a US-based IT enterprise, after due diligence in the second week of September 2000. He informed the stock exchange about this after two weeks.

While deliberately withholding this price-sensitive information, Jain dealt in around 15,000 shares during this intervening period to make unfair profits.

In October 2012, the Indian market regulator SEBI barred Jain from the securities market for two years as a punishment for the insider trading fraud.

Nomura

The over-ambitious Japanese bank, Nomura, faced a setback due to the loss of confidence arising from insider trading scandals. Japan witnessed heavy selling off of shares after a public offering, when share prices dropped significantly. Insider trading and sharing of classified non-public information seemed to be the reason for this trend.

During 2010, Nomura's employees in its institutional equity sales division gave tips to fund managers just before the bank's announcement of shares on three occasions. Based on the tips, the fund managers went short on the shares of issuing companies (and sold shares at a forward date at a predetermined price), expecting prices to go down, and then bought them back after the public issue when prices fell, and thereby made huge profits.

In November 2012, there were further reports of insider trading-related issues ahead of Japanese chip-maker Elpida's public offering.

Old habits die hard!

The bank acknowledged the wrongdoing. Its CEO and Chief Operating Officer resigned in July 2012, following allegations of insider trading in the bank.

Nomura has a history of scandals. In the 1990s, it admitted paying to cover its wealthy clients' trading losses and giving money to racketeers.

Tailpiece

Insider trading is a con game played all over the world. Making quick profits by providing key information and tipping off others by gaining confidential unpublished information are part of the racket to gain an edge over others and play the stock market to one's advantage. It is unlikely that such beneficial buying and selling will ever cease as long as stock markets exist.

BROKERS: BANNED AND DISCREDITED

When one loses money in the stock market, it is bad enough. But what is worse is when a broker one believes is helping in a deal absconds with the money. This is a double-whammy!

Harshad Mehta

In the 1990s, the darling of the Indian stock market was the flamboyant Harshad Mehta, a stockbroker. He was popularly known as the *Big Bull*, owing his pet name to the huge stock market upsurge he brought about during this period. He accomplished this by manipulating share prices. Mehta and 10 others were responsible for creating India's biggest banking and securities scandal of $1.3 billion. Around 10 banks lent millions of dollars to brokers against sham promissory notes, thereby making their loans unsecured. These loans were used to finance speculative transactions of shares. And when fraud was unearthed in mid-1992, several banks were struggling to save themselves from insolvency. The Big *Bull* created a massive *bear* market and wiped out one-fourth of India's market capitalisation!

Harshad, along with his two brothers, Ashwini and Sudhir, was arrested after a decade of the scam in 2001. They were charged with swindling millions of shares of more than 90 companies. Harshad Mehta died while in judicial custody in December 2001.

Ketan Parekh

Ketan Parekh, a broker in India, a former trainee of Harshad Mehta, borrowed INR 8 billion ($130 million) from Credit Swiss Group against false bank drafts. He was involved in engineering and technology stock scams during 1999–2001. Even after being banned from dealing in the market, it is reported that Parekh continued to operate through different *fronts* on a profit-sharing basis. He made significant profits between 2004 and 2008 and apparently used these to square-off some of his earlier debts.

In 2003, Parekh was disqualified from trading in the Indian stock market till 2017 by SEBI. However, according to reports, he continues to operate in the market through *friends*. Parekh is a master operator in the stock market and has the uncanny knack of identifying market pulse.

WHEN BROKERS CHEAT

When brokers cheat, trust is betrayed.

There are several ways in which brokers swindle. They can use clients' accounts without their knowledge. The police suspect some brokers of doing this in the Indian commodity exchange the National Spot Exchange Limited (NSEL)—the scam coming to light in 2014; brokers run away with money—stockbroker Hiten Dalal and two of Andhra Bank's officials siphoned off INR 1.3 billion ($21 million) by executing fake transactions in 1991; brokers help companies corner shares illegally (for example, brokerage firm **Motilal Oswal** helped companies corner shares meant for retail investors in IPOs during 2003–05 by opening 697 demat accounts at the same address).

Peter Bacanovic, the former **Merrill Lynch** broker for Martha Stewart, the founder of Martha Stewart Living Omnimedia, was barred from the industry and banned from working as a broker-dealer by SEC. This was for his aiding and abetting Ms Stewart in lying about her sale of shares in ImClone Systems. It is alleged that she made a profit of $51,000 from *sale of shares one day ahead of the public news* that Erbitux, a cancer drug from ImClone, was being rejected by drug regulators. (Erbitux was thereafter approved by the Food and Drug Administration in the USA.) Merrill Lynch fired Bacanovic in October 2002 after the news broke.

The Financial Industry Regulatory Authority in the USA announced in October 2012 that David Lerner, the founder of **David Lerner Associates**, a broking firm, had been debarred from associating himself with his own firm or any other brokerage firm. The firm was *making continuous misleading statements, a reason enough for such a ban*.

The cases cited above are just a few of several cases where brokers have been banned, debarred or suspended from working till the expiry of the term of limitation placed by the regulatory body or concerned judicial authority on them. The primary responsibility lies with the brokers on abiding by the terms of the limitation placed on them during the embargo. But you need to be careful as well!

Tailpiece

A child described his stock-broking father to his teacher by saying, 'Daddy is a fisherman—every time he hangs up his phone, he rubs his two palms in joy and exclaims, 'Caught another fish'!

Beware! A broker may help you buy low, but may sell even lower!

RAPID TRADING FOR A FAST BUCK

The power of 140 words—a hoax twitter was floated in late April 2013, saying, 'President Obama was injured in an explosion at the White House'. High frequency trading programmes in numerous computers picked up the keywords in milliseconds, *President injured in explosion*, and gave automated sale orders on stocks held. Stock markets crashed in the USA, wiping out $136 billion from the market value. In minutes, the news of the president being safe was known. The markets recovered. The power of fast trading was in full play. This can upset all calculations to make or break investment portfolios.

Fast trading is a high-frequency trading technique used by stock or commodity brokers, investment banks and hedge funds. Shares or commodities are scooped up in a single transaction, only to be off-loaded less than a second or so later before buying more. Millions of transactions can be traded and moved within minutes, if not seconds. These earn minimal profits. However, the sheer volume of the transactions enables fast traders to make money. Computers and advanced software are used to find such opportunities. This involves a split-second automated trading method, which is around 10 years old and is used by both small and large players. It is not illegal, but may alter market dynamics in seconds, as it did when the false news about Obama being injured was circulated in the market. Such is the popularity of fast trading, it now accounts for around half of all trading in the US stock market.

There are now threats of market manipulation by high-frequency traders, since regulators find it difficult to monitor trades due to the often complicated and computerised nature of transactions.

The system uses various types of algorithms, including the use of the computer search mechanism on the Internet, news sites and social media for keywords. It then fires orders within milliseconds to either buy or sell stocks, depending on the position traders are planning to take. This is known as *news aggregation*. The algorithms can also use artificial intelligence systems to predict the market stock movement by analysing historical data.

Insider trading is another area where fraud can occur through high-frequency trading, when sell-side brokers share information with buy-side firms to profit. **SAC Capital Advisors**, one of the world's largest hedge funds, has been found guilty of using information acquired by insider trading to conduct fast trading.

The high-speed stock market witnessed a significant malfunction in August 2012 with one of the major trading firms, **Knight Capital Group Inc.**, losing $440 million in 45 minutes after installing faulty software (meant for conducting frequency trading in line with trends in an evolving market).

In March 2013, the FBI and a new unit of SEC in the USA joined hands to examine hedge funds and firms that were using algorithm-based trading systems and practices.

It is believed that traders using fast trading methods manipulate the market by flooding it with quotes. This is known as *quote stuffing*. This implies placing of millions of orders (that are quickly cancelled) to drive others to trade in ways that benefit their positions. This practice is known as *layering*. It is alleged that it destabilises markets, places retail traders at a disadvantage and discourages them from entering the market.

Tailpiece

Do just 2 seconds count! **Thomson Reuters**, one of the world's top financial data providers, put in place an arrangement to sell new *consumer-sentiment data* to clients paying an extra fee of $6,000 a month, just two seconds ahead of other clients. This enabled high-frequency traders to place thousands of bets in these two intervening seconds. Such is the power of fast trading! (The matter is under probe by the New York State's Attorney General since July 2013.)

DECEITFUL LISTING

Who has not heard of **Facebook**? Would you believe that this highly credible company, which is an integral part of our cyber-related lifestyles, has committed fraud while listing its shares in the NYSE in May 2012? Prior to public issue of its shares, Facebook saw a general slowdown in its sales for the second quarter of 2012, but did not disclose this crucial information to the public, barring a few analysts. The chosen few perhaps avoided buying the offered shares at the increased price. The shares were issued at $38, only to witness a debacle on the first day of trading, with their price crashing to $27. A large number of investors lost millions of dollars!

Banks sometimes play foul at the time of IPOs (Initial Public Offering). They frequently advance money to potential investors for their own shares. Sounds strange, but it happened during **UCO Bank**'s INR 2.4 billion ($40 million) IPO in India in 2003. The shares were oversubscribed on the first day. It was later found that the bank gave loans to some companies to buy its shares. This was a fraud.

Another type of listing fraud is cornering share applications to obtain shares at a cheaper than market price and make a killing on their listing. Yes Bank, a private sector Indian bank, made its debut in the equity market in late 2005. It turned out that there was at least one individual who could beat the system. What he did was simple. He submitted 6,315 separate applications for shares in different names, but from the same address. His objective was to obtain as many share allotments as possible. How did the share depository (in this case **Karvy Stock Broking**) fail to notice this anomaly? This remains a mystery.

When money is sought from members of the public by way of equity or debt, it is important that a company makes fair and adequate disclosure of the state of its business affairs. Wrong, fraudulent or inadequate disclosure results in money being taken from the market without proper information being provided. Such activities can be penalised and may result in civil or criminal (or both) conviction, depending on the nature of the offence.

The first listing of shares in a stock market to raise funds from the public is known as an IPO. This usually provides early opportunities to investors to buy shares and make profits, as for the first time their shares will get market value, reflecting company's future growth prospects. Fraud can occur when an individual corners a large chunk of such shares to the detriment of others.

Purshottam Budhwani cornered the shares of 13 companies, including Suzlon Energy, during the heyday of the IPO scene in India between 2003 and 2005. He opened a large number of demat and bank accounts—all in fictitious names. By applying under different and numerous names, he was allocated shares under the *retail* category, depriving normal retail investors. He then sold the allotted shares in the open market and made large profits. Budhwani was fined INR 15 million ($0.25 million) for the IPO fraud in December 2012.

A textile and clothing maker, **Hontex International Holdings**, in mainland China had an IPO in Hong Kong and raised HK$1 billion ($130 million). On March 2010, the Hong Kong watchdog, the Securities and Futures Commission, froze Hontex's assets as well as those of four of its subsidiaries. The regulator alleged that Hontex had disclosed materially false and misleading information in its prospectus of December 2009. The information was such that it may have induced investors to subscribe for its shares. Essentially, the financial position of the company was materially overstated. Strangely enough, financial statements relating to its IPO were prepared by **KPMG**! Trading in the company's shares was suspended only two months after their listing once the regulator got to know of the fraud.

In another such case, **Onelife Capital Advisors**, hand-in-glove with its merchant banker **Atherstone Capital Markets Ltd.**, managed to hoodwink market investors when its IPO offering took place in September 2011. The shares were issued at a premium, despite the company's poor financial results. Investigations revealed that Onelife had made misstatements in its offer documents. Around three-fourth of the proceeds of the sale of the shares—INR 370 million ($6 million)—was siphoned off to **Fincare Financial & Consultancy Services** and **Precise Consulting & Engineering**. SEBI has banned all the four companies from operating in India's capital market.

Tailpiece

IPOs provide money-making opportunities to many—companies, early-bird investors, consultants, advisors, stock analysts and bankers. With so many entities having an axe to grind, should not care and caution be the buzzword?

CLEVER NORTH AMERICA-LISTED CHINESE COMPANIES

China is a great story to sell all over the world, with its high growth and strong financial indices. Taking advantage of this, several Chinese companies have found a way of raising equity funds by listing their companies in the US and Canadian stock markets.

To raise funds in any market, there needs to be proper disclosure of the state of a company's health. However, several instances have been found where some Chinese companies accessing the North American stock market have been found wanting in their disclosure and corporate governance standards. It is not new that fraud takes place in Chinese companies' stock prices, but this problem of poor corporate governance is aggravated in the case of small Chinese companies with little or no background that want to go for US securities listing.

Many companies involved in fraudulent practices have accessed public funding in the US market through the *reverse-merger* route, a course long used by shady organisations. This route enables their easy access to the stock market, without any significant due diligence being conducted by a local market regulator such as the SEC in the USA. Furthermore, many such companies use small US audit firms, which do not have the wherewithal to audit companies with a significant business presence in a foreign county, in this case, China.

In late 2011, US authorities initiated a crackdown on accounting fraud and other financial crimes committed by Chinese companies listed in US markets. Clearly, lot of investors are angry and feel cheated.

Auditors have now become more careful about what they sign, and some are resigning from assignments where they find there are ethical issues, which they would not like to endorse. For instance, in 2011–12, Deloitte Touche Tohmatsu resigned from **Boshiwa International Holdings**, since the firm was not satisfied with

Boshiwa's treatment of pre-payments amounting to ¥ 392 million ($60 million) to a supplier. Deloitte also resigned as the auditor of **Daqing Dairy Holdings Ltd.** on similar grounds.

Between 2007 and mid-2011, for which the Public Company Accounting Oversight Board made information available, more than 150 Chinese companies with a market capitalisation of over $13 billion entered US markets, mainly through the *reverse-merger-shell* route. Of this, around 50 companies filed for IPOs. Clearly, the shorter public scrutiny avoidance route is preferred by the Chinese.

Let us take a peep into some fraudulent practices undertaken by companies of Chinese origin in the North America region while raising funds from the market.

Inadequate Corporate Governance

A company which proposes to raise funds needs to display a proper corporate governance function and accurately communicate financial information. However, in its listing documents, **SinoTech Energy**, a China-based oil field service company that accessed the US stock market to raise $168 million in November 2010, claimed that it would spend $120 million on hydraulic drilling equipment, but in actuality, it bought much less. Furthermore, the company lied about the equipment it had bought and grossly overstated their value. To top it all, the company's chairperson and controlling shareholder, Qingzeng Liu, stole $40 million from the its bank account. Ernst & Young Hua Ming, the company's auditors, resigned from its role as its auditor in September 2011, NASDAQ delisted the company in January 2012 and SEC sued it for the misdeeds in April 2012.

Serious accounting problems dogged Deloitte, the auditor for **China MediaExpress**. The auditor resigned from its role in the company after having found grave issues with its accounts, including missing cash balances, in mid-2011. The list of concerns enumerated by Deloitte was lengthy and included suspicious bank balance confirmation procedures, the validity of some of the company's customers and the verifiability of its salary payments in cash.

Deloitte, which gave a clean chit to China MediaExpress in 2010, resigned from its role in the company in 2011, having discovered the gory details. It is difficult to understand and believe that how such a long list of misdemeanours could be unearthed in just one year!

A typical instance of poor corporate governance was **China Medical Technologies**, a Chinese company manufacturing medical devices and trading on the NYSE. Since mid-2012, the company stopped answering queries from rating agencies. This forced Standard & Poor's to cut its rating to the lowest category—D (default grade)—and stop dealing with it. It also followed the company's defaults on its payments due on bonds issued earlier. Adding to this, China Medical Technologies faced class action for accounting fraud and using fraudulent shell companies to conduct mergers and acquisition (M&A)-related transactions. While suspending trading of its shares temporarily in June 2012, SEC had clearly stated that there were questions about the accuracy of publicly disseminated information relating to the status of the company's officers and directors, the accuracy of its financial statements and the current status of its financial health. SEC statements said it all! It is the type of company of which one needs to be careful.

Market Manipulation

If it can be shown that the shares of a company are widely traded, more investors are attracted to invest in its shares. **AutoChina International** created a false impression of a liquid and active market for its stocks. The company, its director and some others fraudulently traded in its stock to boost its trading volume. SEC charged the company with fraud, along with its director and 11 investors, with market manipulations in April 2012.

What the company did was simple. Commencing in 2010, and for the next three months, so-called interested parties fraudulently traded in stocks and matched their orders. This involved one account selling shares to another at the same time and at the same price. This is popularly known as *wash trades*, which does not lead to any change of beneficial ownership of shares. SEC alleged that against an average daily volume of 18,000 shares, their average daily volumes increased to more than 139,000 shares between 1 November 2010 and 31 January 2011, giving a false impression of the market liquidity of their stocks.

False Declaration of Non-existent Cash

Deloitte Touche Tohmatsu, the auditor for **Longtop Financial Technologies**, a Chinese financial software company, while certifying its accounts for 31 March 2011, thought to themselves that there was something fishy about Longtop's cash balance. Historically, the company had been providing confirmation regarding its bank balance from the local branches of banks. Deloitte heard from the market, and especially from *bears*, that Longtop's software might not be as good as it was made out to be and its financial results were too good to be true. Something seemed amiss!

In March 2011, Deloitte sought confirmation of the company's cash balance from the bank's head office, instead of its local branch, which had been the earlier practice. Longtop got to know about this. Within hours, it stopped the confirmation process, stating that Deloitte was not its auditor. Deloitte resigned as the company's auditor, convinced that it did not have the reported cash balance, did not report significant bank borrowings in its balance sheet which was phony. A confrontation took place between the two in mid-May 2011.

Longtop was registered in the NYSE with a market capitalisation of around $2 billion. After its confrontation with its auditor, its trading in stocks stopped and it became worthless almost overnight.

This was a case of fraud perpetrated not only by the company, but also by local Chinese banks.

Diversion of Funds

Keyuan Petrochemicals, a China-based petrochemical company, systematically failed to disclose related party transactions and diverted funds. These transactions involved, apart from the CEO, controlling shareholders and entities controlled by the management and their family members. In addition, the company operated an off-balance cash account, which was used to pay for cash bonuses to senior officers' travel and entertainment expenses as well as the rent for the CEO's apartment. The cash account was also used to make cash and non-cash gifts to government officials in China. The company agreed to pay a penalty of $1 million to settle charges against it.

Diversion of funds is a huge problem. In January 2010, **China Natural Gas Inc.**, a China-based natural gas company, and its Chairman Qinan Ji were charged by SEC for defrauding investors by secretly providing loans out of the company funds (totalling around $14 million) to the chairperson's son and nephew. Moreover, the company did not disclose the true nature of the loans.

Diversion of Assets

Funds were obtained from investors in a company that had zero assets. The Chinese coal group, **Puda Coal**, devised a fraudulent scheme in which investors were made to believe they were investing in a Chinese coal company, which was in actuality an *empty shell* entity with no coal-producing assets. SEC alleged that Puda's Chairman Ming Zhao and its former CEO Liping Zhu had initiated a despicable scheme to defraud investors in September 2009.

Puda Coal Inc. had a coal mining subsidiary company, Shanxi Puda Coal, which was the only revenue-producing asset of the Puda Coal Group. Zhao secretly transferred 90% of Puda Coal Group's shareholding in Shanxi Coal to himself. After this was done, funds were raised in the name of Puda Coal Inc. from US investors by conducting two IPOs to supposedly raise capital to enable Shanxi Coal, Puda Coal's subsidiary, to acquire coal mines.

Investors were blissfully ignorant that Puda Coal, in whose shares they were investing, no longer owned Shanxi Coal's only worthwhile asset, since Zhao had already transferred it to his personal name under a secret manoeuvre conducted a while ago. Puda Coal became a shell company with no ongoing business operations, but public funds were raised after being looted through fraudulent disclosures and false promises. Hundreds of millions of dollars were wiped out by Zhao and Zhu, and left gullible investors high and dry.

Overstatement of Assets

Making foreign investors believe they are investing in a Chinese company with substantial assets, whereas it does not represent anything, constitutes fraud. A case in point is **Sino-Forest Corporation**, a Chinese timber company, listed on the Toronto Stock Exchange. The Ontario Securities Commission charged Sino-Forest for overstating its timber resources.

What did the company do? First, it entered complicated arrangements with affiliated companies to inflate revenues by circulating cash within them. Second, it recorded its same forestry assets several times over, exaggerating the value of its timber resources. Third, it fabricated false documents to camouflage actual ownership of the forest resources.

Allen Chen, Sino-Forest Corporation's former chairperson, has been charged with wrongdoing and violating the securities law. It may be pertinent to note that Allen had been once featured in the list of Canada's *greatest chief executives* by the prestigious publication, the *Financial Post*, Canada's national newspaper.

False Sense of Shareholding

You may be shocked to know that foreigners investing in Chinese assets may not in reality own anything. Chinese companies listed abroad often have a dubious structure, known as a *variable-interest entity*.

Basically, this involves the foreign-owned company in mainland China, holding interest in operating companies through profit-sharing licensing arrangements. This effectively distances its foreign shareholders from the asset-holding China-based company. Should the foreign shareholders wish to enforce their rights, the only option they would have is to sue the licensing company, but they cannot lay their hands directly on the operating company. Unusual perhaps, but this is the truth about many Chinese-based companies listed in North American markets.

Several Chinese companies, including **ChinaCast Education Corporation**, the education provider; **VIPshop**, the online Chinese retailer; **Baidu.com** and **Sohu.com**, the popular Chinese Internet companies seeking overseas funding have used this structure.

However, even after such unfortunate experiences three years ago, the shares of several Chinese Internet companies were snapped up in the USA when their IPOs were launched in 2014. Needless to say, these companies were structured as *variable-interest entities*.

Good luck to such investors, since under Chinese legal procedures it may take ages to settle share ownership rights if there is any dispute!

Consultants Making Hay While the Sun Shines

In an environment where Chinese entrepreneurs were selling the China story to investors in the USA, various consultants made merry providing imprudent advice to them. **Warner Technology & Investment Corporation**, a consultancy firm based in the USA, and its owner Huakang David Zhou helped more than 20 companies access US public funds through the reverse-merger route. In late 2012, SEC charged the firm and its owner of various violations of security law, while advising the companies. David Zhou also assumed operational roles in some of these companies.

The list of improprieties perpetrated by David Zhou and his team (mainly during 2007–10) included stealing funds from capital raised to fund his son's condo mortgage payments, collecting money from the issue proceeds of his own bank account and then deciding whom and how much to give it to.

What seems abundantly clear is that David Zhou is only one among many such fly-by-night operators who have sold the American dream to Chinese entrepreneurs, and vice-versa, through shady deals.

Tailpiece: Beware of the Dragon

Allegations of fraud and poor accounting practices have put pressure on the stock prices of Chinese companies listed on the US stock market. The US market regulator SEC has deregistered the securities of around 50 China-based companies and has filed around 40 fraud-related cases against some of them. This has made US funding much less attractive to Chinese entrepreneurs of late. The dice does not seem to be rolling in favour of Chinese dragons any longer.

5

Crime in Our Wired World

A Russian-led posse in Spain ganged up to pump in viruses through the Internet into the computers of unsuspecting users in almost 30 countries in 2011–12. The viruses locked the computers. The fraudsters then sent online extortion messages, called *ransomware*, to the users in the form of fake police warnings, demanding €100 ($120) for unlocking their computers. However, the computers of even those who paid remained locked. This is *cybercrime*. The network was busted by the European Police Agency in early 2013.

Around the world, homes and offices are being broken into every day, not by breaking locks or forcing open windows, but by breaking into computers with a criminal intent by hacking, and using malicious codes and other modes of cybercrime.

Cybercrime is an economic offence carried out on computers via the Internet. It involves the use of a large and ever-changing variety of tricks, and includes illegal downloading of files, data theft and loss, distribution of viruses, *pharming* (redirection of web information to another fraudulent site with a malevolent motive), *phishing* (theft of personal information such as bank passwords and account details) and computer hacking.

Development and progress are accompanied by pain at times. Cybercrime is the latest *kid on the block*, which has infiltrated the world of fraud world unheralded. And with more and more technological *razzmatazz* being thrust into our lives, cybercrime is bound to spread out its tentacles more pervasively.

Cybercrime is now a major risk, demanding immediate attention for any organisation where Internet is part of their business strategy, thus virtually engulfing every enterprise. All that you and me cannot touch and feel, the cyberscammers can.

According to Europol, victims lose a whopping €290 billion ($350 billion) every year due to digital crime around the world. This makes it more profitable than global trade in marijuana, cocaine and heroin combined. An early 2013 study sponsored by Hewlett Packard indicated that companies in the UK and Germany are the victims of at least one successful attack every week.

According to PwC's Global Economic Crime Survey 2014, among all the respondents the firm interviewed, one-fourth had been the prey of some form of economic fraud perpetrated by cybercrime, and one-tenth had suffered losses of more than $1 million. Furthermore, almost half of those who had been victimised by economic crime felt that the risk of cybercrime is growing significantly.

HOW CYBER GOONS OPERATE

The CEO of the giant American retailer **Target** had to resign in May 2014 due to the misdeeds of online intruders stealing 40 million of the company's digital customers' records. The story of how this was done is intriguing. The hackers broke into the computers of the retailer's supplier of heating and air-conditioning equipment, which had access to its login details. Once they penetrated Target's computer system, the cyber criminals installed malware on its point-of-sale tills to capture the debit and credit card details of the company's customers.

The scheming machinations of fraudsters operating in the virtual space are malicious and ever-changing. It is often their expertise in technology that helps these tricksters use to make money, propagate a cause or just disrupt functions for ulterior motives.

Corporate Cybercrime

- *Financial Fraud*
  Technology is frequently used as a tool to steal money. This involves hacking for profit. Phishing and pharming both fall under the ambit of this class of fraud. The latest technology is usually used to fool the unsuspecting and could include extremely credible looking emails and websites.
- *Snooping*
  Theft of critical organisational information for use by competitors or investors or others with a malicious intent constitutes corporate espionage. R&D data, development of new products, product launches, advertising strategies and other important classified data stored in computer systems, if stolen, can do great harm to an enterprise. For example, an employee leaving an organisation and stealing data by using a USB data card to use at his or her new workplace is a type of snooping.

Societal Intrusion into the Internet

- *Social activism*
  This could be a part of terrorism, although it could also have a possible social impact—build a positive public opinion on noble causes including anti-terrorism activities. A case in point is Bangladesh's national movement to build popular public opinion against Islamist fundamentalists in early 2013.
- *Hactivism*
  This involves the use of computer networks to further political ambitions. Fulfilment of political ideology is the aim, rather than making money. The objective of a hacker is to disrupt services and draw attention to a political or social cause. Crashing of several Israeli government sites following the country's aerial attacks on Gaza was an instance of hacktivism in 2012.

Violence and Combat-related Web Activities

- *Terrorism*
  Internet attacks by terrorists, who use these to their advantage and cause, is a huge threat. For instance, taking advantage of Internet mappings, for example, Google maps, could be a possible danger area, since it can help terrorist attacks. Cyber terrorism can cut off distribution of electricity and plunge a city or area into darkness, affect the performance of smartphones and alter their usage for ulterior purposes, adversely impact control systems in prisons as well as shut, maim or destroy potential targets of terrorism.
- *Warfare*
  Attacks on infrastructure can occur through the cyber route, negating or causing damage to state or corporate infrastructure. These are usually state-sponsored or perpetrated by individuals employed by governments. Power and water facilities, air-traffic control mechanisms, railway networks, defence facilities and many other critical national infrastructure are possible danger areas. Cyber warfare may involve in altering sub-marines and ships, and interfere with functioning of satellites. The USA's Intelligence Service revealed in March 2013 that cyber attacks are a more pressing threat to US security than Islamist terrorism.

WHAT'S NEXT?

Incidents of cybercrime and electronic fraud have been rising rapidly over the last two years or so. Globally, in terms of fraud-intensity, after-asset misappropriation, accouting frauds and corruption, cybercrime comes next. The good news is that there is increased general awareness of such crimes, growing media attention and the number of companies setting up cybercrime-related risk-assessment processes is on the rise.

Cyber fraud evolves every day with new vulnerabilities, new criminal methods and new victims. Advancement in technology makes it difficult to address the different kinds of cybercrime, and fraudsters are usually a step or two ahead.

Challenges in addressing cyber fraud will only increase with time, and not become less.

Cybercrime constitutes low-risk, high-reward games. Typically, a fraudster can be anywhere in the world and not be at the forefront to commit a crime, unlike in an asset-misappropriation fraud, where physical presence is usually a necessity.

Finding perpetrators of fraud and punishing them through the legal system is difficult under current legal systems. However, significant developments in the near term are expected in the area of cyber-related legislation to punish fraudsters.

WHO COMMITS CYBERCRIME?

The nature of cybercrime generally denotes that it is committed by *outsiders*. This was confirmed by PwC's Global Economic Crime Survey 2014. However, economic fraud is often committed by corporate insiders as well.

Increasingly, we are seeing the emergence of cyber lingos relating to conspirators or perpetrators of cyberspace crime. *Black Hats* are hackers engaging in cybercrime for money; *White Hats* are cyber terrorists who work on disrupting conventional cyber security; *Freenet* and *GNUnet* are software frameworks used by hackers to pursue their illegal activities.

WHAT ARE CYBERCRIME FALLOUTS?

Apart from financial implications, there could be several other fallouts from cybercrime. These could include reputational loss, a damaged brand image, low employee morale or disruption of services.

A few examples of perpetrators of cybercrime were found in a PwC study of 2011, and make an interesting reading. It included incidents of a disgruntled employee getting hold of a colleague's salary-related information and using it to his advantage; an employee accessing a colleague's email account and sending malicious emails from it, and bullying other members of the staff (cyber bullying); an employee misusing social media and a sensitive information relating to his company and sending it to outsiders; an employee accessing information pertaining to his company's accounts payable department; setting up a dummy supplier account and siphoning off funds.

CYBER SECURITY WORLD: A GLIMPSE

Since mid-2008, a gang targeted web users with invitations to watch a sexy video. Curious Internet users clicking on the link received a message to update their computers' Flash software. Simultaneously, a malware was automatically downloaded and hijacked their web searches. They then received an official-looking advertisement of fake antivirus software. The gang made millions of dollars from unsuspecting users who bought this software. The members of the gang reportedly hid in St. Petersburg, Russia, and announced their luxury holidays in locations such as Monte Carlo and Bali on Facebook. Russia seems to have become a hacker-haven.

- *Europe*

  Europe is a key target for cyber attackers due to its advanced Internet infrastructure and increasing dependence on Internet-based operations. The European Commission announced in March 2013 that companies operating in Europe, including banking and energy enterprises, need to report cyber security breaches or cybercrimes.

  On 1 January 2013, the European Commission established a European Cyber-Crime Centre at Europol. This will be the focal point of the EU's fight against cybercrime. It will help member states build operational and analytical capabilities for investigation and cooperation with their international partners.

- *USA*
  There have been many instances of cybercrime against financial institutions and energy companies in the USA. President Barack Obama highlighted this in his State of the Union address in early 2013, warning that 'our enemies are also seeking the ability to sabotage our power grid, our financial institutions, and our air traffic control systems.'

  US companies have begun buying cyber insurance, protecting risks arising from hacking attacks, computer viruses, data breaches, and so forth, due to their mounting concerns about digital security.

  The FBI is leading the national effort to investigate high-tech crimes, including intrusion into computer and major cyber fraud. It shares intelligence information worldwide to help countries be aware of emerging technological trends. 'We are building our lives around our wired and wireless networks. The question is, are we ready to work together to defend them? The FBI certainly is', claims the FBI.

- *South Korea*
  In March 2013, South Korea alleged that North Korea has committed cyberattacks on the computer networks of three of the former's broadcasters (KBS, MBC and YTN) and three banks (Shinhan Bank, NongHyup Bank and Jenju Bank). They expect further attacks and disruption.

  The South Korean Government has upgraded its defence against cyberattacks by tripling the number of monitors to counter hacking attacks.

- *India*
  Increasingly, India's core infrastructure, such as its power grid, transport network and financial system, is being connected to the Internet, and more and more data is being stored online. This has greatly increased the risk of possible cyberattacks.

  According to reports published in the *Sunday Economic Times* in March 2013, several departments of the Indian Government have been subjected to repeated cyberattacks.

These include the Prime Minister's Office, the Ministry of External Affairs, the Indo-Tibetan Border Police and the Defence Research and Development Organisation.

India is dipping into its talent pool to develop advanced cyber-security capabilities, a practice that is followed by the Chinese as well.

THE ORIGINATORS

TOR is an Internet technology that makes online users anonymous by bouncing data across the world, encrypting and de-encrypting data numerous times so that the original senders cannot be traced. This is just an example how originators of cybercrime can hide behind technology.

With the perpetrators being many a times hidden behind thick veils, it is difficult to find the originators of cybercrimes. The rest of the world casts aspersions on Russia and China for cyberattacks and hacking. While Europe and the USA are the primary targets of cyber attackers, Russia is the 'home of criminals' according to *Spamhaus*, a non-profit organisation based in Geneva and London, which tracks the Internet's spam sources. According to *Spamhaus*, Russia rarely arrests hackers and spammers, even when their identities are established.

Fingers have been pointed at Russia again. Just before the overthrow of Viktor Yanukovich's Government in March 2014, it was found that one of the most sophisticated attacks committed through the cyber weapon *Ouroboros* or snake, infected a large number of Ukrainian computer networks, including government ones. Ouroboros is capable of destroying computer networks, and has serious repercussions for the public.

Can Chinese hackers be far behind where Russians seem to have been successful? *Mandiant*, an American cyber security firm reported in February 2013 that Chinese hackers had broken into the networks of more than a hundred companies in English-speaking countries over many years to steal their intellectual property. *The*

Economist has reported that evidence is mounting on the Chinese Government sponsoring cyber theft of corporate secrets in the West.

However, Russia and China cannot be blamed for all the ills in the cyber domain. *Spamhaus* has alleged that seven of the top 10 spammers in the world are based in the former Soviet Union, Ukraine, Russia and Estonia. Iran has been the source of cyberattacks on financial institutions in the USA and perhaps on Saudi Aramco, mainly as a part of political espionage. Facebook, Twitter and Apple have been breached in recent times and doubts have been cast on hackers in Eastern Europe.

Cybercrimes occur in the virtual domain. It is always difficult to point fingers at the exact source of trouble. However, Eastern Europe and China may remain the dominant source of attackers for some time.

CORPORATE ORGANISATIONS UNDER ATTACK

In September 2012, the Chinese hacked the computer systems of *Telvent*, a monitoring company for more than half the oil and gas pipelines in North America. On discovering this, the company immediately shut down access to its customers' systems. US intelligence agencies are trying to find reasons for this hacking, suspecting motives that could either involve planting of bugs in the system to shut down the USA's power grid if there is any confrontation between the USA and China in the Pacific, or the Chinese may be looking for industrial secrets in the USA's energy domain to use these in own energy companies.

When new laptops were opened from packing boxes on numerous occasions in China, virus hidden in their hard drive was generated. These viruses started searching the Internet of other computers to corrupt them. *Microsoft* is waging a battle against such crimes due to its popular Windows operating system being the prime target for contamination by viruses.

Yes Bank, an Indian private sector bank, was attacked by cyber fraud in one of its customer's bank accounts in Mumbai in February 2013 when the customer complained that INR 10 million

($180,000) was stolen from his bank account by money being transferred through the Real Time Gross Settlement (RTGS) route. (RTGS is an online real-time system that allows money transfer between bank accounts.) The money was moved through several transfers to numerous bank accounts. This was a case of cybercrime involving online theft of money from a bank account.

And the list is unending. *Sony*'s PlayStation Network was attacked and 100 million user records stolen. The Spanish police were able to arrest some perpetrators in mid-2011.

The computer systems of *Lockheed Martin*, the defence contractor, and *Acer*, the computer manufacturer, have been breached. At *eBay*, encrypted customer passwords were stolen by its employee logins being hacked. Even *Apple* Mac users, who thought that cybercrime could not touch them, found their computers being infected by rogue viruses.

WHAT ARE THE PREVENTIVE ACTIONS THAT CAN BE TAKEN?

Cyberspace will never be completely secure.

Most cyber crooks can, however, be kept at bay, simply by allowing only approved programmes to run on companies' systems, patching software, conducting training for employees and constantly monitoring networks.

Cybercrime involves the use of technology, which keeps changing continuously. Therefore, an organisation needs to stay ahead, although it is generally fraudsters who are better at this cat-and-mouse game.

Preventive measures are not rocket science but a matter of organisational discipline and awareness. They include the following:

> *Training*: Making employees aware and training them constitute the fulcrum on which the fight against cybercrime can take place. The battle to win the technology mind-game can be well fought if employees are aware of potential dangers and are given primary training to handle these.

Update: Cyber technology is ever-changing. Data protection and computer security systems should be kept updated to keep pace with changing times. Any lag and fraudsters could take advantage of the lapse.

Response: An organisation should be capable of sounding an alarm and responding immediately as soon as cybercrime is detected. This is best handled by an identified group of trained people who are competent and capable of responding to such incidences.

CIO: CIOs (Chief Information Officer) should hold the primary responsibility for taking effective steps to combat cybercrime, including arranging awareness and training across organisations.

Cyber insurance: Data breaches and cyberattacks can be insured against in most countries. However, there is lack of knowledge the availability of such insurance—only around 30% of US companies have cyber insurance.

Top management: The most important part of an organisation is its top management and its board's awareness of potential threats, mitigating action taken by it and its knowledge of likely cybercrime fallouts. If its senior management is not supportive or lacks awareness, all actions taken by it will fail. The bad news is that according to a PwC survey, a quarter of its respondents indicated that there was no regular formal review of cybercrime threats by their CEOs and boards.

According to *The Economist*, the world spent a colossal $67 billion on information security in 2013. If we could only remember to update software and not forget to install antivirus programmes, we would perhaps remain a bit safer!

Tailpiece

The world is being increasingly digitised—connected technologically and wirelessly. To prevent the ever-growing menace of cyber criminals, we need to be first aware of related dangers and then acquire relevant knowledge to guard against the menace of cyber fraudsters. Otherwise, we should not be shocked to find our bank balance emptied one fine day!

'You can only be as good as this second. Someone is trying to break in', said Ajay Banga, CEO of MasterCard, as reported in *The New York Times* in January 2014. The scenario is unnerving.

6

Accounting: Cheating and Creativity

Some people cheat as they feel they cannot win otherwise. In business, this usually takes place to stay ahead in the game—to earn increased profits, a higher bonus or boost the share price for employee stock option gains. Window dressing of financial results, showing non-existent revenue, eliminating portions of debts are some of the means people use to cheat by hitch-hiking on accounting data.

However, accounting fraud is by no means easy and exciting. It takes quite a while to concoct, unlike back-dating stock options or insider trading, where quick results can be expected.

Accounting chicanery is one of the many modes by which the world of business cheat, as and when they do so.

Why do companies commit accounting-related fraud?

There could be several reasons. Sometimes the management refuses to convey that business is slowing down—fudging sales figures to show growth. Then there are stock price pressures on listed companies—and cooking books is an easy way of showing positive financial figures and keeping a company's share price high in stock markets. There could also be ESOPs, allocated to management—high-stock prices to help employees encash shares given by an employer. There can sometimes be a need to depress profits and pay a lower rate of Corporate Tax, to save outflow of cash. The list goes on and on.

Information generated by accounting is the prime means to decipher the health of an enterprise. How does one know whether a company is profitable or incurring losses? How can one find out whether it has adequate capital to run its business? All this information and others can be found by analysing financial information.

Therefore, if accounting records are fudged, altered or doctored, reports generated will obviously give an incorrect picture, which would normally be rosier than what the reality was.

While most businesses prepare their accounting records to present a positive picture of the health of the business, there are a few that play ducks and drakes with numbers.

Accounting fraud usually begins small—by cutting some corners here and enhancing some revenue there. Usually, the idea is to correct the misdemeanour in the ensuing quarter or year once the business scenario improves.

However, it is like riding a tiger—very difficult to disembark. Once the mischief is done, the next quarter's profits are never sufficient to undo mistakes committed in the past.

Accounting fraud involves improper maintenance of accounting books or non-adherence to generally accepted accounting principles (also known as GAAP). Accounting information should be prepared to convey a true and fair view of a company's commercial dealings and ultimately of its business.

However, if accounting information is given in a manner that it paints an incorrect picture, it amounts to accounting hocus-pocus.

Methodologies adopted by tricksters and fraudsters are numerous. It is almost impossible to describe each of these in this book. Therefore, the only way of getting a glimpse into the world of accounting skulduggery is to look at the common ones adopted by forgers, liars and swindlers.

TRICKY SALES REVENUE BOOKING

During 1998–2001, the management of **United Agri** (a **ConAgra Foods** subsidiary) encouraged an environment in which sales was increased by hook or by crook, to meet its unrealistic profit targets. The company forced recording of *deferred sales* (with actual sales taking place later) in its books of accounts, even when goods were not despatched to buyers. The buyers did not even ask for the deliveries and the risk for the goods remained with the seller. The result was gross over-reporting of sales and fraudulent accounting.

When accounting fraud is committed, what is the most likely area where it could occur? Based on historical evidence it usually involves *increasing sales*.

Propping up sales figures serves the purpose of showing growth in an organisation by depicting an increase in its activity level. It also normally portrays higher profits. If a company's sales are growing, the investing community are usually happy and look positively at it.

Incorrect booking of *sales* means that the revenue should not have been considered under accounting principles, but was booked to show a better than normal picture. This is a fraudulent act.

(The words *sales* and *revenue* are often used interchangeably and both have the same treatment in accounting books.)

Recording Sales Pending Fulfilment of Contractual Obligation

MicroStrategy Incorporated's CEO, COO and CFO concocted the sales figures of this US-based Business Intelligence software-providing company during 1998–99, booking sales against contracts that had not even been signed. Many of the contracts were signed after the end of the quarter, and yet, sales were booked against these contracts much before they were signed. Sales could not have been booked against unsigned customer contracts. Through this misdemeanour, the company showed profits, when it was actually incurring losses.

Revenue should be recognised in companies' books of accounts when obligations undertaken under a contract are fulfilled and not before.

Let us assume that a toothpaste manufacturer has received an order of $1,000 from a distributor. If the manufacturer makes the toothpaste and does not despatch the consignment, but records revenue of $1,000, this will amount to it falsely enhancing its sales.

Let us look at another instance where sales were boosted fraudulently.

In the late 1990s, the Enterprise Resource Planning (ERP) software giant, **Baan Corporation**, found its sales faltering. Its customers' focus on Y2K-related issues took ERP's sales to the background. The financial crisis contributed its bit. Baan panicked. During 1998–2000, it was alleged that the company had practised the fraudulent accounting practice of booking sales well ahead of actual sales. It booked sales of software, which were just getting ready for future supplies and not ready for shipment. It also booked sales of software transferred to related parties, but not sold. This was done to project a better than real picture of the company's financial health.

> Baan, a Dutch company, had its chips down in the late 1990s due to poor sales. Its attempt to prop up its performance through aggressive accounting practices earned it a bad name in the market. Customers stayed away from buying its software. With very little possibility of its revival, the company had to be sold to Invensys in 2000, and ultimately through several intermediate deals, to *Infor Global Solutions*.

Stretch Accounting Period

Normally, a publicly listed company needs to publish its financial results once every quarter. If the period of one quarter can be extended beyond three months fraudulently, then willy-nilly, its revenue figures will get overstated. For instance, a quarter has 90 days. However, if a company can bring forward seven days from the next quarter, its revenue figures will be overstated by one week, and its corresponding profits will also be overstated. This is a fraudulent accounting practice.

Between 1998 and 2000, **Computer Associates** (CA), the US-headquartered software giant, regularly extended its quarter-ending period. This helped it show higher revenue from contracts executed beyond the relevant quarter. The resultant higher profits helped it to meet Wall Street's expected profit projections. The company kept its accounting books open for several days after the end of each quarter to improperly record in that quarter revenue from contracts that were executed after expiration of the quarter ending period. By doing this, its quarterly revenues were inflated between 22% and 53%. This resulted in material misrepresentation of its results.

However, during the first quarter of 2001, CA attempted to correct its past over-reporting of quarterly sales by not recognising sales prematurely from contracts signed after the quarter ended. This resulted in the company missing its quarterly earnings estimates and its stock price crashed by 43% in one day.

In the case of CA, its executives were not involved in creating contracts that were fraudulent, as was the case in Enron. CA had the contracts, but they were acted upon in periods to which they did not belong. Therefore, it borrowed revenue from the next quarter to show good results in the previous quarter.

> The accounting fraud perpetrated by CA was penalised by the US market watchdog, the SEC, which imposed a fine of $225 million on it. Sanjay Kumar, its former CEO, was sentenced to 12 years imprisonment and fined $8 million. The company was renamed as CA Technologies in 2010.

The US-based software company **Peregrine Systems** showed *37 days in a month*. During 1999–2001, the company routinely kept its accounting books open even after the fiscal quarter had ended, and fraudulently recorded sales of software that were not actually made until after the quarter end. On a lighter vein, its employees would internally communicate amongst themselves that sales have been completed on *the 37th of December*! In some cases, transactions did not close for months after Peregrine had recorded as sales for them.

> After the accounting fraud and indictment of Peregrine's top executives, including its CFO, the software company filed for Chapter 11 bankruptcy protection in September 2002. However, within two years, it had emerged from bankruptcy. HP acquired it in 2005.

Tampering with Revenue Recognition Policy

A company needs to normally follow consistent principles in calculating its revenue. Consistency in its policy of recognising sales helps users of its accounting reports compare sales of a given period appropriately with corresponding previous periods. Any change in its method of recognising revenue, should be reported specifically in its financial statements, so that users of these reports are given adequate notice of the change in its policy. Any non-disclosure is a fraudulent act.

To augment sales, **Transaction Systems Architects Inc.**, a company making electronic payment systems (renamed ACI Worldwide Inc. in 2007) changed its revenue recognition policy in 1999 by accounting upfront its five-year contracts with customers. Therefore, while cash would be coming in the future, the company considered its total sale in an earlier period instead of spreading it over the next five years. This helped it incorrectly increase its sales during 1999–2002. It had to restate its sales at a later date.

Incorrect Lease Accounting to Show Higher Sales

It would be nice to acquire capital equipment without paying for it fully. This is known as leasing and involves payment of the total purchase price over a longer period. In view of this elongated payment period, interest is payable by the buyer during this time.

A leasing agreement is like a borrowing arrangement, where the lessee (purchaser) acquires the right to use equipment over the period of the lease, and the lessor (seller) continues to be the owner of the asset. On the expiry of the lease period and payment of the leasing amount (principal plus interest), the terms of the lease determine whether the equipment goes back to the lessor or continues to be under the control of the lessee.

Lease accounting provides opportunities for accounting fraud.

An example of misusing lease accounting rules was practised by **Xerox Corporation**.

Xerox was once one of the most successful brands in the world. Such was the brand's strength that it became synonymous with the generic verb *photocopying*. In its own words, Xerox engaged in *accounting tricks* and *accounting opportunities* between 1997 and 2000 to boost its revenue and profits significantly. It overstated revenue generated by its equipment by $3 billion, and thereby, overstating its profits by $1.5 billion.

Xerox used several fraudulent methods to do this. The two most important ones included:

1. Treating a short-term lease (operating lease) as a long-term lease (finance lease). This helped the company to increase its revenue. The cost of leasing certain equipment was shown as an upfront income by treating it as a long-term lease, as opposed to treating it as regular income during the lease period. Its future revenue was counted as upfront revenue for the year of the sale, bringing forward future income streams to an earlier year.
2. Taking a lower present value rate to enhance revenue. Xerox used the *return on equity* rate, as opposed to the market rate of interest, thereby reducing its discount rate and bringing forward its profits.

By doing this, Xerox was able to meet market expectations of profits, although in reality, its profits would have been either lower or it would have declared a loss for the period.

'For Xerox, the accounting function was just another revenue source and profit opportunity. As a result, its investors were misled and betrayed', said the SEC's Enforcement Director.

> Xerox paid a penalty of $10 million and restated its profits for 1997 to 2000. In June 2003, six of its senior executives, including its former CEO and CFO, who were accused of fraudulent practices, agreed to pay $22.5 million as penalty. KPMG, its auditor, was fined $22.5 in 2005.

Mark to Market to Enhance Revenue

In the case of assets or liabilities, where market prices are volatile, these are shown in the balance sheet on a *mark to market* or *fair value* basis. It means that if the market value is higher or lower than the procurement value, the cost of the acquisition of the asset needs to be replaced by the market value, which is fluctuating in nature. This method of valuation (to prepare balance sheets) is usually used in cases of stock-in-trade (i.e., equity shares held for trading), FX or commodities. Fluctuations in market prices affect the profits or losses of companies, being the unrealised profits or gains.

Let us assume that a company purchased 100 equity shares of a particular company to resell them, as on 31 March, for $10 per share. The stock-in-trade will be shown in the balance sheet at $1,000 (100 shares × $10 per share). On 30 June, the market price of shares becomes $9. These 100 equity shares will be shown at $900 (100 shares × $9 per share). This will imply that $100 ($1,000 less $900) will be booked as loss in its P&L account for the June Quarter. This is a typical *mark to market* concept of valuation.

This valuation concept has often been misused to show fraudulent profits. This is especially practised when the market price is not objectively determinable or there is difficulty in finding a comparable product to which the market price can be compared.

In many cases, companies make use of financial models to show future potential cash flows, and fraudulently come to conclusions regarding potential market values.

The concept of *mark to market* is applicable even on long-term contracts, where companies have outstanding derivative contracts (including energy-related ones, as in the case of *Enron*). Such contracts may need to be adjusted to their fair market value, resulting in the necessity to book unrealised profits or losses in their income statement.

It may be noted here that in the case of some long-term commodity contracts such as gas, it is difficult to estimate market prices, since normally, market quotes are difficult to obtain on a long-term basis.

Companies can take advantage of this lack of information on market prices and make their own estimates to falsely bolster their profits by showing increased long-term market prices through esoteric valuation models by making assumptions that may or may not fructify in the future.

The undisputed king of accounting fraud, **Enron**, among many fraudulent actions, engaged in juggling *mark-to-market* accounting concepts for long-term gas contracts and derivatives. This accounting method helped it show increased revenue, but did not produce cash. The method allowed Enron to show the entire revenue of 20-year gas contracts, upfront on the first year.

Enron entered long-term contracts for delivery of energy and showed the accumulated profits for future years upfront in its P&L account, as though these profits had been earned in the first year. This was, of course, without affecting actual delivery of the energy or gas, which would take place in the future.

Not only did Enron take future gas supplies as an upfront income, it also estimated through its own financial models what would be the future price of the commodity. Therefore, by a slight of hand, and by making some assumptions, its profits multiplied manifold. While the energy industry was by and large following the concept of recognising income from energy only when it was delivered and based on contractual prices, Enron changed the game almost overnight.

Enron was created in 1985 through the merger of Houston Natural Gas and InterNorth after natural gas pipelines in the USA were deregulated. The merger resulted in huge amounts of debt and its ancillary costs, and the company began searching for additional means to increase its income to show a better than actual business performance. Its basic business model was to create a

> *gas bank*, where it would buy gas from a group of suppliers and sell it to a group of consumers, guaranteeing both price and supplies. Enron charged a fee for services rendered as well as for absorbing associated risks such as price fluctuations. It thereby became an energy trader and correspondingly created energy-derivative products. In order to show improved results, it entered numerous fraudulent transactions and structures, some of which were complicated and convoluted. When its fraudulent practices came to light, Enron's shares plunged and the company had to file for bankruptcy in late 2001. Its remaining assets were held to compensate those who had incurred losses. In September 2008, the concerned US District Court awarded $7.2 billion as compensation to Enron's shareholders whose holdings in the company had become worthless when it collapsed due to the scandal. Kenneth Lay, its former CEO, died while awaiting his sentence. Jeffrey Skilling, its former CEO and COO, was sentenced to 24 years in prison.

Tampering with Revenue Allocation Method for Multiple Products

Have you noticed that razors are sold relatively cheaply compared to blades? It is a pricing ploy used by manufacturers to sell the main product cheap, so that they can make profits by selling its co-products. Companies sometimes sell co-products, where the sale of one product helps that of the other. In the case of mobile companies, they may sell the handset free or at a nominal price, and recover the cost and revenue through the sale of a long-term mobile contract with the customer.

The revenue from the two products needs to be recognised in the companies' books of accounts, based on the allocation assumption of their revenue. This implies that handset revenue recognition should be based on its contractual price (upfront revenue) and the mobile service contract revenue over the period of the contract (spread-over revenue).

If the basis between the two product revenue allocations can be tampered with, there is a possibility of up-fronting revenue to earlier years rather than spreading it over a longer period. Such irregularities can be carried out by altering the allocation method or contractual terms in the case of co-products.

In 2006, **Softbank**, the Japanese telecom company, changed its method of revenue allocation for its mobile phone business (which it acquired during the year from Vodafone) between its handsets and the monthly mobile service it provided in such a way that it allocated more revenue to handsets. This enabled it to bring its revenue upfront. This was done suddenly to take its operating margin from 3% to 11% just after acquiring Vodafone's mobile division, although there was no visible improvement in its business.

Bill and Hold: Book Sales before Goods Are Shipped to Buyers

It is common sense that revenue can only be booked after shipment of goods to the buyer or when the title of the goods has been transferred from the seller to the buyer. If the seller continues to hold the goods and bears the risk on them, no sales can be booked.

Sometimes sales are booked in accounting books, prior to the shipment of products. This arrangement involves invoicing by the seller to the buyer of the goods, but the seller holds the goods on behalf of the buyer, without shipping the goods to the former. This is commonly known as a *bill-and-hold* transaction.

If bill-and-hold arrangements are recorded as sales, (i) the buyer should have asked for the goods to be held by the seller on its behalf and not vice versa, (ii) the risks and rewards for ownership of the goods have passed to the buyer, (iii) the ordered goods must be segregated from the seller's inventory and (iv) they must be complete and ready for shipment.

It is important to check what happened to past bill-and-hold arrangements and whether they were converted into sales within a reasonable period. This concept can be used in accounting fraud to show higher than normal sales.

The bill-and-hold concept was extensively used by the Canadian manufacturer of telecommunication equipment, **Nortel Networks** during late 2000–early 2001 to fraudulently pull forward revenue of more than $1 billion to meet its sales revenue targets. This helped the company steer its results for 2000 according to the equity market's expectations and show a sizeable increase in its revenues.

What did Nortel Networks do? When its management realised that the company could not meet its revenue targets at the end of 2000, it devised a devious method. It started working on providing a solution for the millions of dollars of inventory that was sitting in its warehouses. In November 2000, the company's salesmen contacted customers who had placed their orders earlier and obtained from them bill-and-hold letters. Nortel also incentivised its customers by offering them discounts in prices, deferment of interest and extended their billing terms. The management's objective of meeting its sales targets was achieved though by phony methods.

> Nortel perpetrated a number of accounting fraud during 2000–03, including by enhancing its bill-and-hold revenue and using its *cookie jar reserves*. In October 2007, it paid $35 million to settle charges on the accounting scandal.

Channel Stuffing: Shipping Goods When Buyer Has No Intent to Pay

The investigating director of SEC said, 'For 2 years **Bristol-Myers Squibb Company** (BMS) deceived the market into believing that it was meeting its financial projections and market expectations, when, in fact, the company was making its numbers primarily through channel-stuffing and manipulative accounting devices.' BMS, the pharmaceutical giant, inflated its profits by stuffing its distribution channels with excess stocks of products during 2000–01 close to the ends of quarters. This was done to meet its targets selling its pharmaceutical products to its wholesale dealers ahead of their asking for these. Bristol-Myers made improperly sales of $1.5 billion to two of its largest wholesale dealers. It compensated the dealers with extra storage and the carrying cost of the excess inventories. Needless to say, the excess wholesaler inventory resulted in a material risk to the company's future earnings potential, since its later period sales were lower as its sales have been pulled forward to earlier periods.

> After its accounting scandal in 2000–01, Bristol-Myers paid a fine of $150 million and promised to undertake various remedial measures.

To inflate sales, a popular method is for a seller to dump goods with the buyer, as **Peregrine** did. Booking of sales where goods have been shipped without any clear understanding or possibility of receiving the payment within a reasonable period is also a fraudulent practice. *Channel stuffing* is the term used for this phenomenon.

In order to recognise shipment of goods as sales, one of the criteria is clearly that customers should pay for goods delivered to them. If buyers (i) are not able to pay, (ii) have no intention of doing so or (iii) have an understanding that they can return the goods shipped whenever they want, such shipments cannot be treated as *sales* under accounting norms. Several companies have followed this method of boosting sales.

Even **IBM** booked sham sales. In 2000 and 2001, the company booked revenue of around $280 million, a substantial portion of which involved the use of *side letters*. (*Side letters* are confidential arrangements entered by two parties with the intent that the contents will normally *not* be disclosed to the outside world including auditors.) IBM gave its customers the right to return equipment shipped through such side letters. It followed this practice around the world. For example, in December 2000, its retail store solutions recognised sales in connection with sale of printers to a business partner, granting it the full right to return the printers through a side letter; $9 million was improperly recognised as sales and enabled IBM's retail store solutions to exceed their full-year sales target.

> During these two years, 2000 and 2001, IBM maintained inaccurate books of accounts, which included several cases of misrepresentation. It agreed to pay a penalty of $7 million.

Another example was *gallon pushing*, which is nothing but *channel stuffing*, practised by **Coca-Cola** in Japan in 1997 to pull its sales forward into an earlier period. To accomplish this, its Japanese bottlers were offered extended credit terms to attract them to purchase quantities of the beverage concentrate, which the bottlers would have not normally purchased until the following quarter. As a result of this *gallon pushing* (Coca-Cola sells gallons of concentrates to its bottlers and hence the acronym!), Japanese bottlers' inventories increased at a rate that was more than five times higher than their normal sales requirements.

In eight out of 12 quarters during 1997–99, Coca-Cola engaged in channel stuffing practices, to ensure that its earnings estimates were met. It did not disclose its gallon pushing practice in its periodic reports.

To top it all, in early 2000, the company announced that it would be taking steps to reduce its world-wide inventory, and this would have an impact on its future quarters' earnings. This was untrue. It was not reducing inventory but had decided to correct its misdeeds of the past two years.

> Coca-Cola agreed to the SEC's decision in 2005 on the issue of accounting fraud through channel stuffing, without admitting or denying the findings (which is the usual practice) to settle the proceedings by consenting to a cease-and-desist order, and taking action to strengthen its internal review process to prevent future violations.

Round Tripping and Providing Cash to Buyers

The senior management of **Krispy-Kreme**, the doughnut seller, had an *incentive plan*, which kicked in after it met its Earning Per Share (EPS) target. The target of this incentive was EPS guidance provided to the market, plus 1%.

Beginning 2003, the company saw slowing down of sales. This triggered an accounting fraud. Its management conjured up a grand plan of *round-tripping*.

During 2003–04, Krispy-Kreme hiked the price of acquiring a franchise operation. The excess billing was used by the franchisee to purchase future supplies from its Principal, Krispy-Kreme.

From the accounting treatment point of view, this arrangement worked perfectly for Krispy-Kreme. The amount billed extra on acquisition of a franchise was the *capital cost* to the franchisee and not deducted from its income. The excess amount charged by Krispy-Kreme (the seller) to the franchisee (the purchaser) to acquire the business was used by the franchisees to purchase supplies in the future from Krispy-Kreme. The amount paid by the franchisees was shown as an *income* in the company's books. This constituted a *round-trip* transaction and a fraudulent act.

What did Krispy-Kreme do? In June 2003, it entered into an agreement to acquire Texas operations of a franchisee for an agreed price of $65 million. Instead, it paid $65.8 million—an excess of $0.8 million. The extra amount, $0.8 million, was used by the franchisee to procure goods from Krispy-Kreme, and this amount was shown as an income by the company in the June quarter of 2003. This helped to improve its financial performance. In October 2003, in another such acquisition, its excess billing came back to Krispy-Kreme as a *management fee*, which was also recorded as income in its income statement, boosting its third-quarter results. Both were round-tripping and illegal transactions.

> Krispy-Kreme restated its financial statements, correcting its false reporting of profits by $11 million for 2003 and 2004.

Why is round-tripping fraudulent? Buying and selling should take place on an arms-length basis. Buyers should not be under the influence of sellers, be able to decide on the purchase price independently and be in a position to pay for this from their own resource base. However, if sellers fund buyers for purchases, directly or indirectly, fraud can be perpetrated as the sellers would have control over sales, based on finance provided by them. This will negate the presence of *arms-length* concept in the arrangement.

The usual purpose of such transactions is to show higher sales revenue for the sellers, and the buyers hiding the funding provided to them. *Round-tripping* therefore involves money provided by sellers to buyers, which comes back to the sellers on completion of sales. How deceitful can a company be to structure such deals? But, it takes place.

AOL and Time Warner

Around mid-2000, when the AOL and Time Warner merger was pending, the stock prices of Internet-related businesses crashed. Among other factors, sales on online advertising declined and the rate of growth of new online subscriptions suffered.

During this period, AOL engaged in *round-trip* transactions to boost its revenue and profit numbers.

The essence of these transactions involved AOL using its own money to create false receipts of advertising revenue, which enabled it to meet its internal revenue targets and analysts' expectations. It helped AOL mask the slow-down (also faced by other Internet companies) in its business.

AOL practised several round-tripping methods. One of its techniques involved foregoing discounts on purchases that were exchanged for new advertising revenue. While buying goods and services from vendors, AOL either inflated its purchase price or arranged to forego discounts negotiated. In exchange, the vendors purchased online advertising for the same amount as the mark-up or discount foregone. For example, on purchase of computer hardware for $250 million, AOL secured a discount of 15% or $37.5 million. In order to inflate its online advertising revenues, it agreed to forego the discount and paid $250 million for the equipment. In exchange, the vendor agreed to purchase $37.5 million of advertising. Consequently, AOL increased its revenue from advertising fraudulently.

> AOL, an Internet service company, and Time Warner, a media-entertainment company, announced their merger in January 2000. AOL Time Warner Inc. was formed by their merger in January 2001. The implied market value of the merged company was around $200 billion—at that time the largest merger in history in the US, if not in the world. It was hailed as a business masterstroke for the marriage between the old and the new age. But the bursting of the dot-com bubble and failed synergy benefits after the merger resulted in the deal collapsing and the company suffering the biggest ever corporate loss of $100 billion in 2002. In October 2003, the merged company dropped the name AOL from its prefix and changed it to Time Warner Inc. The merger of AOL and Time Warner turned out to be the biggest corporate disaster in the US.

GE

Even companies such as GE have over-reported their sales by arranging funding and despatching goods.

What GE did was something like this.

GE's transportation systems unit wanted to show enhanced sales. It approached its group company, GE's Capital Markets Group, seeking help to sell a significant number of its products (locomotives) to railroad end users in the fourth quarter of 2002 and 2003, and asked many of its customers to defer their purchases to later quarters. GE Capital Markets arranged so-called buyers in the form of *financial intermediates* (who were doing business with the GE Capital Markets group) to whom GE Transportation would sell locomotives. These financial intermediaries would then resell the locomotives to its railroad customers in ensuing quarters. The financial intermediaries were not supposed to profit by selling the locomotives at a higher price, but by charging GE certain upfront fees. GE also issued *side letters* to the intermediaries, agreeing to reimburse funds tied-up, storage and insurance on the locomotives.

How can a seller be responsible for a buyer's cost of storage and insurance?

Clearly, these sales to *financial intermediaries* could not be considered as revenue, since the so-called *customers* (the intermediaries) did not take titles and did not assume the risk of owning the locomotives. The inclusion of these *structured* sales helped GE Transportation unit overstate its sales and profits.

> These ill-conceived structures were corrected by GE in July 2007 by adjusting and restating its historical financial statements for the relevant quarters in 2002 and 2003.

Tyco International

Of the several fraudulent accounting acts perpetrated by Tyco between 1998 and 2002, one was funding sales. While purchasing security monitoring equipment, the company increased its purchase price, so that it could be correspondingly invoiced to the vendor, thereby offsetting the increase in the purchase price.

For example, assume that the normal purchase price of the equipment was $100, but this was increased to $120 through a special understanding with the vendor. The extra $20 purchase price was set off against a sales invoice of the corresponding amount of $20 to give a better picture of the company's revenue figures. Tyco overstated its revenue by $567 million during this period.

> After the SEC's findings about its serious accounting fraudulent acts, Tyco split itself into three independent companies in 2007—(i) TE Connectivity Ltd. (data and power connection, and protection), (ii) Covidien Ltd. (healthcare products) and (iii) Tyco International Ltd. (fire and security systems). The company agreed to pay $3 billion as penalty levied by the SEC. Its CEO and CFO were both sentenced to imprisonment. PwC, its auditors, also agreed to pay $225 million to settle investors' claims. Unfortunately, Tyco did not learn from its mistakes and committed further accounting fraud during 2006–09 and had to pay a penalty of $13 million.

Sales of Non-consolidating Subsidiaries

The easiest way to project an impression of a company is to somehow show that revenue figures are galloping. Sales growth numbers augur well for investors.

Of the several methods of accounting juggleries that can be employed to fulfil this goal of enhancing sales, one way is to include the sales of subsidiary companies, even when they are not to be clubbed with that of the parent. Normally, if the parent company holds more than 50% of the shares in the subsidiary, the latter's sales and results need to be consolidated. However, if the parent's shareholding is less, clubbing is generally not permissible.

A fraudulent practice is to include sales of subsidiaries, even where only minority shares are held by the parent. Thus, by wrongly including the sales of other companies that are not controlled or owned by the parent, a false picture can be given of its financial health.

During 2000–02, **Royal Ahold**, the Dutch company, perpetrated a major fraud by including in its revenue figures the sales and operating profits of JV companies in which it had neither a majority shareholding nor control. Ahold fully consolidated several JVs in its financial statements despite the fact that it owned less than 50% of the shares and clear agreement for joint control by Ahold and its JV partners.

In order to justify full consolidation of these JVs, Ahold provided its auditors falsified *side letters* for the JV agreements. These were signed by Ahold and its JV partners and stated that the company controlled the latter. Since these side letters were fakes and to protect the JVs, as soon as they were signed, Ahold gave *rescission letters* to the JVs, stating that the contents of the side letters were invalid. The rescinding letters were, however, not shown to the auditors.

This enabled the subsidiary companies' sales and profits to be included in Ahold's financial results. The company materially overstated its sales by around $26 billion and its operating profits by $1 billion for the financial years 1999–2001.

> Ahold agreed to settle the SEC's charge of fraudulent accounting, without admitting or denying them, as is the normal practice.

Deceptive Barter System

Sale of goods or services involves exchange of money or its equivalent. Receipt of payment by a seller from a buyer through non-monetary methods may not be out of place as long as it is measurable in money. However, if the payment for goods and services is fallacious and deceptive, *sales* made in non-measureable payment terms cannot be considered in income statements.

Peregrine Systems, a San Diego-based software company, between 1999 and 2002, used various deceptive methods to increase its revenue. One of these was a misleading *barter* system. The company entered non-monetary transactions (barter or swaps) with some its customers. While it is true that under certain circumstances non-monetary transactions can be recognised as revenue, Peregrine included revenue on transactions that did not satisfy applicable revenue-recognition rules under accounting principles. In fact, Peregrine recorded sales against its own software received back from customers sold earlier. How could *revenue* be recognised when neither money nor any money-equivalent was received it, which could be measured and evaluated? If a company's own goods or services are received back, its original sales would need to be reversed and it cannot book fresh sales. What a scam!

Showing Bogus Sales: *Back-to-Back* Arrangement of Goods Return

One of the basic principles of *revenue recognition* in companies' books of accounts is that delivery of goods or services must take place. However, if there is a hidden arrangement between a seller and a buyer that goods supplied will be returned, no sales can be recorded.

If the arrangement of goods being returned by a buyer can be kept under wraps, their original delivery can be fraudulently shown as sales.

General Motors spun off Delphi, its auto parts-maker, in 1999. Once **Delphi Corporation** became an independent entity, it began perpetuating several fraudulent accounting acts between 2000 and 2004.

One of these was to book sales when there was a corresponding arrangement to take back the goods later. In the fourth quarter of 2000, Delphi booked sales worth $270 million. However, it simultaneously agreed to repurchase the inventory it had sold for the original sales price in addition to interest and structuring charges in the following quarter. In spite of its back-to-back agreement to take back the goods, Delphi recorded sales of $270 million in its income statement, thereby overstating its sales in the fourth quarter of 2000. This was deceitful.

Showing Fake Sales: 'Reciprocal' Arrangement with Buyer

How can sales be recorded when there is a corresponding arrangement to buy something of a similar value from the customer? It is a bizarre plan, when there are no disclosures about it.

The telecommunications company, **Global Crossing**, was in the business of acquiring global fibre-optic networks and selling fibre-optic capacity and telecommunications services on a network to other telecommunications service providers. During the first half of 2001, it sold telecommunications capacity to other carriers. This was linked to its purchase of capacity from the same carrier and amounted in essence to *reciprocal transactions*.

In view of difficult market conditions during this period, Global Crossings began increasingly relying on reciprocal transactions as a substantial source of its revenue. It did not disclose these sales and corresponding reciprocal agreements, but booked sales in its financial records to falsely indicate that it had achieved its sales targets. Without these reciprocal transactions, Global Crossings would not have met securities analysts' figures for the first half 2001. This also helped the company improve its cash flow position during this period, since it realised much of its sales in cash. It spent this on reciprocal purchases in a later quarter, but did not disclose the amounts.

This kind of fraud has several fallouts. First, cash flows from sales are not permanent and need to be used soon on reciprocal purchases from the same customers. Second, the sales volume and growth is not sustainable, it is only a short-term measure. Third, and the most important, sales shown are not bona fide.

> Global Crossings was issued a seize and desist order in April 2005 for violating its future accounting figures. The company's CEO, CFO and Vice President Finance had to pay $100,000 as personal civil penalties.

Tailpiece

Businesses are set up to sell their products and make profits from their economic activities. When efforts to produce positive results fail to match expectations, sometimes human minds get diverted towards unsavoury acts. Showing non-existent *sale* is the numero uno mode—to fool the unsuspecting.

CREATING SALES OUT OF THIN AIR

For self-aggrandizement, the President and Finance Director got together to conspire falsification of books of accounts of **Posterscope**, a large outdoor advertising company, which is a part of the **British Aegis Group**. It made false entries of $20 million between 2004 and 2009, either by entering phony sales data or showing artificial rebates received on goods and services it had purchased.

While money does not grow on money plants, some corporate organisations do create *sales* out of the thin air. Posterscope was such an instance.

A phony or sham sale is where no sales actually takes place. No goods or services are transferred and no orders are placed by any buyer on seller. And consequently, there is no income. However, sales or income is booked in a company's income statement. An out and out fraud.

Some instances are cited below, which indicate how companies try to project a better than actual image of their financial positions. And while you are reading this, many more must be going on somewhere in the world.

Showing Sales without Despatching Goods

Innovations which are hallmark of **IBM**, worked even in the accounting areas. IBM sold to itself during 2000–01 and showed it as genuine sales. It also transferred goods to its self-controlled warehouses and booked these as sales. This involved booking of sales on goods stored in its own warehouses instead of those of its customers. The amount involved in such *phony* sales was around $170 million during the two years. These sales were shown to increase a particular quarter's reported earnings and were corrected in one of the ensuing quarters. This fraud was detected internally.

Sales is a commercial activity involving transfer of ownership of goods or services from a seller to a buyer in return for a consideration, usually money. Sales cannot generally be recognised unless delivery of a product has taken place. *Delivery* is considered to have occurred only when the customer has taken the title and assumed the risks and rewards of ownership. However, when none of this happens, but sales are shown in a company's accounting books, this amounts to creation of bogus sales.

When phoney sales are entered in the books of accounts, there needs to be another corresponding entry made. Sales are made to a customer. Therefore, when fraudulent sales are recorded, the other side of the so-called transaction is also recorded, which is falsified too. [When *revenue* is increased through a credit entry in a P&L Account, correspondingly *debtors* need to be enhanced too (debit entry to increase the asset side of the balance sheet), or else, the double entry system of book-keeping will remain incomplete.]

Companies such as Peregrine and IBM that have falsified their accounts through phony sales normally enhance debtors. However, there have been instances, for example, **HealthSouth Corporation**, where the corresponding *debit* entry (increasing the asset side) was made to *fixed assets* instead of giving effect to the debtors' accounts. This avoided unnecessary enhancement of the debtors' outstanding figures in an effort to escape the attention of those analysing dues from customers.

One of the USA's largest healthcare service providers, HealthSouth Corporation, became a public company in 1986, and since then has been tampering with its sales figures to artificially maintain its stock price at a high level. However, between 1999 and June 2002, the company either overstated its sales figures or decreased its expenses by $1.4 billion by making false entries. Correspondingly, under double-entry bookkeeping, wherein it was required to make a second entry, it artificially increased its *fixed asset* figures. While an increase in sales should correspondingly enhance debtors' outstanding figures, in this case, the company falsified the fixed assets figures, ostensibly to avoid the attention of investors. Its overstatement of income falsified its actual reported profit figures by as much as 4,700% in 2001!

> HealthSouth, a healthcare company curtailed the size of its operations after discovery of its accounting fraud, but continues its operations and is listed on the New York Stock Exchange.

Syntax-Brillion Corporation

The management of Syntax decided to increase the company's sales between 2006 and 2008. Syntax was listed on the NASDAQ stock exchange and the purpose of the fraud was to artificially inflate its stock price, so that its senior management team could profit by insider trading in its shares, based on its inflated financial performance.

Strangely enough, when Syntax's management wanted to falsify sales, it took the help of its auditor. Robert Chiu was a Partner in the audit firm and decided to advise the company's management in its fraudulent activity. (There are not many instances of auditors actively participating in wrongdoing—passively, however they have done sometimes—as is evident from instances mentioned elsewhere in this book.)

Chiu and Syntax's management worked out a scheme that involved (i) creation of forged shipping documents and fake sales invoices and (ii) round-tripping money between Syntax, its primary manufacturer (Taiwan KOLIN Co.) and a so-called customer in Hong Kong (abbreviated name SCHOT).

Since its sales were fake, some payment had to be received by Syntax to indicate the genuineness of the sales. This was done by the company sending money to Kolin under the guise of making deposits for *tooling* or moulds for TVs. Kolin in turn paid to SCHOT and SCHOT to Syntax, so that the funds flowed back to Syntax as payment towards sales invoices.

The fake customer, SCHOT, was set up in Hong Kong so that large sales could be explained away on the pretext that the huge demand for the product in China was attracting sales. No one doubted that China was not a major market, and therefore, the increased falsified sales figure, even when it was sometimes 60% higher than the previous year's similar quarter, was not questioned.

> Syntax-Brillon, headquartered in Tempe, Arizona, was a marketer of TVs under the *Olevea* brand. It mainly sold TVs in the USA and supposedly in China. The accounting fraud fell apart due to the company's very high and unsustainable accounts receivables and its inability to generate adequate legitimate sales in Asia. After discovery of the accounting fraud, the company filed for bankruptcy in July 2008. Emerson Radio Corporation acquired the Olevea brand from Syntax for $1.3 million in May 2009.

Reebok India

It was alleged that the CEO and COO of the Indian subsidiary of the Adidas Group tampered with the company's financial figures. These allegations included bogus sales and sales returns not being deducted in its accounting books. Thus over-stating of sales figures.

In addition, there were four undisclosed warehouses, where goods apparently stolen from Reebok outlets were stored and sold to personally benefit the company's CEO and COO—estimated by the Indian police at INR 110 million ($2 million).

The German sportswear company Adidas reported that it had corrected its earlier overstated sales for 2012 by INR 15 billion ($270 million) in March 2013.

> The CEO, COO and three others from Reebok India were arrested for the fraud. The Serious Fraud Investigation Office is investigating it.

Creation of Sham Insurance Premium Income

Insurance companies (*insurers*) receive insurance premiums from enterprises or people who are provided insurance cover (the *insured*). The premium amount is an income for the insured. Settlement claims paid under any insurance contract are costs borne by the insurance companies.

Fraud can be committed by insurance companies by recording false income for premiums, which in reality could be loans or deposits from someone else.

AIG and **Gen Re**, two insurance companies, structured two sham reinsurance transactions of $250 million each. Their objective was to enable AIG to book $500 million ($250 million in 2000 and $250 million in 2001) by manoeuvring its accounting books, improving its income and creating a *loss reserve* to avoid analysts' criticism of its declining loss reserve position. (*Loss reserve* is technically a fund created to utilise payment of future losses, if any. The higher the reserve amount the better is the financial position of an insurance company, since its future losses, if any, can be funded from the reserve and will not affect its current year's income.)

So what did the company do? AIG obtained two reinsurance businesses from Gen Re (i.e., by AIG supposedly reinsuring Gen Re's risks) on paper. To do this, Gen Re took on the obligation to pay AIG $500 million, although it did not pay the latter this amount.

Since the transactions were a sham, AIG did not absorb any risk. If no risk was assumed, AIG could not have shown $500 million as a *loss reserve* addition. In reality, there was an understanding between the two, that neither party was taking or sharing any risks. The loss reserve addition treatment was fraudulent and misrepresented the true nature of the transaction.

These convoluted and circuitous transactions were handled through the respective subsidiaries of AIG and Gen Re, so that it need not be disclosed. The misrepresentation of showing higher reserve account (for absorbing potential future losses) was carried in the books of accounts of AIG till 2005, when its financial accounts were restated to reflect the correct position.

> Gen Re, one of the world's largest reinsurers, is a subsidiary of Berkshire Hathaway Inc., whose primary shareholder is Warren Buffet. Gen Re agreed to pay a penalty of $90 million for helping AIG manipulate its financial statements through its fraudulent scheme from 2000 through 2004. It agreed that its senior management was engaged in the scheme to falsely inflate AIG's reported loss reserves.

Using Subsidiaries to Book Phony Revenue

Parent companies generally retain good control over their subsidiaries. According to accounting rules, transactions between parents and their subsidiaries need to be at arm's length. This means that the parent should not influence its subsidiary engaging in activities that are not prudent or proper.

A recalcitrant parent can, however, meddle with its subsidiaries' operations and pressurise them through its controlling interest. One of the methods could be to decide to show or not show sales between the two companies. Common sense tells us that sales need to be booked when goods are shipped. But, if it is played with, fraudulent accounting practice can be experienced.

Ulticom Inc., with one of its Group Company **CNS-Israel**, had a gala time in playing with the sales numbers. Between 1998 and April 2001, Ulticom engaged in improper revenue-recognition practices between itself and CNS-Israel in an effort to demonstrate its steady revenue growth to investors.

Whenever Ulticom wanted to suppress sales, it would instruct CNS-Israel to reject the materials shipped, when in reality, they were perfectly acceptable. Similarly, the companies would just decide to skip booking invoices, irrespective of shipments from Ulticom. It was mayhem.

The companies' sales figures were adjusted at their will on transactions between the two group companies to meet their objective of meeting their targeted sales figures. If sales exceeded their target, they would not record a few. If they were in deficit, those not recorded in previous quarters would be drawn upon to make good the deficit.

> Ulticom agreed to desist from entering fraudulent accounting treatments without agreeing or disagreeing with the complaints raised.

Loans Taken from Banks and Shown as Sales

Loans are debts that are liabilities and need to be returned. Anything that is a *liability* and repayable cannot be treated as an *income* in accounting books under any stretch of imagination.

However, since loans taken involve inflow of funds, fraudsters sometimes align this with sales realisation and falsely show it as their *revenue*.

In the fourth quarter of 2001, the US-based auto-parts supplier **Delphi Corporation** solicited a lump sum amount of $20 million from an IT company in return for the former providing new business to the company. Delphi agreed to repay the amount with interest over five years.

However, in order to meet its targeted financial results for the quarter, Delphi treated the loan as a *non-refundable rebate* on past business rather than a *liability*. This meant that the quarter's income was overstated by $20 million by fraudulently accounting a loan taken as income from additional rebate.

Tailpiece

'A fake smile can be bad for your health ... a phony smile to hide unhappiness can further worsen your mood', was *The New York Times*' comment, summarising a research report. Similarly, recording phoney sales in financial statements, while providing a temporary respite, do catch up with reality in the future.

BOOKING FALSE VENDOR REBATES

While purchasing goods and services, vendors often offer rebates and discounts, which are usually based on the volume of off-take. The purchaser needs to buy goods at a competitive price, add value to the goods procured and then sell them at a price that is higher than their cost in order to earn profits. This is the normal business process. Discounts help to reduce cost of procurement.

Rebates can be booked in accounting records only when they *accrue* or when purchases have been made and terms for obtaining rebates fulfilled.

Let us assume that a vendor provides a rebate of 5% only when purchases exceed $10 million in any quarter. Assuming the purchase value is only $6 million in a particular quarter, no rebate can be claimed. However, if the purchasing company books the rebate wrongly on the basis that the purchased amount has reached $10 million (although it has not), the amount can be over-reported by $0.3 million (5% on target purchase of $6 million).

Fraudulent accounting can take place either by bringing forward the ensuing period's purchased quantities or by improperly booking rebates, irrespective of shortfalls in their volume.

One such fraud was perpetrated by **Ahold NV**, which used several accounting tricks, including booking false income from non-existent rebates. As part of its global expansion strategy, the Ahold group acquired a food-distribution company in the USA, **US Foodservice**, as a 100% subsidiary in 2000.

US Foodservice was already sick when it was taken over, and was apparently already in the habit of cooking its books of accounts.

The Ahold scam related to *promotional allowances*—a rebate suppliers paid to customers for making a commitment to purchase certain threshold quantities during 2000–02. The wholesale food business was very competitive, and one of the methods of earning revenue was to obtain extra rebates from vendors on achievement of certain volume of purchases. This is where the scam occurred.

US Foodservice, in collusion with its suppliers, increased the quantum of promotional allowances receivable. Foodservice's employees would contact vendors and insist on them signing and returning false confirmation letters about rebates and allowances to be given. On several occasions, US Foodservice's executives would issue side letters to vendors assuring them that in reality they did not owe the company amounts confirmed through confirmation letters. The amounts involved were double that of normal promotional allowance figures. What this meant was that these allowances were a form of *income* and the false confirmation letters from vendors enabled Ahold's management to falsely double the rebate amount.

> The Ahold Group was established in 1887 in Amsterdam, primarily as grocery stores, and then became a global supermarket chain.
>
> On completion of its 100th year in 1988, the Queen of the Netherlands bestowed the prefix *Royal* to the company and it also became known as *Royal Ahold*.
>
> However, the company's ambitions led it to commit serious accounting fraud between 1999 and 2002 to project better financial figures. It became known as the *Enron of Europe*.
>
> Ahold agreed to settle the US SEC's action and consented to permanent entry of the judgement, which instructed the company to stop violating the legal provisions of security-related laws. The Dutch authorities also filed prosecution suites and the company paid the fines in 2004. It has resumed its operations after restructuring its management.

Tailpiece

Many companies have followed suit, giving false rebates to vendors. **Marriott International**, the famous hotel chain, was accused of unfairly pocketing vendors' rebates. **OfficeMax**, one of the largest retailers of office supplies, dismissed several of its employees when it found improprieties in rebates given by a large supplier in its accounting books. **Collins & Aikman**, an auto-parts company, filed for bankruptcy protection over supplier-rebate controversies. And the tale is unending.

TINKERING WITH THE PAST: RETROSPECTIVE CHANGES IN THE SALES RECOGNITION POLICY

Strange things happen in the world of accountancy. In order to show better sales and profits, historical figures are sometimes tampered with.

One way in which organisations do this is by revising their sales recognition policies with retrospective effect. Their purpose is to show that their sales figures were over-reported in the past and they are now correcting this. What this implies is to reduce their reported sales and profit figures for an earlier period, ostensibly to correct their so-called sales figures for the current period to give a better picture for now. Merely by the flick of a pen, the sales figures of the past get undone and new figures emerge for the future.

Such organisations' general belief is that investors would have already given credit to past sales and profit figures and that this cannot be changed. They therefore transfer some figures from the past and move these forward to fool investors. This is bizarre accounting and rather cunning. This can be better understood by looking at what *Vestas* did in the recent past.

The Danish company, **Vestas Wind Systems**, manufacturing, selling and installing wind turbines across the world, realised in the third quarter of 2010 that it was likely to incur losses. Being the largest wind company in the world and having made commitments to investors earlier, it was difficult for company to report losses. Hence, they turned to accounting intervention, or was it invention!

Essentially what Vestas did was to take portions of sales and profits earned between 2006 and the second quarter of 2010 and shifted these to the third quarter of 2010. This was done for wind turbines that were under shipment, but not supplied and installed at customer locations. By making this transfer, its EBIT (Earnings Before Interest and Taxes) loss of €59 million was converted into an EBIT profit of €52 million. That was a 180 degrees swing!

How did this happen? Vestas declared that they were changing their sales recognition policy from the *percentage of completion method* (accounting standard in the construction contract industry, known in the accounting world as IAS 11) to the *transfer of goods method* (accounting standard for *sale of goods*, known as IAS 18) method for their supply and installation projects. Wind turbines are put together at the site of a project and take several months, if not years, to manufacture and complete. Therefore, it is normal for many wind turbine- manufacturing companies to use the *percentage of completion* method to recognise their revenue and profits. This means that as wind turbine projects move towards completion, proportionate sales and profits are recognised in companies' accounting books. For example, a 1-MW wind turbine supply-and-installation project has a sales price of $1 million, and if 40% is completed in the first year, 20% in the second year and the balance in the third year, sales will be recorded as $0.4 million in year 1, $0.2 million in year 2 and $0.4 million in year 3. However, the company decides to change its method of sales accounting from the percentage of completion method to another method such as the transfer of goods method on year 3. Since the project (including supply of the wind turbine) was transferred in full to the customer only in year 3, and not earlier, the company decides to only show sales when delivery takes place. To implement this change, it reduces its past period sale of $0.6 million (sale in year 1 and year 2), and adds this to its year 3 sale, which then becomes $1 million instead of $0.4 million under the old method. With a stroke of pen, the sales figure gets jacked up! Isn't it very original? It also helps to transfer proportionate profits forward. However, since it had not recorded its sale in year 1 and year 2, its inventory figures will need to be correspondingly enhanced, since the work-in-progress wind turbines will be shown as stock items.

What happened in Vestas? Exactly this, except that the figures were much larger. Loss in year 3 equivalent, which was nine-months ending 2010, got converted into profits.

So what is the problem? In 2013, investors demanded an independent inquiry, accusing Vestas of using an accounting change method to boost its financial results in 2010 and avoiding issuing a profit warning. Had the accounting change not taken place, there would have been a loss in the third quarter of 2010 and perhaps a loss for the full financial year 2010, which would have necessitated the company issuing a warning to investors.

Retrospective accounting treatment leads to companies' losing their shareholders' confidence, which affects the former's share price adversely. This was the case with Vestas.

Tailpiece

The world of accounting is sometimes bizarre—where real figures are hidden to report another, costs are misrepresented and camouflaged, a second set of records are maintained and past records are changed where possible. Accounting fraud usually involves cutting in slivers or increments. Rarely it is a one big fraud, but often a matter of a small falsification here or an inflated profit there. The challenge is always to find out the accounting shenanigans even if it is pint-sized and teeny-weeny at the onset.

MANIPULATING PROFITS WITH ONE-TIME EVENTS

When a company is evaluated through its financial reports, these are expected to reflect the true state of affairs of its business, transparently and truthfully. When it declares its profits, these are expected to be from regular sources, unless specifically stated.

Hiding information on how profits accrued, especially those arising from *one-time* or *exceptional* reasons, is a fraudulent practice. For example, a company makes a profit by selling a portion of its business. This is a one-time event. Profits arising from such activities should be highlighted separately and not hidden within a plethora of accounting information.

Misreporting *Special Earnings* as Regular Income

Misrepresentation of a company's factual position is due to the unethical behaviour of its management and mars its image in the sphere of good corporate governance. Any special kind of earnings, which may not occur regularly, should be specifically disclosed in its accounting reports. Non-disclosure amounts deception and deceit.

A company such as **Dell Inc.**, a Fortune 100 company widely known for its superior quality computer products, was found to have engaged in serious fraudulent practices during 2002–06. Unbelievable as it may seem, it misreported its revenue and falsely communicated to the outside world that it was in the pink of health, which it was not.

During the 1990s, Dell's share price trebled and it became the darling of the stock market. However, after the bubble burst, it began juggling its accounts to give the impression that it was continuing to do well.

Dell entered an arrangement with Intel Corporation to use the latter's central processing units (the famous *Intel Inside* ads were meant for this purpose) in its own computers and not to use Intel's competitor's chips—AMD processors. This was in exchange for exclusivity payments made by Intel to Dell. Intel paid large sums of money during this period to Dell to keep its competitor's AMD chips out of the market.

Dell did not disclose to investors the large exclusivity payments it was receiving from Intel. Its business was not doing well during this period, but it met, quarter after quarter, its expected profit targets, only due to payments made by Intel and not due to company's operations. Its poor business performance was not communicated to the investors, and the special payments received from Intel were kept hidden and not separately reported in its financial statements.

Dell's Chairman, Michael Dell, was involved in these fraudulent disclosures along with his CEO, Kevin Rollins, and CFO, James Schneider. What they represented to the outside world was that the company's increasing profit margins were due to its cost reduction initiatives and the declining cost of components, rather than revealing that these were from compensatory payments made by Intel. Complete misrepresentation of facts as one can clearly observe.

> Several former executives and Dell's founder Michael Dell agreed to pay more than $100 million in penalties (with Michael Dell paying a $4 million penalty) in July 2010 to settle the SEC's charges on its lack of disclosures and accounting fraud.

Showing One-time Income as Regular Income

To evaluate a business organisation, one of the important areas to look at is how stable is its *regular* flow of income and whether it is growing. Stability, consistency and growth are the hallmarks of a successful enterprise. However, this is precisely the reason why accounting fraud takes place—to give a false picture if an enterprise is not able to prove its consistent growth story.

In difficult times, corporate organisations often look for one-time gains in addition to their regular income.

One-time income usually arises from sale of assets or by restructuring of businesses. It should not be treated as a regular revenue income stream, but a one-time capital gain or exceptional income, depending on the type of transaction.

Showing one-time gains as part of their revenue income is another way in which companies dupe the unsuspecting investor community.

The world-renowned IT company **IBM** did this. In 1999, its employee, Kevin Collins, conjured a scheme for an accounting fraud through a sham transaction. This was not only to help IBM, but also **Dollar General Corporation**, a US chain of variety stores.

IBM wanted to increase its revenue by at least $10 million in 2000 by selling its new electronic cash registers to Dollar General and replacing the latter's old registers. However, there was one problem. If Dollar General replaced its old equipment, it would need to write off its book value as an expense in its books of accounts. (Assets need to be written down if they are junked or disposed-off at a loss, since their resell value is no longer equal to the book value shown in the asset side of a company's balance sheet.) The *book loss* had a negative implication on Dollar General's earnings for 2000.

What did IBM do? Through a sham transaction, it agreed to buy the old registers at their book value for $11 million in December 2000 and agreed to pay for this in January 2001. Thereby, Dollar General avoided a book loss, since it no longer needed to junk the old worthless registers at no value. IBM then billed for its $10 million machines at $21 million to recover the original $11 million paid to Dollar General for the old useless machines, and gave it time to pay this over the next five years.

So who benefited and by how much? Dollar General did not have to write down in its books the value of the old useless cash registers and its financial accounts (financial-year ending January 2000) showed enhanced earning figures of $11 million. IBM could show additional sales of $10 million (after netting the $11 million returned to Dollar General in January 2000 from the invoiced amount $21 million) in its books of accounts in the financial year ending March 2000. Its employees, including Collins, who were involved in the sham deal, received a bonus on $21 million (gross value of sales). Win-win scenario for all with IBM help to structure the sham deal.

Goodwill in Acquisitions to Slow Down Depreciation Costs

In case of acquisition of another company, if the purchase consideration is apparently paid more than what is logical, the excess is due to *Goodwill*. (Goodwill constitutes the excess of the asset value paid by a company to another company in an acquisition.)

For example, let us assume that company X buys company Z for $10 million. Assets of Z company were $15 million and liabilities $5 million. The acquisition price paid was the exact difference between their assets and liabilities—$10 million. Therefore, there was no goodwill. However, assume that their assets amounted to $12 million and liabilities at $5 million. Normally, the cost of the companies should have been $7 million. However, if $10 million had been paid instead of $7 million, the extra $3 million would have been considered as Goodwill.

Goodwill, like any other asset, needs to be depreciated or written down over a period of time. Amortisation or writing off of Goodwill under various accounting GAAPs is usually at a slower pace than in the case of normal assets. Therefore, if the value of the assets taken over is shown at a lower value and that of Goodwill at a correspondingly higher value, writing down or amortisation charged in the P&L account in future years will be lower. This is a way in which companies reduce their future costs.

Vodafone's mobile business in Japan was acquired by **Softbank** in April 2006. At that time, the value of its fixed assets comprising its network, transmission towers and other infrastructure amounted to $9 billion. However, Softbank had other ideas of valuing the assets it had acquired in its own books. It valued fixed assets at half their value. Without providing an explanation, it wrote down the fixed assets and correspondingly enhanced the amount of Goodwill. The advantage was Goodwill is written off in 20 years (under relevant accounting standards) against fixed assets, which are to be written off in 10 years. A longer write-off period meant a reduced annual depreciation charge. Its future profits were therefore enhanced through one accounting entry.

Tailpiece

According to the NYT, 'Praise is fleeting, but brickbats we recall', summarising the human trait of recollecting bad events in the past and forgetting good times. The corporate world is no different.

Negative trends dominate analysis. Therefore, corporate managers are usually looking to find succour—sometimes by hiding bad news by overplaying even one-off good ones.

FUDGING OPERATING INCOME AND LOSSES

Exaggerating *operating income* is a ploy companies sometimes use to reflect a better picture of their financial health. It reflects revenue earned from regular business activities. The other side of the spectrum is *non-operating income* customarily not arising from regular business operations. These include income from sale of plants and equipment, prior-year adjustments, one-time bonuses received from vendors and income from changes in accounting policy.

Shifting Non-operating Income to Operating Income

In business, consistency of performance is very important. A roller-coaster ride depicts uncertainty, insecurity and ambiguity. If we look around, consistency helps to evaluate a situation better. Be it a football team, a car or a student's result in class, performance needs to be steady and somewhat predictable.

Appraisal of operating income enables us to gauge whether a business is a consistent performer. Operating income arises from the regular operations of the business and is recurring in nature. This includes sale of products dealt with by the company. Non-operating income includes revenue flowing from irregular sources.

If operating income shows a slump, some companies tend to classify non-operating income as operating income. Such reclassification may involve falsification of accounting disclosure.

Cardinal Health, Ohio-based company, did exactly this. Since it followed a strict regimen of meeting market expectations of its quarterly results, it would push and cajole its employees to make this happen. In fact, the company met or beat profit guidance given to the market for 77 consecutive quarters. This was an unbelievable achievement and should have led to verification of whether a company could have such an uninterrupted and consistent performance without resorting to under the board activities. And it did carry out accounting wickedness.

Cardinal, a provider of healthcare products and services made accounting adjustments to show that its operating income in a better position than what it actually was between September 2000 and March 2004 to misguide investors. It materially changed its reporting of its income by inflating its operating revenue figures by misclassifying over $5 billion of bulk inventory sales as operating revenue, whereas this should have been shown as a non-operating income stream.

What was its fraudulent practice? The company disclosed two types of sales revenue. The first was on buying drugs, storing them and then selling them at a profit (shown as operating revenue). The second was pure brokerage, which was a negligible margin business where bulk drugs were ordered from manufacturers and generally shipped within 24 hours to customers' warehouses without any risks being taken and a negligible margin being earned (shown as non-operating revenue).

Cardinal's profits were from its operating business and not its brokerage business. The company knew that investors focus on operating revenue.

In order to show higher operating revenue, Cardinal ensured that most of its bulk drug brokerage business had a gap of 24 hours or more. Even when the drugs were supposed to move before 24 hours, stocks were held for more than 24 hours. Internally, and without making any disclosure to the shareholders, the company classified that its products had a 24-hour gap between purchase and sales as operating income instead of bulk or non-operating sales. This did not increase its sales. It only shifted its non-profit generating bulk sales to its operating income. By doing this, its operating revenue growth was shown in excess of around one-third over its real growth percentage during the three-year period.

It should be noted that by showing bulk sales as its operating income, the company needed to show higher than actual profits. This is because low-margin bulk business was shown as a high-margin operating income business. The company committed other accounting fraud to show false profits.

> In 2007, Cardinal agreed to pay a penalty of $35 million to settle charges on accounting fraud committed over four years.

Shifting Operating Losses to Non-operating Ones

It is comforting to know that a problem is only temporary. However, *operating losses* in an organisation are generally expected to recur to the discomfiture of investors.

Companies therefore tend to shift their operating losses or costs to the non-operating sections in their income statements. These incorrect classifications result in deceiving investors by giving an incorrect picture of their business.

To sight an example, **SafeNet**, the information security company, misclassified and excluded a significant amount of recurring and operating expenses from its earnings statement in the third quarter of 2004 till the second quarter of 2005 to meet or exceed its quarterly profit targets.

SafeNet improperly classified its ordinary operating expenses (recurring costs) as integration expenses (non-recurring costs) in its books of accounts. The operating expenses it misclassified included costs such as expenses for the foreign advertisements, travel, meals and entertainment of its international subsidiary company.

> SafeNet made several accounting misstatements between 2000 and 2006. This included backdating its options and earnings management. The company paid a civil penalty of $1 million and its senior management members were subjected to personal fines.

Tailpiece

Every investor's dream is to hold stakes in companies showing a steady growth in their operating income. Many companies do not dishearten them. They achieve this by cooking their account books!

SUBSIDIARIES, JVs AND AFFILIATES: AN OPTION TO HIDE PROBLEMS

Do we not sometimes wish that our problems could be passed on to someone else? How wonderful it would be if our shortcomings could be hidden? This is precisely what corporates do when they use their subsidiaries or JV partners and push their problems to these lesser mortals. It is literally hiding things under the carpet! The reverse is also sometimes true. How you wished that in a game of basketball some of your opponent's scores could somehow be included in your team's score? Similarly, if the sister company of an enterprise is doing well, although it has no effective control over it, it sometimes steals its subsidiary's improved financial results and makes it its own.

All these are frauds—accounting deceptions, to be precise!

Incorporating Non-consolidating Subsidiaries as Part of Parent to Improve Its Position

There are occasions when subsidiaries are performing better than its parent. However, if the parent does not control its subsidiaries or does not own more than 50% of their shares, it cannot take their revenue figures into consideration while preparing its own financial results. Sometimes, to disguise the poor performance of the parent, subsidiary numbers, which cannot be consolidated, are included to camouflage the former's actual business performance.

Vivendi Universal turned its disastrous financials upside down, showing a brilliant performance and cash flows by piggy backing on its subsidiaries fraudulently. The media and telecommunications company held a 44% stake in the *Cegetel Group* and 35% in *Maroc Telekomunikacja* (Telco) during 2001–02. Both were profitable and cash-generating companies. However, since Vivendi had a less than 50% shareholding, it could neither access their surplus cash nor could it consolidate their financial results.

In March 2002, Vivendi's management declared that it had generated operating free cash flow of €2 billion in 2001. This was untrue. Not only did it do this, but its management declared a dividend payout of €1 per share in May 2002 because of its so-called brilliant results in the previous year. This sucked out €1.5 billion in cash its subsidiaries.

What did Vivendi do? It borrowed funds on a short-term basis from Cegetel to pay the dividend and promised to repay the loan by July 2002, which the management knew it could not. Not only this, though Cegetel and Telco could not be consolidated, Vivendi took their performance into consideration to paint a rosy picture of its own operations, although it was incurring losses. Its cash position improved due to the short-term loan, which it did not show as a loan, but as its own funds. A complete fraudulent treatment!

Vivendi SA, with substantial holdings in the USA and Europe, became a conglomerate with its merger with Seagram and Canal+ in December 2000. When this merger took place, Jean-Messier (the company's CEO) announced that it would generate an annual profit growth of 35% during 2001–02. This announcement was the starting point of doctored accounts during the ensuing downturn when the dot-com boom bust and markets crashed. In July 2002, Messier and Guillaume Hannezo (the CFO) resigned from their positions, and Vivendi's new management disclosed that it had experienced a liquidity crisis and its accounting information had been doctored.

Messier was convicted by a French court on criminal charges in January 2011, a three-year suspended sentence and fined €150,000 for misleading its shareholders

Inter-company Expenses Shown as Customer Receivables

There could be several legal entities or companies, belonging to a single group, conducting a common business. In such cases, it is usual that one company incurs expenses for another. However, it needs to pass on the cost to the company to which the expense belongs.

Accounting manoeuvres take place by not executing appropriate accounting treatments for such inter-company costs.

This type of fraud took place at the **Interpublic Group of Companies**, an advertising agency that had **McCann Erickson** as its flagship concern. McCann Erickson fraudulently misstated its financial results by recording its inter-company costs as receivables instead of expenses (that is, deducting from income). Keeping pace with market expectations, it cooked its financial results. Its accounting problem started in 1997.

The basic issue was that McCann Erickson would incur costs on behalf of Interpublic. These needed to be charged (passed-on or debited) to Interpublic. However, McCann, instead of passing this on to Interpublic as an inter-company charge, accounted these as debtors (*debited* debtors) as a balance sheet asset. This had the effect of reducing implications of expenses incurred (by reversing or crediting the expense incurred) and showing this as receivables from customers.

Had the inter-company accounts between McCann and Interpublic been periodically reconciled, they would have got caught. But their managements failed to ensure reconciliation of their intercompany accounts for at least six years. In fact, at times, they purposely delayed reconciling the inter-company accounts, since they knew that any reconciliation would reveal their wrong-doings and require them to book their costs.

> Interpublic restated its accounts for the period 1997–2002 by $180 million by booking additional expenses it had not booked earlier, and agreed to pay a $12 million fine in May 2008.

Tailpiece

Hiding a problem is often considered synonymous with fixing it. In the corporate world, this technique is adopted over and over again.

HIDING PROBLEMS BY UNDERSTATING COSTS

Who does not want to hide bad news? Businesses are no different.

Commercial activities are undertaken to generate a surplus. When sales exceed costs, profits are generated. The cardinal principle for doing well in business is either to enhance sales or curtail costs.

If costs incurred can be suppressed or concealed, the end objective of beefing up surplus can be achieved, though fraudulently.

Capitalising Normal Revenue Expenses

Sales, distribution and marketing costs constitute revenue expenditure. These are expenses incurred to run an organisation on an ongoing basis. In 1995 and 1996, advertising costs incurred by AOL, the global web-services company, to acquire new customers were capitalised and not shown as a revenue cost item. AOL capitalised advertising costs of $385 million by September 1996 when it corrected its wrongdoing. It was penalised $3.5 million for its misdemeanour.

Let us examine the implications of revenue expenses shown as capital costs.

Expenses pertaining to regular running of businesses are known as *revenue expenditure* or *operating expenses*. The expenses, which result in acquisition or making improvements in assets is known as *capital expenditure*.

Revenue expenditure is deducted from sales in the period during which expenses are incurred to arrive at profits or losses. Whereas *capital* expenditure is not subtracted from sales, since it results in a long-term benefit, this goes to the asset side of the balance sheet. Capital costs are however subjected to periodical depreciation, which is a revenue cost. Examples of revenue expenses include raw material used to manufacture end products, salaries and wages given to employees, advertisement cost of sales promotion, and so forth. Examples of capital expenses include purchase of plants and machinery, furniture and fixtures, and so forth. Therefore, profit figures can be enhanced fraudulently if any expenditure constituting revenue can be treated as capital expenditure.

Such fraudulent actions make a significant impact on the financial statements of a company because (i) transfer or reclassification of cost reduce its operating costs and affect its net income positively, (ii) the value of its assets is overstated by the amount reclassified and (iii) its net worth in its balance sheet is correspondingly increased due to enhancement of its asset side. This is a fraudulent accounting practice and is often practised in the business world.

Greed overtook sanity—gross over reporting of profits was undertaken.

WorldCom, providing a broad range of communication services, including Internet services, incurred *line costs*. This included the various fees the company paid to third-party telecommunication carriers for its rights to access third-party networks to serve its customers. Under accounting rules, these should be treated as operating costs.

During the third quarter of 2000 till the first quarter of 2002, WorldCom transferred, without any backup, line costs from its operating costs to capital costs, thereby understating its costs, overstating its assets and correspondingly its net worth.

During these six quarters, the company's costs were understated, with its profits being overstated by a staggering $5 billion. This misreporting had the effect of converting some of its loss-making quarters into profit-making ones. By showing fraudulent profit figures, WorldCom falsely projected itself as a profitable business.

> WorldCom filed for bankruptcy in July 2002 when it came to light that its accounts were forged and profits grossly overstated. Its top management was found guilty of fraud and filing false statements. Some of the members were imprisoned, including its CEO, Bernard Ebbers, who was sentenced to prison for 25 years. Its shareholders, who lost a large amount of money due to the fraud, were offered a settlement of $6.1 billion. The company reorganised itself as MCI Inc., and emerged from bankruptcy in August 2004. MCI was bought over by Verizon Communications Inc. in January 2006.

Banks' Failure to Write Down Bad Loans

Banks, where we deposit our savings, lend the money gathered to those who require it. They gain from the interest and other income they earn on the money they have lent. To any bank, a loan advanced to someone is an income-generating asset till it is repaid. The quality of loan granted is dependent upon the borrower's ability to repay or make timely payment of interest. Accordingly, the loan amount shown in a bank's balance sheet needs to be evaluated regarding its worthiness.

Let us take an example. A bank has lent $200 million to a borrower. However, the borrower did not repay it on time. The bank needs to assess the recoverability of the loan and begin writing down its value. In the first year, it decides to write down the loan amount by 20%. If this is so, at the end of the first year, the loan will be shown on the asset side of the bank's balance sheet at $160 million, i.e., after it writing down 20% of $200 million ($40 million). In the first year, the bank will need to show in its income statement (P&L Account) a cost or charge of $40 million, and accordingly, its profits will go down to this extent.

At the end of the second year, the bank will again need to evaluate this account, and if need be, write down further the loan outstanding amount if the borrower is still not meeting his or her obligations. Such evaluation of the loan account will need to be done at the end of every quarter.

It should also be noted that a complete write-off of a loan account may not be required, since the bank will have the right to recover part of its loss through sale of assets that would have been taken as a mortgage against the loan granted.

Banks or financial institutions not writing down their *bad* loans or not reflecting their true value give a rosy picture of their financial health in their balance sheets.

Not only do banks provide loans directly, but they may decide to sell or pass them on to other financial institutions to free their own ability to lend. This amounts to trading of bank loans in the market. When such trading takes place, accounting becomes a bit complicated, and there is a potential for fraudulent practices.

Let us look at an example where there was improper accounting.

The business model of **Fannie Mae**, the US Government-sponsored mortgage finance company, practised buying mortgage-backed (asset backed) loans from banks and assume its risk for payment of interest and principal. In return, Fannie Mae would be entitled to a fee.

While carrying out such transactions (especially between 2002 and 2004), Fannie Mae juggled its accounts to boost its profit figures. During this period, interest rates were on a downward momentum. Therefore, on many occasions, Fannie Mae purchased a loan portfolio with a higher rate of interest at a premium when the market rate of interest was already lower. To obtain such loans, Fannie Mae needed to pay a *premium*, and this premium needed to be amortised over the remaining period of the loan.

For instance, Fannie Mae acquired a loan portfolio of $100 million from a bank carrying an interest rate of 5% p.a., at a time when the prevailing rate of interest was already 4% p.a. Since it would normally earn only 4%, if it decided to lend in the market it could acquire a loan portfolio of $100 million with a 5% p.a. interest. To do this, Fannie Mae would need to pay a premium of say $2 million. Such a premium is a cost and needs to be amortised over the lifetime of the loan. However, a loan can be paid earlier by the borrower (known as prepayment), and consequently, the premium write off (or amortisation) will need to be hastened. If a $100 million loan had a balance repayment period of five years, the $2 million premium charge would need to be amortised over five years, or at $0.4 million per annum. However, assuming that the loan was to be prepaid in two years by the original borrower, the premium charge would need to be accelerated and amortised in two years (perhaps at $1 million per annum.) instead of the earlier five years. Such an adjustment would affect the profits of Fannie Mae, since the charge (cost) would go up.

Between 2002 and 2004, Fannie Mae did not make such adjustments and avoided charging its income statement with enhanced costs, which accounting rules required. This was an accounting fraud committed to show better than usual results.

> Fannie Mae paid a civil fine of $400 million to settle the accounting scandal case against it.

Failure to Write Down Excess or Obsolete Inventory

Most of us accumulate junk, be it in the office or at home.

An enterprise is no different. Inventory is an asset of any company. Over time, some inventory gets accumulated that is either useless or obsolete. Worthless inventories should be written down in value, since it is likely that its market value will be less than what is reflected in the accounting books. If these obsolete inventory continue to be shown as an asset and not written down (that is, not shown as a cost in a company's income statement), the financial results will give an incorrect picture.

Similarly, inventory that is not in existence, but is shown in the books of companies, should also be written off. Inventory deficiencies are usually observed during a stock-taking exercise, where physical stocks are verified and compared with book stocks. Shortages may occur due to theft, shrinkage, short-receipts or over-usage in manufacturing, which was not recorded earlier.

Rent-Way, Inc. is an example where this writing-down was not done. An expert in juggling its accounts, the company made a physical inventory of merchandise parts in September 1999. It showed that the actual inventory in hand amounted to $0.4 million, whereas its books of accounts showed a balance of $1.4 million. The shortage of $1 million needed to written off, but, the company failed to do this. This resulted in its understating its cost by $1 million.

Failure to Write Down Non-collectable Debtors

Debtors are created when sales are made on credit. It is presumed that customers will eventually pay on expiry of credit period. But what happens when the debtors (that is, customers who have not yet paid) either deny payment or there is reason to believe that they may not ever pay. If money is not received against sales made, income shown earlier when sales took place need to be corrected. This reversal (correction) can happen by showing as a cost the debts that are likely to remain uncollected. This is known as *bad-debt provision* and implies that certain debtors are likely to go *bad*.

In order to perpetrate fraud and show an enhanced business performance, many companies do not have adequate bad debt provisions, which results in their income continuing to be shown at higher than reality levels.

Vivendi Universal, the French company, with operations in the USA and Europe, fudged its account books between 2000 and 2002. Among the many methods it adopted to give a positive picture of its revenue figures, was not making adequate provision for bad debts—not showing as a cost the likely quantum of debtors that may not pay.

One of Vivendi's subsidiaries, **Cegetel**, would make provisions for bad debts, based on its experience. For example, it may have experienced that on an average 5% of debtors usually do not pay and go bad. And in such cases, they could make, as a matter of financial prudence, a provision for the bad debts of 5% of its debtors every year.

In mid-2001, Vivendi became worried that it might not be able to meet the profit targets it had set. During the second quarter of

2001, its management departed from its historic methodology for determining the level of its reserve for bad debts. This resulted in Cegetel making a lower provision for bad debts during the quarter than its historic methodology required and led to its provision for bad debts to become €45 million less than it should have been.

This helped Vivendi, Cegetel's parent, to improve its overall profit figures. The decision to reduce the provision for bad debts was taken at a time when Cegetel was facing difficulties in collecting money from customers. This was due to ongoing difficult market conditions on account of the dot-com bust.

Vivendi did not disclose that its basis of providing for bad debts had changed during this period, and was silent about the change in its accounting method. It was a poor accounting practice.

Failure to Write Down Bad Investments

Most of us have made bad investments. If this is the case, we should not consider the bad investment at its so-called original worth, but at a much lower value, based on what it is currently worth.

This is also the case in business acquisitions. When a company is acquired, sometimes the acquisition price exceeds the value of the target company's identifiable assets. Let us assume that the net value of assets of company A is $100 million, and is being acquired by company B for $120 million. The excess is paid, since company B believes that the future cash flows of company A will compensate for the higher price it had paid. The difference of $20 million is therefore Goodwill and needs to be accounted as such. However, if company A's profitability declines for whatever reason, the Goodwill value will need to be written-down or impaired in company B's books of accounts.

European companies are facing a problem currently due to their past over-priced acquisitions prior to 2008. The pan-European market regulator is questioning them why adequate impairments are not being reflected in their books of accounts. Listed companies are usually required to undergo an *impairment test* once a year.

According to reports published in the *Financial Times*, 235 European companies have been surveyed by the European market regulator. These companies had €800 billion as Goodwill at the beginning of 2011, but only wrote down 5% (€40 billion) in 2012. There seems to be too much Goodwill hanging around in Europe!

Failure to Record Invoices Received Late from Vendors

One of the ways in which companies show improved profits is by reducing their costs. How do they do this, if these costs have been incurred? It is simple. They do not record or recognise bills received from vendors during the current period and push these to a subsequent one. This helps them improve their financial results during the current period (quarter or year).

Irrespective of whether payment is made or not to a vendor, the monetary value of goods received or services consumed should be recorded in a company's books of accounts as a cost (and a liability to be accrued) for the period when either the goods were received or services used.

Rent-Way engaged in fraudulent accounting. To improve its profits, invoices it had received from vendors, but which were not processed for payment by its accounts department by the year end, were pushed to the next financial year. Unrecorded expenses ($5 million) at the end of 1999 were deferred to 2000. Its unrecorded expenses at the end of 2000, pushed to the next year, were even higher at $9 million. Very effective way was found by Rent-Way to improve business performance by some strokes of a pen.

Receipt of Sham Cash Received from Vendors to Reduce Costs

Showing reduced costs to boost profit is a popular way in which companies fraudulently prop up their financial position. One way could be to show that vendors have given cash rebates or funding for exclusive sourcing arrangements. These so-called fund receipts from vendors can be used to offset expenses incurred by the companies. Such receipts should be disclosed separately and not set off against recurring expense items.

Let us take an example of this. The operating costs of **Dell**, the computer technology company, were growing. It devised a dubious method to project a rosy picture of the costs it had incurred.

Between 2002 and 2006, the company wrongfully set off its growing operating costs against special payments received from Intel. It entered an arrangement with Intel for exclusive use of the latter's central processing units instead of also using its competitor processors (e.g., AMD) on receipt of an exclusivity payment. Dell should have shown these special payments received separately. However, it used this to set off its recurring costs and communicated to the outside world that it had taken special cost reduction initiatives to save costs.

Failure to Record Expenses Incurred or Reversing These

The top management of **Medaphis**, a business management service company, who were masters of accounting fiddling game, directed one of the company's wholly owned subsidiaries to reverse a cost accrual into income for employee bonuses, though eventually payable in the first quarter of 1996. The effect of this directive was to reduce its expenses and liabilities, and increase its income on its books. Similarly, in the second quarter of 1996, one of the subsidiaries of Medaphis was expected to incur an additional cost of $1.4 million to enter certain software development and consulting contracts. However, in order to protect its financial results, the company ignored this cost as its potential liability and showed enhanced profits for the quarter.

Accounting norms require that costs incurred or accrued are recorded in the books of accounts of companies during the same period. If costs have been paid, the expense head shows an increase in cost and cash is depleted, since it is utilised to make the payment. If the expense is yet to be incurred, a *liability* needs to be created for the payment obligation.

Incurrence of expense goes to reduce income. Once an expense is incurred, it cannot be reversed unless a company's liability to pay has been extinguished.

Another such example was **Tyco International**—a story of corporate plunder and cost-concealment. It involved self-serving and clandestine misconduct of three of its senior-most executives. Between 1996 and June 2002, Dennis Kozlowski (then CEO) and Mark Swartz (then CFO), and between 1998 and 2002, Mark Belnick (then Chief Corporate Counsel) appropriated hundreds of millions of dollars in secret and unauthorised improper low interest or interest-free loans and compensations from Tyco. These transactions were kept hidden and not recorded in the company's books of accounts. The extent of their self-aggrandisement extended to highly profitable related-party transactions with Tyco, lavish perquisites and massive appropriation of corporate funds. None of this was shown as a cost in the company's income statements and no disclosures were made by the company. It was a loot!.

Tyco practiced all sorts of corporate burgle, including paying *fees* to one of its directors on an M&A transaction without any disclosure. It acquired the CIT Group in 2001 for $9 billion and paid Frank Walsh, a director, a *finder's fee* of $20 million, but did not make a cost entry in its books of accounts. The company's unethical practices went to the extent when it fraudulently made a disclosure that except to its own investment bankers for the acquisition, no other finder's fees or commissions were to be paid. Not only that, Walsh participated as a board member in the meeting that considered the acquisition of CIT by Tyco, but he did not disclose that he had been instrumental in recommending the acquisition or that he would receive a finder's fee.

Failure to Record and Report Depreciation

Expense incurred is a cost. But if a company books the incurrence of an *expense* as asset creation, this has the implication of not enhancing its cost, but increasing its assets.

This sort of incorrect accounting is often done in the case of accounting of depreciation (i.e., amortisation charges on assets held and used), where instead of increasing the depreciation account as an expense head, the company's asset account (as a non-cost head) is enhanced. In simple language, its expenses are hidden by stashing it against some assets in the company.

Rent-Way, a rental merchandise company, knew that its largest cost head was *depreciation*. During each accounting period, the company needed to recognise expenses for depreciation on its rental of merchandise. This would entail a corresponding reduction in its merchandise rental asset account (since its assets are getting depreciated due to usage). The company manipulated its merchandise rental account to artificially limit its recognition of its quarterly merchandise rental depreciation expense. The company artificially increased its merchandise rental asset account to hide its current depreciation.

Apart from the above, Rent-Way also artificially inflated its merchandise rental asset account and made a corresponding entry to inflate its miscellaneous income. This implied an increase in its assets as well as in its *other income* heads. The impact of this manipulation was understating its expense by $6 million in 1999 and $36 million in 2000.

Tailpiece

Hiding wealth amassed by corrupt means is challenging. In China, a Lieutenant General hid his ill-gotten wealth, by making a gold statue of Chairman Mao Zedong, the father of the Chinese revolution. A raid on his house in January 2014 revealed his novel way

PLAYING WITH INVENTORY TO GENERATE PROFITS

Simple tricks sometimes generate extraordinary results. A relatively innocent, but highly illegal way of doing this is by exaggerating the value of inventory. Closing stocks, the other name for inventories, includes raw materials, work-in-progress and finished goods. This is a hot bed for accounting fraud.

Let us take an example. Assume that an enterprise purchases goods worth $100 and sells products worth $80 at $70. Its closing inventory would normally be $20 ($100 for its purchases less $80 as the cost of goods sold). The loss would be $10 ($70 being the sales price of goods worth $80). Now, in order to give a better picture, the company fraudulently values its closing stock of $20 as $50. This enables it to change its the actual *loss* position of $10 into a false *profit* of $20 (purchases of $100 *less* sales of $70 plus closing stock of $50). The swing of profit is $30 (from loss to profit change) can be made by valuing the company's inventory upwards from $20 to $50 by fraudulent means. A significant accounting bluff practised in the corporate world.

Valuing LIFO to FIFO Cost of Sales to Augment Profits

If the cost of inventory used for manufacturing (also known as cost of goods sold) can be reduced, it helps to show sham profits.

During inflation, one of the methods is to value *goods used for sales* using the First In First Out (FIFO) method, compared to the Last In First Out (LIFO) or average cost mode. When prices are rising, goods coming in first should normally be less expensive. If goods that have arrived earlier are shown to have been used for production, as opposed to those coming in last, the cost of goods sold is automatically shown as low and a company's profits are boosted.

An instance of juggling with the cost of goods sold took place in **Exxon Mobil**, an oil and gas company, although this was to deplete its profits and not to enhance them. In 2006, the company used the LIFO method to value cost of the goods sold by it. This helped it to use higher cost goods that came in last to convert these to petroleum products. This helped it to show decreased profits and consequently pay a low Corporate Tax rate.

Converting Inventory into Fixed Assets

Profits can be boosted by fraudulently showing increased inventory figures. However, the problem is that showing higher than usual inventory levels can attract the attention of investors and analysts. To hide this, companies sometimes convert excess inventory into fixed assets. Since norms for levels of fixed assets such as plants and equipment are difficult to fix and evaluate, conversion of excess inventory into fixed assets seems a safer bet.

Both inventory and fixed assets are assets shown in a balance sheet, and therefore, it is easier to make the switch between the two heads fraudulently through false accounting entries and documentation.

To show enhanced profits, **Comptronix Corporation**, an electronics company, fraudulently increased the value of its inventory between 1990 and 1992. When its false inventory figures became too high, its executives panicked. They converted a major part of it into *purchased equipment* or *fixed assets*. This was done through a series of phony transactions and helped them show fixed assets higher from $35 to $54 million. Comptronix was caught, confessed to the fraud and restated its accounts.

Tailpiece

Leo Tolstoy said, 'It is amazing how complete is the delusion that beauty is goodness'. Similarly, doctoring inventory to pep up profit is a good idea till it catches up in the next period—when closing stock becomes the opening stock the next time!

COOKIE JAR RESERVES AND ILLUSORY PROFITS

Dell did it; so did Microsoft and GE.

A well-known computer company such as **Dell Inc.** was involved in wide-ranging accounting fraud including maintaining *cookie jar* reserves it used to cover shortfalls in its operating results between 2002 and 2005. By releasing reserves it had created in an earlier period, Dell misrepresented its operating expenses as a percentage of sales, quarter after quarter, for three years. The company showed that it was improving its cost trend although in reality it was going up or at best remaining steady.

What are *cookie jar reserves*?

We store readily accessible food in our refrigerators. These can be taken out any time we feel hungry. Corporations sometimes follow this principle to store *goodies* so that these can be drawn upon at times of a dip in their profits.

How are these *cookies* created in the corporate world?

This is done by suppressing real profits to release portions of it in the future when a company's actual profits are inadequate.

Let us take an example to illustrate this. A company's annual profits are usually around $25 million. In 2011, they are significantly higher at $70 million (due to exceptionally good market conditions or accrual of extraordinary income). The company should report its abnormally good financial performance and the reasons for it. However, an enterprise with a fraudulent intent could show, for example, $30 million (and not $70 million as its real profit). This will help it create a secret reserve of the balance of its unreported profit of $40 million ($70 million real profit less $30 million reported profit). It can use this reserve in the future. For instance, in 2012, its profit is $10 million (instead of the usual $25 million). It can draw upon its secret reserve (of $40 million created in 2011) and can draw (i.e., reverse) $15 million from this amount. The profit it reports in 2012 will again be $25 million ($10 million real profit plus $15 million drawn from the earlier created secret reserve). By showing its profit in 2012 as $25 million instead of $10 million (its real profits), investors and others are being misled into thinking that all is well with the company, when its financial condition is deteriorating with its falling profits.

Secret reserves can be created in various ways, for example, by creating a *liability provision* under an expense head, knowing well that such liabilities will not arise. For instance, a liability provision can be created on grounds of 'provision for doubtful debtors'—amount set aside for likely non-receipt of payments from certain customers, knowing that debtors are unlikely to become bad for payment. When such provisions are created, this is shown as a cost in the company's P&L account, which has the effect of reducing its profits. The excess liability provision created becomes a secret reserve and is reversible in full or in part when required.

This reversal of a liability provision has the effect of increasing a company's profit. Conversely, when the liability provision was created in earlier years, it had the effect of reducing it.

Creation of a reserve has the effect of creating a cookie jar by saving cookies in a jar when there are excess cookies. These can be used in bad times when there are no cookies available for consumption. Creation of secret reserves is also known as cookie jar reserves.

Enron

The master of fraudulent accounting, from the third quarter of 2000 through the third quarter of 2001, Enron used cookie jar reserves from one of its businesses, Enron Wholesale, which was making profits. This business earned windfall trading profits, especially from California's energy market.

The large profits earned by Enron Wholesale were underreported by it to avoid reporting large losses in other areas of its business and preserve its earnings for use during later quarters. Enron Wholesale's undisclosed reserve accounts reached over $1 billion by early 2001. They were used in later quarters (till 3Q 2001) to bolster profits in Enron's other non-performing businesses, especially losses in its Enron Energy Services (EES) Business Unit, to project a better than real picture to investors.

Sunbeam Corporation

In July 1996, the financially ailing company Sunbeam appointed a new CEO, Albert Dunlap, and CFO, Russell Kersch, to restructure its operations. The newly appointed CEO and CFO had negotiated hefty pay packages to increase the company's share price and then sell the company at a much higher share price. This incentivised them to improve the company's performance in 1997 disproportionately after joining it in 1996. This was the starting point of their cookie jar policies.

What did they do? Having joined in 1996, the duo depressed the company's profits in 1996 with the intent to show a better than usual performance in 1997. On successful implementation of this policy, this would have the effect of enhancing its stock price in early 1998 (after its 1997 financial results were published) and they would be able to sell the company at a much higher stock valuation. Therefore, they created *cookie jar reserves* by showing excessive *liability* provisions against non-existent costs including excessive litigation costs and restructuring liabilities.

What did Sunbeam do with the cookie jar reserves? Did the plan to create reserves work? In 1997, the cookie jar reserves were released quarter after quarter. Since the liability or reserves created in 1996 were either in excess or against non-existent potential costs, it was easy for the company to reverse part of the reserves and *cook its books* to show a better than real financial performance.

The cookie jar reserves it created in 1996 worked in 1997 and through the first quarter of 1998.

However, when the company's sales continued to falter and market estimates of its anticipated financial performance could not be met, the value of its stocks tumbled from the second quarter of 1998. It filed for bankruptcy in February 2001. Its purpose in creating cookie jar reserves did not work beyond a few quarters, since the amount reserved was not sufficient to cover all its future profit-related shortfalls.

> Sunbeam Corporation was an American electric home appliances company. Its then CEO Albert Dunlap perpetrated a massive fraud by over-reporting its sales and profits. In 1997, out of its reported profit of $189 million, almost $60 million was shown by manipulating the company's accounting books. When Sunbeam's accounting violations came to light, the company filed for Chapter 11 bankruptcy in 2001. In 2002, it emerged from bankruptcy and was renamed American Household Inc. (AHI). In September 2004, Jarden Corporation acquired AHI.

Krispy-Kreme

For fiscal year 2003–04, Krispy-Kreme accrued its senior management incentives (cash bonuses on attaining certain target business performance criteria) on a quarterly basis. However, the accrual was usually in excess of what was to be the likely payout. The difference between the actual cost and the excess liability provision made for its management incentive plan helped the company build its cookie jar.

The secret reserve created was released in future quarters, based on the shortfall in Krispy-Kreme's business performance. In good quarters, the company made excess provisions of incentive costs, and in poor ones, it released the excess provisions made earlier. By creating a variable incentive provision in its books (irrespective of probable payouts) and by writing back a part of the earlier excess incentive provisions it had made whenever required, the company *managed* its profit numbers.

> Since 1937, Krispy-Kreme, a US corporation has been in the business of making and selling doughnuts. The company listed its shares in the New York Stock Exchange in May 2001. After this, it provided guidance on its likely quarterly EPS. In fiscal year 2003–04, the company followed the policy of exceeding its EPS guidance by 1 cent ($0.01 per share—no more and no less). No business in the world can ever fulfil, quarter after quarter, its earnings guidance by a particular percentage. Krispy-Kreme created a cookie jar reserve to adjust its profits and declare a pre-determined growth number on its EPS. This began its downfall. In January 2005, when its accounting fraud came to light, the company had to re-state its results of 2003 and 2004. It restructured its businesses in 2005 to avoid bankruptcy by closing several of unprofitable stores and changing its management team. Krispy-Kreme, currently operates in various countries in the world.

Microsoft

Who can imagine that Microsoft Corporation, the world leader in software, services and solutions, has juggled its accounts books? During 1995–98, the company maintained undisclosed reserves without any clear requirement to make provision for any future liability. Normally, it maintained between $200 million and $900 million as cookie jar reserves at the corporate level to help fiddling with earnings reporting. It created these reserves in good times, and in bad or not so good times, these were released to show steady growth in the company's profit.

Now, let us look at one of the ways in which Microsoft created these cookie jars. The accounting con was to *accelerate depreciation* with *retrospective* effect. To charge depreciation, the company retrospectively reduced the useful life of its personal computers from three years to one year. One can understand prospectively reducing the life of computers from three years to one year, but to do it retroactively is preposterous. Microsoft accounted for its PCs in 1996 and 1997 showing these had always had a life-span of one year.

The difference in the value generated between the old and new useful lives was charged to the company's depreciation expense. It retained this amount in its accelerated depreciation account, which was its cookie jar reserve, without making any specific disclosure in its financial statements.

GE

In the first quarter of 2002, GE wanted to correct an accounting jugglery it had earlier perpetrated (of $1 billion) by creating a corresponding corrective accounting entry of $844 million. Not only did the company not disclose its billion dollar incorrect accounting, but also decided to retain the difference of $156 million as a reserve for its future usage. It used at least $42 million from this reserve to top up shortfalls in its profits in the ensuing second and third quarters of 2002.

> GE, perhaps one of the world's most respected companies in the world, has not been immune to accounting mischief mongerings. It used to pride itself in not failing to meet the earnings estimates of analysts. Between 1995 and 2004, GE either met or exceeded the earnings estimates, quarter after quarter. The company was the darling of the stock market. There are hardly any companies that can show, quarter after quarter, such high growth in their earning and match the expectations of stock market analysts. In hindsight, it is clear that certain accounting jugglery and improprieties in which the company engaged helped GE to return superior financial performance for a decade.

There are several other illustrations of companies using their cookie jar reserves to manipulate their profits. **ConAgra Foods**, the US-based international food company, used its reserves to meet unrelated and unplanned-for costs in legal and environmental matters during 1999–2001. **W.R. Grace** manipulated its quarterly and annual earnings to meet its internal profit targets by using its secret reserve use during 1991–95. The list is unending.

Tailpiece

Children have piggy banks. Accountants maintain cookie jar reserves. Both need to be broken open during emergencies.

However, while children learn to be thrifty by saving their little nest egg, accountants sometimes resort to sordid trickery. Both have similar concepts but completely differing ethics.

WHO KNOWS THE FUTURE: WRITING OFF FUTURE COSTS IN CURRENT YEAR

Natural tendency of management, who are mentally attuned to committing accounting juggleries, is to show higher profits in the current or the immediate succeeding reporting period. This they do by either showing increased sales or reduced costs. But can they take a contrary stand? Does any management ever show increased costs to indicate reduced profits in its current period of financial reporting? While this sounds illogical, there are organisations that adopt this approach to fulfil their objectives.

By showing an increased cost at present, companies can show turn-around financial results tomorrow. To make this clear, let us assume that a company spends $100 million on R&D, whose benefits will be evident over the next few years. Normally, the company should show a cost of $20 million over the next five years to amortise its costs over the ensuing benefit accrual period. However, the company can choose to charge the full $100 million in its income statement as a cost in the first year and thereby reduce its profits for the year. The implication would be that in future years, its profits will be enhanced, since the amortisation cost of R&D of $20 million for each of the next five years will not be shown as a cost.

The company may do this for several reasons. One reason could be that a new management team has joined the company. They *charge-off* the so-called amortisable cost (in this case R&D cost) in the first year to show a below standard business performance for the year. In this case, its financial results will be shown as better than the usual picture in the future, since its first year's results, when the new management took charge, were artificially shown at a depleted level.

Several companies have made use of such ruses, depending on their intent and objectives.

During the period 2000–01, **Cisco Systems** wrote off a significant portion (an excess of $2 billion) of its inventory, since it was useless and not saleable. However, it did sell these written down stocks in 2001 and 2002 to show increased profits.

Toy "R" Us also wrote down its stocks of toys to a negligible value and sold it later to postpone announcing its profits to a later period.

The intent of both these accounting chicanery was to make extraordinary profits from inventory written down earlier to sell these at a later date.

In addition to showing increased costs in the current period, so that their business performance can be shown in a better light in a future period, companies create *cookie jar reserves* (discussed earlier) as an alternate method of accelerating cost depiction. Secret creation of reserves is also a way in which the financial results of an earlier period can be reduced so that the reserves created can be used at a later period of time when better business results need to be shown or costs need to be doctored.

Tailpiece

'Cheer up! The worst is yet to come!', said Philander Johnson. Accountants juggling accounting books to show an enhanced future picture may be also thinking 'the future is purchased by the present', as famously stated by Samuel Johnson.

DECEITFUL ACCOUNTING OF DERIVATIVES

Life is full of uncertainties. The future is uncertain. And business is no different. If one can predict the imminent or have a crystal ball for gazing into the future, life would have been so much simpler. But that is not to be.

In view of the uncertainties of the future, several mechanisms have been developed, to protect organisations from the vagaries of general uncertainties. One of the several ways in which attempts can be made to protect the foreseeable is by using *derivative* products such as hedging, options or swaps.

Derivative transactions are sometimes so complicated that even professional accountants fail to understand their mystery. It is the haze around these products that is often taken advantage of to perpetrate accounting deception.

A company that prides itself for its high ethical standards and consistent business performance is **GE**. Between 1995 and 2004, it met or exceeded final consensus analysts' profit estimates quarter after quarter. This was an amazing run of business performance.

Unfortunately, even a company of GE's standing was not immune to fiddling with its accounting records to meet its objectives. During 2002–03, GE played with accounting principles to increase its revenue and earnings for the four quarters to avoid reporting negative financial results.

One instance of improper accounting was in GE's financial services business, where there was improper application of accounting principles to its Commercial Paper (CP) hedging programme, to avoid unfavourable disclosures and reflect a reduction in its earning of $200 million. During that time, GE mainly sourced short-term maturity funds (for 1 to 270 days) from CPs and used this to provide loans and leases to its customers. Since the CPs were for a short duration, their interest rates fluctuated, depending on prevalent interest rates, whereas the loans given by GE had fixed-term interest rates.

Thus the issue of CPs exposed GE to fluctuating interest rates to fund fixed priced financial assets and exposed it to interest rate risks. To protect itself from this interest mismatch risk, GE hedged through interest rate swaps (a type of derivative). The structure of the derivative converted variable rate CP interest rates into fixed rate interest payments and reduced GEs exposure to changing interest rates. During 2002, a portion of the company's long-term loans (issued to its customers) was not appropriately covered for risk on the interest rate differential, since all the loans given to customers did not have a corresponding CP loan, which was hedged. The mismatched portion resulted in GE losing $200 million in 2002. The company hid this fact and did not disclose it when declaring its 2002 results. This helped it meet analysts' expectations of its business results.

Tailpiece

Credit default swaps, collaterised debt obligations, interest-rate swaps, futures and options—forms of derivatives—are Latin to many. These become more complicated when some are used as instruments of deceit. Impediments are magnified when certain contracts, known as derivatives, are formed to beat the law, for example, gambling is sometimes called a future contract, a form of derivative! This is ludicrous. Care and caution need to be exercised to avoid getting into the clutches of these apparently harmless creatures created by certain financial wizards!

Warren Buffet once said that 'Derivatives are financial weapons of mass destruction'. We can add to that and say—derivatives are also financial weapons of mass deception!

BLUFFING THROUGH OFF-BALANCE SHEET FINANCING

A balance sheet is like the curriculum vitae of a business organisation. It is a good way of sifting the good from the bad. Therefore, businesses are always keen to project a favourable image of themselves through their profiles—their balance sheets.

Debt, an item in the balance sheet of a company, is usually not viewed kindly by the investing community unless it is within prudential financial norms. Therefore, whenever there is an overload of debts, efforts are often made to keep it outside balance sheets. Such debts are known as *off-balance sheet financing*. These structures are not necessarily illegal or improper. There is proper off-balance sheet funding for running a business, which is not reflected on a company's balance sheet.

The purpose of a company keeping its debts away from its balance sheet can be several. One reason is to maintain a sound debt-equity ratio. (Debts can be doctored to show them at a level, for example, not exceeding twice the company's equity value—a desired ratio.) Another could be to maintain debts within banks' *covenant* targets. When banks give loans, they normally have a maximum cap on debt figures in relation to companies' profits.

The broad purpose, as is evident, is to avail loans, but not to reflect this on a balance sheet. It is a win-win situation—a company takes a loan, but does not show it to avoid adverse implications.

Let us now look at some instances of off-balance sheet-financing techniques used by companies to fraudulently or illegally show a better than reality picture of their balance sheets.

Pushing Loans, Expenses and Losses to Non-consolidating Subsidiaries

Normally, the financial results of a subsidiary or daughter company need to form a part of the parent company's accounts, i.e., P&L accounts and balance sheet. This is known as consolidation of accounts, where the financial figures of subsidiaries are consolidated with that of their parent. This gives the true picture of the company, including that of its subsidiaries. Various countries have different rules for consolidation, the most common being that if a parent company holds more than 50% of the equity shares of the subsidiary, the latter's accounts should be consolidated with that of its parent.

However, if any part of the business faces adversity, and if there is the possibility of it pushing this on to a subsidiary company, whose accounts are not consolidated with the parent enterprise, then window-dressing of the parent company's accounts can occur. For instance, let us assume that the parent company already has very high debt figures (compared to its profit or equity figures). Any further acquisition of debt by it may be looked at adversely by the investing community. In such cases, the parent company can take steps to structure the debt in a way that it is pushed out to a subsidiary company, whose accounts are not being consolidated with those of the former. Consequently, the parent company's accounts (and balance sheet) will look better than the real picture. This is a fraudulent practice.

PNC Financial Services

PNC is an American group with a banking arm. The Bank had several underperforming corporate loans and sold some of these (valued at $760 million) to three partnerships (formed with AIG, an insurance company) to avoid writing down its bad loans.

When loans are turning bad (i.e., due to borrowers not paying interest or the principal in time), they need to be written down, depending on likely losses.

PNC should have written down its bad or non-performing loans, but it avoided this by shifting these to its partnership organisations. Consequently, during the second to fourth quarters in 2001, its profits were overstated by $155 million. When the matter came to light, the company's accounts had to be restated in July 2002 to correct its overstatement of profits. This resulted in a crash of its share prices and its shareholders faced a huge loss of around $1 billion.

> PNC settled the matter by paying $115 and AIG paid $44 million.

Biovail

Biovail, a Canadian drug maker, played a nice game to provide an appearance of achieving its earnings target by overstating its profits between 2001 and 2003 and hiding its losses.

What did Biovail do? It improperly moved its financial statements to a special purpose vehicle (SPV) of around $47 million for expenses incurred on R&D of it products.

However, in spite of its wrong accounting and pushing expenses to a SPV, the company still faced a shortfall in its earnings. It made up a story that its earnings had suffered due to a truck carrying its drugs having met with an accident. Though there had been an accident, this had no impact on its business performance. The company not only cooked its books of accounts, but also gave bizarre explanations for shortfalls in its targeted earnings.

> Biovail agreed to pay a penalty of $10 million to settle the case of wrongdoing against it in 2008.

Olympus Corporation

The fraud perpetrated by the well-known Japanese camera-maker, Olympus, hit the headlines of newspapers for days. The company had engaged in activities that led to a huge scam, which lasted more than two decades.

The fraud was discovered by Michael Woodford after he was appointed the company's CEO in September 2008. He realised that its former Chairman had perpetrated a massive cash extraction fraud, although at that time, efforts were being made to make Olympus Corporation's balance sheet more accurate. However, it emerged that the Chairman had not stolen the funds, but was trying to clean up fraudulent transactions conducted in the past, so that the company's reputation was protected.

The fraud commenced around 1985 when Japanese currency was rather weak. Japanese companies, including Olympus, made several speculative investments as a matter of business strategy. However, these investments incurred huge losses, while Japanese currency continued to strengthen. It is not known how its losses accrued, but Olympus wanted to hide them. This is where its problems began.

The company continued to carry investments at cost, although these should have been written down as the market value of the investments were much lower than their acquisition cost, but this was not done. Olympus hoped that its losses would be made up with further risky investments. But it was not to be. Ultimately, the losses grew to $1.7 billion.

Till 1997, Olympus was making losses without any disclosures till accounting rules changed in Japan to enforce companies to record their investments in their books of accounts on a *marked to market* basis. If the company had done this, the sordid tales of its past would have been exposed.

What did Olympus do? It set up shell subsidiaries to *sell* its loss-making investments at their original cost, and thereby avoid writing down of its investment values. At that time, the accounts of shell companies were not to be consolidated with their parents' balance sheets under Japanese law. Since subsidiaries did not need to be consolidated, their losses could be hidden. Companies sought to wipe out their losses either by making additional investments or through over-priced acquisitions. If there could have been more over-priced investments, the loss in the value of investments could have been shown in their balance sheets as Goodwill and then written off over a period of time (an accounting issue, which is rather complicated to execute) and their balance sheets could have been corrected slowly.

In 2007, accounting rules changed in Japan. It became compulsory for shell companies to be consolidated. Olympus needed to close its deals with shell companies before 2008. However, some of its transactions got into trouble. A shell company, demanded payment which had earlier accepted some securities from Olympus, with promise to exchange the securities for cash in a few years.

In July 2008, a Japanese newspaper reported that excess payment had been made by Olympus on investments. At that time, its new CEO, Woodford, a British citizen, had taken over. He thought that the Chairman had stolen funds after seeing the reports in Japanese newspapers. He confronted the Chairman and was fired. He leaked the matter to the press. In September 2012, the company admitted that it had tried to conceal its investment-related losses by using fraudulent accounting methods since 1990.

> In September 2012, Olympus and three of its former executives, including its Chairman, pleaded guilty for the accounting cover-up in one of the biggest corporate scams in Japan. They were charged with inflating the company's net worth for five years up to the financial year 2011. Furthermore, in December 2012, the FBI arrested a former bank executive for receiving funds to play an international *shell company* game in the US to allow Olympus to keep a massive accounting scam going for years. The scandal was exposed by Woodford in October when he questioned the board about deals that were later found to have been used to conceal losses incurred by the company in earlier speculative investments.
>
> After the scandal broke, calls were made for implementation of external scrutiny over boards and corporate governance reforms in Japan, as had happened in the US after the Enron scandal, but no sweeping reforms have taken place in Japan till date.

Showing Controllable Subsidiaries as Not Being Controllable by Non-disclosure

A company can have one or more subsidiaries. These could either be controlled through majority shareholdings (i.e., more than 50%), control over the majority of the board of directors or through operational and management control.

Now the crux of the issue arises. A parent company can either transfer bad news or loss-making businesses to its subsidiaries or make them handle sub-optimal or risky businesses to isolate the parent from the vagaries of any unpleasant developments.

The crucial issue, however, is that subsidiary accounts should not be consolidated with a parent's accounts. This can either be done legally (when a shareholding is less than 50%) or through sheer non-declaration that the subsidiary is a controlled one. The latter is obviously a deceptive action.

Boston Chicken practised this mischief. In 1993, the company (with around 35 stores) had an Initial Public Offering (IPO), raising $65 million by selling its shares to the public. However, by late 1994, the price of Boston Chicken stocks had declined to as low as $15 per share against the post-IPO price of $26 per share. Its top management members were worried about the bad performance of the company's stocks. They knew that the low stock price would make it impossible for them to raise further funds for expansion, which was basic strategy. The real problem with Boston Chicken was that its new stores were performing poorly. The only way out for it was to report strong sales and profit growth, and at the same time open many new stores. This was the starting point of the deceitful acts.

To achieve its objective, Boston Chicken's management concocted an ingenious scheme. The members decided to open new stores through the concept of financed area developers, which were actually franchisee operations. Many of these area developers were also related to Boston Chicken's directors. The company made a commitment to fund 70% of the cost of opening the new stores.

Since 1994, Boston Chicken, commenced opening numerous stores using majority funding by lending hundreds of millions of dollars, although most of its stores incurred losses. In these loan agreements, the company included a condition that the loans could be converted into equity after two years. (Conversion of loans into equity shares enables the lender to become part owners, since equity holders are treated as owners of a company.) Boston Chicken's plan was to keep these area developers as separate entities until such time when they became profitable and could convert the loans into equity, and then add in its own financial statements the earnings of these entities.

How did this scheme help Boston Chicken? It removed from the company's consolidated financial results the hugely loss-making stores owned by area developers, since these enterprises were not technically subsidiaries of Boston Chicken, since the company was still a lender and not an equity holder till the conversion. Moreover, this gave it the option of acquiring the franchisees only when they became profitable, thereby improving its earnings without having to ever show losses during the start-up phase. This provided the company the opportunity to conceal the operating losses of its franchisees and give the impression that its store operations were successful and had extremely favourable prospects, since the expansion was leading to enhanced financial results. Not only this, Boston Chicken also lent money to these area developers, who paid it back to the company, which booked these receipts as franchisee fees to inflate and further overstate its reported revenue and earnings.

What did Boston Chicken achieve? It raised around $800 million from fresh sale of securities to the public between June 1995 and April 1997, without disclosing the truth about the disastrous performance of its area developers. The fresh funds raised allowed the company to lend more money to area developers to enhance its growth further in spite of the stores losing cash.

Boston Chicken could raise vast sums of money from the public through this sham scheme and by concealing its actual business performance between 1994 and 1996. When its business performance continued to suffer and its cash flows dried up in May 1997, the company was forced by the SEC to disclose that its results were falsified and it had initiated public issue of securities without adequate and true disclosures about the performance of its businesses. This led to its share price collapsing to $1 per share.

What went wrong for Boston Chicken from the accounting point of view? First, in view of the structure of its loss-making franchisees to which 70% of funding was provided by the company by way of debt (and not equity) was not consolidated with its balance sheet. This was technically correct, since the area developers or franchisees were not owned (no shareholding but only debt) by Boston Chicken. Second, however, Boston Chicken should have written down the loans given by it, which were not recoverable in the short term, due to huge losses made by the franchisees. The loans given to the area developers should have been evaluated on their recoverability and appropriately impaired. (Impairment is a charge or cost in a P&L account, and has the effect of reducing declared results.) Third, non-disclosures time and again of the losses, been incurred by franchisees where large sums of money have been pumped were incorrect. And fourthly, and most importantly, the company raised funds from the public without adequate disclosure of the losses being incurred at the area developers' level. This was the most crucial bit.

The key learning from this is that while consolidation of subsidiaries or franchisees may not feature in the parent's balance sheet due to the legal position of consolidation rules, material facts of business performance need to be communicated truthfully and appropriately to avoid the liability of non-disclosure of material facts. Similarly, loans given to non-performing subsidiaries or franchisees should be evaluated and written down if non-recoverable.

> Boston Chicken Inc., a chain of restaurants, was renamed Boston Market Corporation in 1997. After the discovery of the accounting scam, it filed for bankruptcy in 1998. In 2000, McDonalds acquired the company. In August 2007, the chain was acquired by a PE firm, Sun Capital Partners.

Tailpiece

Playing the balancing trick in the matter of balance sheets is all about balancing an imbalance. To provide succour to the weak is natural. But balance sheets that are frail and fragile, due to relatively high debts, are often nurtured to demonstrate might and muscle—not through milk and honey but through application of steroids that could be immensely harmful. Off-balance sheet structures are sometimes application of wonder drugs with colossal side effects.

CREATION OF NON-EXISTENT CASH-IN-BANK

Who does not love cash—you, me and everybody. Any enterprise with an adequate cash balance or free flowing cash is the darling of the investing community. No wonder funds available with businesses are often played with to present an appealing picture.

Cash in any form, in hand or in banks, is the most liquid of assets. *Cash in hand* is normally verified by auditors by a physical count at periodical intervals. *Cash in bank* is usually confirmed by the auditors by sighting banks' certificates.

If certificates from banks can be forged, it is a great method to show an asset which actually either does not exist or is much less than what is shown in its books of accounts. In order to avoid forgery, auditors do counterverify this with banks and try to broadly reconcile their cash flow statements with the bank balances shown by them.

However, if a company and an auditor is hand in glove or the auditor does not carry out his task of verifying the salient details appropriately, fraud can be committed.

Over-stating cash balance is one of the most serious scams that can happen.

Satyam: When Truth Lied

During the period 2001–08, Satyam Computer Services Limited, an Indian IT outsourcing company, perpetrated a massive fraud by misreporting its non-existent cash balance of over INR 50 billion ($0.8 billion), along with other scams including over-reporting of sales, profits and debtors' understatement of liability and depiction of accrued interest that was non existent. It was one of the largest corporate accounting scandals ever exposed in India.

Strangely, the fraud came to light when the Chairman of the company, B. Ramalinga Raju, confessed on his own volition by writing to his fellow board members (with a copy to the Indian market watchdog SEBI and the stock exchanges) on January 2009.

Please note that the fraud did not get detected by a third party or by the auditor, but came out into the open by the confession of its perpetrator. From his various statements, it appears that the fraud was mainly committed to show customers, the stock market and the outside world that the company was very large and growing at a fast pace. The main motive perhaps was to impress global customers and incentivise them to give new orders to Satyam and not to its competitors such as Infosys, Wipro or TCS in a scenario where the Indian IT sector was growing rapidly in a highly competitive environment.

In order to meet Raju's objective of painting a rosy picture of the company's operations, false sales and bogus profits were shown on its books. These sham profits were either parked as a cash balance or as debtors (i.e., customers' outstanding amounts). Since there was no real cash involved, Satyam's cash balance was shown in the form of fixed deposits in banks.

When its auditor, Price Waterhouse, enquired about confirmation of the company's cash balance at the end of every quarter, Satyam would provide false certificates from banks.

Satyam means truth in Sanskrit and the paradox is that a company with such a name committed one of the largest corporate scams in India.

1. After the scam, the Mahindra Group, an Indian conglomerate, took over Satyam Computers under its IT arm, Tech Mahindra, in April 2009 and renamed it Mahindra Satyam. The new company was formally merged with Tech Mahindra in mid-2012..
2. The key accused to the crime was Raju, his brother, the company's CFO Vadlamani Srinivas, two Partners from PwC, along with five other Satyam employees; They were all arrested after the scam broke out and then granted bail in 2012.
3. In April 2011, the SEC and the Public Company Accounting Oversight Board in the USA fined PwC, India, Satyam's statutory auditors, $7.5 million. This is the largest penalty ever levied on a foreign accounting firm in the US.
4. The Accounting Oversight Board has barred the two PwC India Partners from taking part in the audits of US companies. This is because they refused to cooperate during the investigations.
5. On completing its probe in July 2014, the Indian market regulator SEBI ordered Raju and his key accomplices to return INR 18.5 billion ($300 million) of their unlawful gains with interest.
6. Raju, his brother, two PwC Partners and six others were found guilty by a court in April 2015 and jailed for seven years. Raju's brothers were also fined INR 50 million ($800,000).

This was an accounting fraud of colossal magnitude perpetrated to pander to the greed of a very ambitious individual, and was carried out with the connivance of the company's auditors, revealed through self-confession.

Parmalat

This Italian food giant, faced a severe cash crisis in 2003 in spite of it showing a huge cash balance in its balance sheet of €4 billion ($4.8 billion). Its Italian bankers and investors were puzzled by this situation about how a company with such a large cash balance could be in trouble. What transpired was it had shown a forged bank certificate of Bank of America for funds presumably received against non-existent sales to an off-shore customer. The bank account was shown as held by an off-shore entity in Cayman Island, where the money was purportedly paid to the company for supplying 300,000 tons of non-existent milk to a Cuban customer.

In order to prove the authenticity of the transaction, Parmalat created a fake customer who presumably purchased milk and paid a large amount of money. The money was shown to be held by an off-shore entity that was shown to be the supplier of the milk. To prove that this was so, the counterfeited bank certificate was passed through a fax machine several times and the document that emerged looked like a copy of an original bank certificate that had been directly faxed by the bank. But it was a forgery, which was prepared by the company in-house.

> Parmalat Finanziaria S.p.A., an Italian company, was founded in 1961 by over ambitious Calisto Tanzi. The company is known for introducing the concept of shelf-stable milk (in tetra packs). It had ambitions to go global and acquired companies across the world by borrowing from banks.
>
> Since Parmalat's business was not doing well, and was in fact incurring losses, its books of accounts were purportedly cooked between 1990 and 2003 by falsifying its sales and justifying its debts. By the end of 2003, the biggest corporate fraud in Europe came to light when it became clear that a €4 billion bank certificate had been forged by the company and claims of its liquidity were false. Furthermore, its actual loan was found to be around €14 billion—double the amount disclosed in its balance sheets.
>
> When the scam came to light, Parmalat was placed under an extraordinary administration procedure between January 2004 and September 2005. The administration entered a scheme of composition with the company's unpaid creditors through an exchange of equity for debt (known as a swap) by which Parmalat's outstanding creditors became part owners of the new company by

their ownership of its equity shares, and Parmalat Finanziaria was converted into a new legal entity called Parmalat S.p.A.

Tanzi was sentenced to 10 years' imprisonment. The new Parmalat S.p.A. was established on 1 October 2005 and listed on the Milan Stock Exchange.

Peregrine Financial

The US-based brokerage firm submitted false reports to the US Commodity Futures Trading Commission, between February 2010 and June 2012. It falsified bank statements and lied to the regulators. The bank accounts, meant to hold customers' funds, which was supposed to have a balance of over $200 million, held in fact only $5 million.

Russel Wasendorf Sr, the CEO of Peregrine Financial, confessed to stealing its clients' funds and defrauding banks.

Wasendorf's confession was made under strange circumstances. He knew that he had been caught in a web of cheating and deception, and attempted to commit suicide by hooking a tube to his car's tailpipe after writing a long suicide note. However, his attempt to commit suicide failed. He was found unconscious in his car outside his Cedar Falls, Iowa office's car parking lot. His mechanisations were brought to light through his own confession. Unfortunately, Wasendorf will have to face the consequences of his very own confessions.

Peregrine Financial has since collapsed.

Tailpiece

'Cash is exactly like sex; you thought of nothing else if you did not have it and thought of other things if you did', said James Baldwin, an American novelist, defining the mystique of money! No wonder, cash is the aphrodisiac which corporates use sometimes if there is lack of self-power.

BOOSTING OPERATING CASH FLOW TO GIVE A ROSY PICTURE

'Cash is king' goes the popular maxim. However, cash is not the king—*profit* is the real king. While the debate on who came first—Adam or Eve—is yet unanswered, but regarding cash, profit clearly precedes it. When profits wane or vanish, creative accounting often takes over to show cash—mainly operating cash.

Adequacy or otherwise of cash flows can be evaluated from companies' operating cash flow statements. Those with healthy cash flows always find favour with investors. Consequently, fraudulent techniques are frequently used to boost the cash flows of organisations.

Vivendi Universal precisely did that. Vivendi had minority holdings (with a shareholding of less than 50%) in some of its subsidiaries. These included the *Cegetel Group* and *Maroc Telecom*. Both these companies were profitable. However, since Vivendi only had a minority holding in these subsidiaries, it did not have access to their surplus cash flows. It needed to pay a dividend and project a positive cash surplus scenario to keep pace with market expectations due to certain earlier commitments made by its management. This occurred between 2000 and 2002.

Vivendi played a trick. It took a temporary debt, known as an *inter-corporate loan,* from Cegetel and showed it as its own cash flow. Vivendi neither disclosed that it was a loan nor did it reveal that Cegetel's cash was not accessible to it. However, by a sleight of hand in its accounting, it turned the table to project a false picture of good health in mid-2002 when it disclosed its financial year's results for 2001 and declared a dividend.

Tailpiece

'Money makes the world go round,' sang R Kelly, 'how important money is—making the whole world spin'. Therefore, in business one should not be surprised to discover that businesses frequently fudge the four-letter fantasy word—*cash*.

MANIPULATING REPORTING ON BUSINESS SEGMENT TO CAMOUFLAGE POOR PERFORMANCE

Some enterprises are involved in multiple business segments. In such situations, there is need to show segmental results, to show how the various business components of some critical size are performing. Investors are not only interested in knowing about a business entity's overall performance, but they also want to know how its various businesses are functioning. This helps them identify the decaying or rotten eggs in the basket.

In order to give a better than real picture, companies sometimes merge or demerge their businesses deviously so that non-performing ones are hidden from investors and analysts.

Enron, the master of accounting deception, used this cloak of disguise. One of its businesses, EES, was incurring huge losses. In order to hide problems in EES during the first quarter of 2001, a large portion of its loss-making business was moved to Enron Wholesale, which was doing very well at that time. This was done under the guise of reorganising its business segments. This helped Enron hide EES' losses by setting these off against the profits of Energy Wholesale's business. This move had no commercial significance, but to camouflage EES' poor financial performance.

Tailpiece

Investors, financial advisors and fund managers love information on segment-wise performance of corporates. It helps to unravel some critical information which would otherwise be hidden from the probing public eyes. It is a good source to know some decisive details of what lies behind the corporate curtain. That is why the backstage is often stage managed.

WHO WANTS TO PAY TAX? MANIPULATE TO AVOID

How we wish that there were no taxes to be paid! Companies are no exception—they are also subjected to taxes on their profits. Their tax liabilities are generally based on the tax laws prevalent in the particular jurisdiction where a business is situated.

Profit that is taxed is known as a *taxable profit*.

Payment of tax to the government can be avoided by showing an enhanced cost that may not ordinarily be deductible for the purpose of calculating tax or by avoiding disclosure of income.

Incorrect interpretation wrong calculation, erroneous cost booking, can all lead to lowering of tax liability. It is a ripe place for fraud.

To sight an example, **ConAgra**, the company making agricultural commodities, made inappropriate profit calculations when it sold some of its subsidiaries. Sale of subsidiaries, when made at a price that is higher than their *book value* attracts Capital Gains Tax (tax calculated on sale of capital assets).

In order to lower the tax liability from the sales proceeds of its business, ConAgra subtracted the value of its assets without netting off its liabilities. This resulted in reduced calculation of its taxable profit.

Let us take an example. Assume that a subsidiary has assets worth $10 million and liabilities of $4 million. Its net asset value will be $6 million ($10 million assets less $4 million liabilities). If its business is sold for $ 8 million, its taxable profit will be $2 million ($8 million sale proceeds less $6 million net assets) and tax will be calculated on $2 million. However, if the subsidiary's liabilities are excluded, there will be a loss, since its assets (valued at $10 million) were sold at $8 million.

There was a similar issue in the case of ConAgra. In 2004, the company juggled its accounts and showed a capital loss of $243 million. In reality, it made a taxable profit of $85 million. What a huge swing, just due to tax-related accounting hocus-pocus!

Accounting: Cheating and Creativity | 235

Tailpiece

Accountants searching for loopholes in tax laws is an age-old practice. There is no jurisdiction where loopholes cannot be taken advantage of. Most companies search for ways in which they can minimise their taxes. Intelligent minds and sharpened pencils work for optimising taxes. Whether such tactics lead to manipulation is a matter of conjecture. *Tax magicians* are ever-ready with a few tricks up their sleeves to display their manoeuvres whenever desired!

MANIPULATION OF ACCOUNTS PRIOR TO M&A

Most of us have heard the term M&A. It appears in business newspapers with regularity. It is the short form for mergers and acquisitions. When company A and company B join their operations to form company AB, it is merger. When company A buys company B such that the latter seizes to exist, it is an acquisition.

The shareholders of the respective companies need to be compensated by the new or acquiring entity in M&As. The compensation depends on the historical performance of the companies as well as their future potential and possibilities.

The past performance of a company is reflected in its financial statements. If these are doctored, compensation to the respective companies will probably not remain fair and transparent.

There are several examples where the figures of one of the companies or both were doctored to fill the coffers of interested few.

HFS and CUC Merger

Two high-profile CEOs, Henry Silverman of Hospitality Franchise Systems (HFS) and Walter Forbes of Comp-U-Card (CUC) International, decided to have a merger at the end of 1997. Their merger led to the formation of **Cendant Corporation**, franchiser and direct marketer, and the owner of the Avis car rental company and the Days Inn hotel chain. A huge fraud was discovered in CUC's accounts just after the merger when the accounts of the new company were being prepared in April 1998 by transferring their accounting data.

What transpired was that CUC had inflated its revenue by $500 million over a period of three years. The market price of its Cendant shares collapsed by 75% once news of the accounting fraud reached the public domain.

What did CUC do? It (i) converted its liabilities into revenue, both being *credit* entries by reversing its *liabilities* account and replacing it with its *revenue* account; (ii) a long-term future fee income shown as its current revenue; (iii) customers' rejections and charge-backs, neither recognised nor deducted from its revenue and (iv) recording fictitious and false revenue with fabricated customer names.

The incorrect and fraudulent accounting treatments are a bit technical in nature and it does not matter if their details are not understood. The broader issue was that one of the parties to the merger fudged and overstated its profits for the earlier period and was caught by the accountants of the merged entity.

The lesson is that if a company's accounts have fudged and falsified figures, it should not enter into M&As, since the possibility of getting caught increases.

> Walter Forbes, CEO of CUC, was sentenced to 12 years imprisonment for the accounting scandal in 2007. Cendant was broken up in 2006 and its constituent businesses sold.

McKesson-HBOC

McKesson Corporation acquired HBOC in January 1999, and changed the company's name to McKesson-HBOC. Soon thereafter, in April 1999, post formation of the new entity, a fraud was detected.

What transpired was that Charles McCall, the CEO of HBOC and Chairman of the newly formed combined company, participated in fraudulent schemes to inflate HBOC and McKesson-HBOC's revenues by more than $100 million.

What McCall did was to show *contingent software sales* as part of *sales*. These sales were contingent on customers accepting the software and should not have been booked as revenue. McCall perpetrated the fraud in the two quarters of 1998 (prior to the acquisition) to get a better value for the company. He continued this practise even after the new company was formed.

> In January 2005, McKesson agreed to pay $960 million to settle a class action lawsuit on accounting fraud at HBOC, which bought McKesson in 1999. The pre-acquisition accounting fraud resulted in McKesson's shareholders losing around $9 billion in one day (28 April 1999), which was nearly half the value of their holdings. The share prices tanked after McKesson declared that HBOC had booked sales improperly and that it would have to restate its financial results. In 2010, McCall, CEO of McKesson-HBOC, was sent to jail to serve a 10-year prison term.

Hewlett-Packard–Autonomy

In one of the worst corporate blunders ever, Hewlett-Packard (HP), a computer-maker, acquired the British software maker Autonomy PLC for $11 billion in October 2011, but has been mired by accounting loss recognitions, controversies and accusations ever since.

In 2012, HP took an accounting charge and wrote down $8.8 billion out of the acquisition price. The write-down was essentially the *Goodwill* booked in acquiring Autonomy.

Autonomy's accounting had been under criticism for a long time by certain short-sellers, but HP did not pay heed to this and acquired the company. In November 2012, HP accused Autonomy of cooking its books. It seems HP came to know about Autonomy's accounting improprieties after one of the latter's senior finance executives alerted HP's management about emails and memos that purportedly detailed fraud committed prior to 2011 before the company's takeover by HP.

HP's allegations mainly relate to how Autonomy has (i) shown buying and selling of personal computers look like sales of valuable software, (ii) hidden costs as marketing expenses when this should have been reported as the cost of goods sold and (iii) round-tripping sales to boost its sales and profits.

Mike Lynch, Autonomy's founder, who was fired by HP after the takeover, responded by saying that his company's accounting was fine. 'If Autonomy lost its market value post acquisition, it is because HP mismanaged the company', was his stand.

Now let us look at the role played by the Big Four auditing firms. Autonomy was audited by Deloitte and HP by Ernst & Young. HP hired KPMG to perform due diligence on Autonomy in connection with the acquisition. PwC was brought in by HP to conduct a forensic audit on Autonomy.

How did such huge accounting issues arise when the Big Four were involved in the transaction? Are accounting rules so nebulous that a multi-billion dollar M&A transaction can be thrown off-gear?

> The accounting issues discovered in Autonomy's operations are being investigated by the US investigating agency SEC. Britain's Serious Fraud Office ended its investigations in January 2015, without coming to any specific conclusions on conviction of any executive. Further, HP filed a $5.1 billion suit in March 2015 directly against two former top executives, the CEO and CFO of Autonomy, alleging accounting abuses

Tailpiece

A balance sheet is like a painting on a canvas. If the painting is shoddy, the artist alters it by painting over it. Fixing a balance sheet is no different. It is also an art used to manage the earnings of companies. Prior to acquisitions, companies' accounts are sometimes fiddled with to either clean up their past messes or to improve their share-exchange values to pocket good returns. Behind the scene machinations and *creative* accounting are ingredients sometime used for cooking an M&A arrangement. One needs to be careful of possible hidden intrigues in M&A deals.

SHODDY ACCOUNTING

Accounting manipulations have been happening since the birth of accounting.

Through its sheer high-handedness, **Medaphis Corporation** instructed one of its subsidiary companies to improperly reduce its income by $2.5 million by decreasing its revenue and increasing its reserves in the first quarter of 1996. It did not have any reason for doing this. In the second quarter of 1996, Medaphis instructed the subsidiary to reverse the $2.5 million reserve into income. Therefore, the original creation of the reserve was improper and so was its subsequent reversal. This resulted in it showing both the quarters' results incorrectly.

Why do accounting? In the olden days, people used to maintain dairies. Nowadays, we put down everything in laptops, tablets or mobile devices. This is to maintain records, so that we do not forget tomorrow about today. Accounting records are no different.

It is necessary for books of accounts to be maintained according to general accounting principles to truly and fairly record business transactions.

Why engage in improper accounting? Common sense says that if accounting books can be doctored, it is possible to project a holier than thou image. Many companies do it. The following are some examples of shoddy accounting:

During 1999–2001, **Peregrine Systems** failed to maintain adequate accounting books and records to support its financial statements. For example, it did not maintain detailed accounts receivable sub-ledgers (with customer-wise details of its outstanding) that reconciled with its general ledger (showing its total customer outstanding). The company used the *back of the envelope* system to track and record customer sales and receivables.

Let us take an example to illustrate improper maintenance of accounts. In the case of Peregrine, its general ledgers and sub-ledgers did not tally. General ledger provides the *total* of an account, while the sub-ledgers provide the *details*. For instance, if its customer outstanding totals $100, this will be reflected under its *debtors account* in its general ledger. There should also be a corresponding list of customers' names from whom sales realisation needs to be collected. For example, an organisation may have its dues from Mr A ($50), X and company ($30) and Y Company Ltd. ($20). These three customers' details should appear in the company's sub-ledger. The total outstanding of $100 (appearing in the general ledger) must add up in the sub-ledgers. If these do not tally, something is amiss.

Peregrine's case is preposterous. How can a company not maintain detailed customer records? How can it only maintain a rough tally? If this is the case, financial statements cannot be relied upon. That is precisely what happened with Peregrine. In 2002, it was found that its accounts were falsified.

Moving to recent times, **Liliput Kidswear**, the Indian retailer of children's apparel, wanted to raise money from the public. The company decided to have an IPO of INR 8.5 billion ($140 million). In October 2011, its two owners with a total share of 45%, Bain Capital and TPG Capital, accused the company of fudging its accounts before its proposed public issue. Its auditors as well as four independent directors resigned. Since that time, the company has been in a huge financial mess. Allegations of accounting fraud have been dragged to the Delhi High Court. Bain Capital sued EY, the auditor for Liliput Kidswear, for $60 million, citing its negligence in issuing accounting statements.

Tailpiece

A section of the corporate world continues to mislead investors and fill the coffers of an interested few by pushing accounting rules, manoeuvring accounting principles and using financial skulduggery to prop up earnings. However, the good news is that investors punish corporations transgressing the principles of truthful disclosures when they find financial statements are not what they should be. Accounting trickery cannot trick all shareholders all the time!

LAX INTERNAL CONTROLS

The Public Company Accounting Oversight Board in the USA pulled up the *Big Four* accounting firms in late 2012 saying, '1 in 6 of the audits into internal controls did not do enough work prior to approving the annual accounts of its clients.' Reviewing 2009 audits of 309 sample corporates, it found that around 15% were negligent 'in obtaining sufficient audit evidence to support their opinion about the adequacy of internal control over financial reporting'. The number increased to a frightening 22% in 2010. An Accounting Oversight Board member rang the alarm bell by saying, 'If auditors don't get the internal control piece right it is very likely that they will not get the financial statement audit right.'

This is a problem around the globe. Not only are internal controls neglected on many occasions, auditors seem to be turning a blind eye on many occasions.

Think of roads without traffic signals. Visualise trains running without their timing being adjusted amongst each other. Envision our society without the rule of law. Virtual mayhem and chaos will prevail if there were no systems and processes in our lives.

A business organisation is no different. Its *internal control* mechanism is its rule of law, which establishes systems and procedures, and run the business in an organised manner.

Internal control systems entail presence of *four-eyes* principle—two of the *maker* and two of the *checker*. This necessitating the work of an individual or entity being vetted by another before payments are made or accounting entries recorded. Internal controls act like a moral prophylactic.

In July 2012, the largest financial institution in Europe, **HSBC**, admitted to major internal control weaknesses in its operation for not being able to detect money-laundering activities in the USA. Its CEO, Stuart Gulliver stated, 'Our anti-money-laundering controls should have been stronger and more effective, and we failed to spot and deal with unacceptable behaviour'.

In another instance, a Senate report, investigating multi-billion dollar trading losses at one of the largest banks, **JPMorgan Chase**, reported that 'the bank ignored internal controls and manipulated documents as it accumulated trading losses in 2012'.

Lax control is a serious issue. A huge rogue trader-related loss took place in the **Société Générale** during 2005–07 due to serious lapses in the internal controls of the bank, which allowed illegitimate trading to take place.

After allegations of widespread bribery were made at **Walmart**'s Mexican outfit in 2012, the company reported that it had 'beefed up its internal controls to make sure it was complying with the Foreign Corrupt Practices Act', which prohibits US companies from bribing foreign officials to obtain business. Lack of proper internal controls could lead to a section of an organisation resorting to bribery.

Improper distribution of products could be due to lax internal control. In June 2013, **Walgreen Company**, the USA's largest pharmacy, admitted that it had failed to control sales of narcotic painkillers at some of its outlets, through which its drugs were dispensed and made their way to the black market.

Internal controls were inadequate at **Fannie Mae**, the US Government sponsored mortgage-backed securities trading house during 1998–2004. In spite of it being an institution of national importance, it neglected its internal controls. This turned out to be devastating for the company and its investors. It lost its credibility in the market, had to ultimately restate its earnings by $6 billion and its senior management were accused of manipulating its business results to earn increased bonuses.

The US pharmaceutical giant **Cardinal Health** reported profits for 77 consecutive quarters by manipulating its books of accounts during 2001–04. Its internal control system was so inadequate that this accounting jugglery by a section of its management and accounting staff was not caught.

Weaknesses in the internal control systems of organisations can lead to serious consequences in business. The examples given here are just a glimpse into what can go wrong if the lax controls in organisations are not strengthened.

Tailpiece

Internal controls are levers that help companies' operations run on track. Otherwise, they might run amuck and interpret things the way it suits them. Presence of control ensures efficient operations, compliance with applicable rules and regulations, reliable financial reporting, safeguarding of organisational assets and assessment of risks before decisions are taken.

Internal control is the fulcrum on which the efficacy of an organisation rests—its non-existence usually results in accounting fraud, improprieties and dishonesty.

ACCOUNTING RED FLAGS: ALL IS NOT WELL

Red flags fluttering! Aha! It is a warning signal, an alarm bell for some suspicious circumstances. There is no standard definition of red flags. It is subjective and circumstantial. Red flags are usually a danger signal indicating potential problem areas, the possibility of a fire burning somewhere, a risky situation, a hint of probable trouble and a warning signal.

Signs of potential red flags may not be obvious at the beginning or easily perceptible. Therefore, bit of understanding of how to identify probable fault-lines is helpful.

While reviewing financial statements, there are a few accounting numbers or ratios which wave a red flag.

1. **Growth in revenue, but stress on cash flow**

   It is simple—increased revenue should mean an enhanced cash inflow. However, if a company has significant cash flow difficulties, there could be the possibility that its revenue-recognition policies are improper. For instance, **Syntax-Brillion** forged its sales data between 2006 and 2007 without corresponding cash flows. It had to file for bankruptcy in 2008.

2. **Fluctuations in cash flow ratio**

   Sales ultimately need to convert to cash. If there are bogus sales booked, cash flows will show a fluctuating trend. Cash flow trends can be analysed by calculating *cash flow yield*. This can be done by dividing cash flows from operations by a company's net income. Operating cash flow normally refers to the cash generation from its business operations before capital expenditure and pay-out of dividends.

   The following could be red flags while assessing cash flow yields:

   (a) Negative trends over a few quarters or years.
   (b) Positive net income, but negative operating cash flow yields.
   (c) Very high operating cash flow, but low or shrinking net income (could be a case of falsification of cash balance). For instance, **Satyam Computers**, went into a tail-spin when it showed a non-existent cash balance of over $1 billion.

3. **High cash balance, but equally high debt**

   If a company's debts are high, but it has surplus cash, there is something amiss. **Geodesic**, a software company in India, showed a cash balance of INR 11.4 billion ($185 million), but had a debt of INR 11 billion ($177 million) and paid an interest of INR 0.8 million ($13 million). The company went under debt stress. Why did it have such a huge debt when there was nearly a corresponding figure in its cash balance?

4. **Debtors high in comparison to sales**
   Customers need to pay their debts someday. Therefore, any abnormal increase in debtors is an area of concern. Sales shown fraudulently will either sit in accumulated debts or reduced cash inflow. Debtors are seen as number of month's sales. If the average credit period is one month, any debtors outstanding beyond eight to nine months must be viewed with a pinch of salt. A case in point was **Kendall Square Research Corporation**, which booked sales when it was clear that its customers did not have the ability to pay. The company went bankrupt.

5. **Goodwill to total assets high**
   Entries of Goodwill in the accounting books of companies is usually made when acquisitions are made at prices that are higher than value of the net assets taken over. Instances where the value of Goodwill is disproportionately high, compared to a company's total assets, are suspicious. One reason could be that such acquisitions are made at a significantly high value. Another could be that Goodwill lying in a company's books of accounts is not adequately amortised. (Goodwill needs to be written down over a reasonable period of time.) For instance, when **Softbank** acquired Vodafone's Japanese mobile business in 2006, the former undervalued the fixed assets and showed the difference as Goodwill so that the depreciation charge could be reduced.

6. **High inventory**
   Inventories are held for conversion into sales and ultimately into cash within a reasonable time frame. However, very large inventory is a cause of concern. If the industry norm for holding inventory is around three months on an average, any holding beyond 9–12 months should be a red flag. High inventory can be shown to depict enhanced profits by including bogus or non-existent stocks. For instance, **PwC**, the auditor of **Warnaco Group**, was penalised when it allowed the company to overstate its inventory during 1996–98.

7. **Excessive operating margins**
   Reporting very high operating margins could be a figment of the imagination. It could occur due to bogus sales being booked. A sudden spurt in an organisation's operating margins is an area of concern and could imply creation of fraudulent sales. For example, **GE** over-reported its sales and profits during 2002–03, but rectified this in 2007.

8. **High prepaid expenses**
   If the ratio between a company's prepaid expense to its operating expense is very high, it could imply that a major part of its operating or regular expenses are not being shown as a cost in its income statement. These may be shown under the *prepaid* head (a balance sheet item). For example, in 2000, **Rent-way** classified its insurance premium as *pre-paid insurance*. Two of its executives were jailed for this.

9. **Deferred creation of tax assets**
   Excessively high *deferred corporate tax assets* could be a red flag. Asset creation helps a company enhance its profits, unless the calculations are genuine.

10. **Fluctuating sales returns**
    Sales made, but returned by customers for whatever reason, including quality-related issues, are a common phenomenon. However, if there are severe fluctuations in returns from customers, this needs to be taken note of. It could imply that bogus sales reported earlier are being corrected in the particular quarter without any specific and separate disclosure. The figure to be looked at is the company's percentage *sales returns* to its *total sales* and any fluctuations thereof.

11. **Debt not in sync with interest expense**
    Debts are often understated to project a better picture, either by using the off-balance sheet financing mode or by using fraudulent means to suppress these. How can this be detected? The interest cost or financing charges are shown in the company's income statement. Estimating approximate debt figures from its financing cost will give an inkling of

the real debt. For example, the interest figure in a company's P&L account is $10 million, and if the average cost of financing is around 8%, the debt should be around $125 million. The liability side of the balance sheet should then be checked to verify the debt figure shown. If it is grossly different, say $80 million or so, then reasons to worry exist.

Tailpiece

Neither all corporates are holy-cows nor do all enterprises have poor corporate governance. There are some black sheep that we need to identify either through the colour of their behaviour or the way they generally conduct themselves. It is both an art and a science. It is good to know the tricks of the trade which tricksters use to trick us.

NON-ACCOUNTING RED FLAGS: POOR CORPORATE GOVERNANCE

It is common sense that a company with good corporate governance is attractive to investors as opposed to the one which shows deficiency. The challenge is to identify the rotten egg in the basket.

Ability to identify red flags is a good weapon to fight the potential demon of corporate greed, lurking round the unknown crevices and corners.

Accounting-related red flags are one of the many ways to identify the recalcitrant.

There can be several concern areas, existence of which could lead to trepidation of probable inappropriate corporate governance practices by an organisation. Some instances are as follows:

1. *Very high compensation given to senior management for change of control:* M&As are part of business strategy in the modern world. However, companies sometimes have *parachute*

clauses for their senior management. This entails enhanced compensation for them if there is any change in the ownership of a company. However, if the compensation clause is unreasonably high, this is a cause for concern. For example, in the case of **Shaw Group Inc.**, there was a clause that its Chairman, J.M. Bernard Jr., would be paid a whopping $24 million termination fee should there be a change of control in the company. The Shaw Group was taken over by Chicago Bridge & Iron Company in early 2013. Since Bernard was the Founder Chairman, it was easy for him to strike a deal and siphon out a huge amount of cash.

2. *Related-party transactions:* Care needs to be taken to examine the nature of related party transactions. These are usually disclosed as notes to accounts. Such transactions imply that a company is buying and selling to and from parties or companies, respectively, in which either a board member is interested or the company has a share. For example, **Adelphia Communications** failed to disclose the extent of its related party transactions and its auditor, **Deloitte & Touché**, was penalised for this in 2005.

3. *Constant litigation:* A steady flow of litigation against a company is huge area of concern for it. Let us take the example of **Monsanto Company**, a leading producer of genetically engineered seeds. The company is under regular threat of litigation from farmers and has liabilities that are hard to quantify at any point in time. This is a company with a red flag.

4. *Stock options not based on company's performance:* Options for a company's shares are usually given when its share price attains a predetermined *strike price*. This encourages its employees to enhance their performance and help the company's share price rise in due course. However, if stock options are linked to expiry of time and are not based on the performance of the share price, this is a bad news. For instance, the CEO of the retailer **Abercrombie & Fitch Co.**, Michael Jeffries, was awarded a flat sum of shares as stock

options at the 1999 price, irrespective of the strike price, in 1999. This was a dubious way of sharing the company's profits, rather than an incentive to raise the price of stocks at a future date.
5. *Lack of internal controls:* If an audit report includes adverse comments or there is any reason to believe that there are inadequate internal controls in a company, this is a huge red flag. Unless there is an adequate control mechanism in the company, this could lead to havoc due to fraud, cheating and scams. Some organisations openly acknowledge that they have inadequate internal controls. For instance, **General Motors** has repeatedly admitted that its internal control systems are inadequate. In its filings for an IPO in 2010, the company's spokesperson reported, 'We have determined that our disclosure controls and procedures and our internal control over financial reporting are currently not effective.' This is a serious red flag.

Tailpiece

Why does a company fail to take cognitive action when there is a red flag? In *Wilful Blindness: Why We Ignore the Obvious at Our Peril*, Margaret Heffernan, the author, argues that 'such failures are part of a human phenomenon to which we all succumb in matters little and large'. She writes that 'part of the reason is that the brain's cognitive limits do not let humans absorb everything they encounter'. Therefore, in spite of known dangers, red flags may not always be red alerts for action!

Accounting fraud has been in existence since accounting was invented. How do we pay heed to the inner voice of the 'fudge factor—the delicate balance between the contradictory desires to maintain a positive self-image and to benefit from cheating?' questions Dan Ariely in his book, *The (Honest) Truth about Dishonesty*. He goes on to say, 'When the rules are somewhat open to interpretation, when there are gray areas, and when people are left to score their own performance ... traps for dishonesty will exist'. Companies are no exception. Accounting fraud is not going away in haste. Therefore, every reader of financial statements would do well to remember the old and perhaps clichéd adage—discretion is the better part of valour.

7

Checkers Could Be Cheaters

Ernst & Young (E&Y) was the auditor for **Bally Total Fitness**, a health club operator. Since 1997, E&Y had allowed Bally to falsify its books of accounts. Post Enron scandal exposures in 2001, matters became more sensitive for E&Y and the firm got worried due to the then ongoing enhanced US market regulator SEC's scrutiny of such matters. Therefore, in 2002, E&Y woke from its slumber and forced Bally to stop recording its revenue in an improper manner, which allowed the company to claim higher sales and profits earlier than it was allowed under accounting rules. However, when taking such corrective action, E&Y prevented Bally from disclosing its past incorrect reporting, and in fact issued a 'preferability letter' stating that the company was switching between two accounting policies and both were legal. The firm had allowed incorrect accounting practices in the past and repeated its misdemeanour. E&Y tried to hide the past, so that it was not questioned about previous improper audits. Ultimately, the SEC found out its wrongdoing. It imposed a fine of $8.5 million on the firm and censured its six partners. SEC stated, 'E&Y and its partners violated their fundamental duty to function as public watchdogs'.

Moving the clock a decade forward, misdemeanour repeats.

A grave tussle broke out in mid-2011 between **E&Y**, the auditor, and an investment research firm *Muddy Waters Research*. The company in question was a Chinese forestry organisation, **Sino-Forest Corporation**. The auditor gave a clean-chit audit opinion, but Muddy Waters announced that Sino-Forest was a cheat, a fraud and its shares trading on the Toronto Stock Exchange were worth nothing. Sino-Forest's primary asset was forest, whose value was certified by E&Y, as shown in its books, as appropriate. Muddy Waters responded with the allegation that neither the trees nor the forest existed. Sino-Forest's share value collapsed by over 70% when these allegations came out in the open. Its shareholders filed a suit against the auditor—E&Y agreed to settle the charges for $116 million, although it denied that it was liable. Auditors do not pay up unless they know they are guilty! The company filed for bankruptcy protection in March 2012. Sino-Forest was a hoax, which the auditors could not identify.

The saga of auditor-related problems continues.

A senior **KPMG** partner, Scott London, sold confidential client information to his golfing buddy. In exchange, London received a pittance—a few dinners, occasional cash payments of $1,000–$2,000 and a discount on a watch. The information pertained to *Herbalife*, which promotes clean living, and for *Skechers USA*, a lifestyle footwear company. London would disclose the company's financial details a few days before public announcements. London's golfing partner used the information to trade in the company's shares. This was insider trading. KPMG resigned from both the assignments in April 2013 on grounds that its independence had been impaired. The auditor breached its fiduciary duty to maintain the secrecy of client information.

Auditors are the eyes and ears of shareholders and their boards. Their financial statements are relied on by the outside world to take a view on a company's state of affairs. Auditors verify whether accounting information and reports have been prepared accurately. They are looked upon as protectors of the interest of shareholders, creditors and governments. However, on certain occasions, they belie this trust and miss out in doing their duty fairly.

Many a time, auditors fail to acknowledge that they have the responsibility of detecting impending disaster in a corporation and highlight an ongoing fraud or financial disaster in the making. Time and again, auditors tend to wash their hands off on the plea that they were led up the garden path by the management, and they believed in what they were told and showed.

PwC was the auditor for *Satyam*, the computer giant that went bust because of its misdeeds. Following detection of the $1 billion fraud perpetrated by the company, PwC's chairman said, 'It was a massive fraud conducted by the management, and our partners were clearly misled'. Two PwC partners were jailed. In the case of *JP Morgan*, where a massive derivative trading loss of over $6 billion could not be identified in time, its CEO Jamie Dimon agreed that its trades were 'flawed, poorly reviewed, poorly monitored', yet its auditors PwC escaped from any responsibility.

Auditors have time and again failed to provide advance notice of an impending debacle. No warning bugles were blown before *Lehman Brothers* collapsed or *Bear Sterns* folded up. Neither leading banks fiddling with Libor rates nor AIG were cautioned by their auditors about their misdemeanours.

Auditors have failed themselves on certain occasions. **Arthur Anderson**, once one of the world's most venerable audit firms, collapsed, causing 28,000 of its employees to lose their jobs. It was indicted and found guilty for playing a central role in questionable accounting practices and obstructing justice in its audit of the now infamous energy company, *Enron*, in 2002.

The good news is that auditors are increasingly being brought under the scanner for not raising timely alarms when businesses fail. In March 2014, **Deloitte Haskins & Sells**, the auditor for *Financial Technologies*, the promoter of the failed and fraud-hit *National Spot Exchange*, was questioned by India's accounting regulator for alleged lapses.

It is reported that all the Big Four accounting firms are re-examining their internal training, monitoring compliance programmes to identify gaps that may allow an auditor to trample on system weaknesses and enhance internal controls to improve the quality of service delivery.

Taking responsibility for economic disasters caused by corporates, being liable to be questioned deeply in shareholder meetings, compulsorily rotating auditors at shorter intervals, more focus on fraud reporting and making complete disclosures about selling additional services to clients are some measures that ought to be implemented in the accounting world to make auditors the guardians of the investor community in reality.

There are many instances where auditors have been found wanting in delivering their duties and responsibilities. Some such incidents are highlighted in this chapter to give you a glimpse into problems in the audit world.

KPMG

Falsification: IPO Document Data Manipulated

Strange as it may sound, KPMG helped to prepare the accounts of **Hontex International Holdings**, a Chinese textile and clothing company, which launched an IPO in Hong Kong. It transpired that its IPO prospectus (in December 2009) was falsified and financial results overstated, which helped to attract investors to subscribe to the issue.

Falsification: Over-reporting of Profit

KPMG was censured by the US market watchdog SEC on grounds that the firm helped **Xerox Corporation** manipulate and distort its financial statements between 1997 and 2000. The audit firm incorrectly certified that Xerox's reports were consistent with accounting rules. Xerox over-reported its profits by $1.5 billion during these four years. KPMG signed off on this over-reporting. The firm agreed to pay $22.5 million towards settlement, without agreeing or denying to the wrongdoing. A director in SEC stated, 'This is a case about gatekeepers and the failure to do the job that the investing public expects auditors to do'.

Falsification: Bogus Expense Claims

A group of hospitals, apart of **HCA**, a healthcare company in Florida and Kentucky, were helped by KPMG to submit fraudulent expense claims for reimbursement of medical insurance. Costs that were not eligible for reimbursement were misrepresented. Expenses were overstated from 1990 through 1993.

Illegal Action: Tax Shelter Products

As a tax-related service, KPMG structured certain tax-saving schemes for clients having an income of over $20 million a year. Between 1996 and 2005, KPMG put together tax shelters known by various acronyms such as BLIPS, FLIP and SOS. Its purpose was to show phony tax losses. Two former KPMG managers were sentenced to imprisonment of eight to ten years and levied a fine for using illegal tax shelters. The judge commented that 'the concerned men's behaviour was extremely offensive, and a brazen act'.

Dereliction of Duty: Inadequate Write-down of Collaterals

The SEC filed its first case against auditors in January 2013 as a fallout of the financial crisis in 2008. KPMG Partner, John Aesoph, and a senior manager in the firm, Darren Bennett, were accused of inappropriately giving a clean chit to one of their clients—**TierOne Bank**. This involved auditors allowing an inadequate write-down by TierOne on the value of real estate development loans given by the bank. TierOne, a savings bank, gave loans to developers, with exposures increasing with plummeting property prices. The bank failed in 2010. KPMG was not named as a defendant in this case. The SEC complained that 'auditors must adhere to professional auditing standards and exercise due diligence rather than merely rely on management's representations'.

E&Y

Conflict of Interest

Between 1994 and 1999, E&Y as **PeopleSoft's** auditor, was also marketing (through the firm's consultancy arm) its client's software. This was *conflict of interest*. E&Y, being an auditor and a marketer at the same time, entered a settlement with the SEC, with a three-year probation period, due to its business relationship with PeopleSoft. During the probation period, E&Y's accountants attended sessions on ethics and independence. The SEC commented that the construct of E&Y's agreements with PeopleSoft was 'well concealed in lawyerly bombast, but fantasy just the same'.

In another incident, E&Y's Dutch accounting firm (then known as Moret E&Y Accountants) had a joint business relationship with its audit client, **Baan Company NV**, a business software company. From 1995 to 1997, E&Y and Baan jointly developed software implementation tools and coordinated their efforts to implement Baan software for third parties. Baan used E&Y as a subcontractor to service its clients. This seriously impaired the auditor's independence, since E&Y was an auditor and marketer at the same time.

Improper Tax Shelter Products

Tax shelters are structured schemes to help high-income people to save income tax. E&Y did not register tax shelters properly, nor did it maintain a proper list of people buying the products. The firm was fined $15 million and four of its partners were indicted in May 2007 for tax-fraud conspiracy. E&Y's tax shelters included an equity compensation strategy, whereby taxes can be deferred on executive's stock options for 15 years. Earlier, PwC had settled a similar case. One of E&Y's customers was the infamous Dennis Kozlowski, the much maligned and indicted former CEO of Tyco.

Misreporting of Profits

E&Y had to pay $335 million in December 1999 to settle accusations involving false certification of financial statements and for inflating the earnings of **Cendant Corporation**, which operated Ramada Inn Hotels and Avis Car Rental Agencies. The firm gave the excuse that it had been led up the garden path by Cendant. According to an accounting watchdog agency, 'auditors are supposed to be smart enough that they don't get duped'.

Sales Overstated

'The audit partners in E&Y... failed to fulfil their bedrock responsibility,' said the Chairperson of the US Public Company Accounting Oversight Board. The auditor failed to properly audit the annual financial statements of **Medicis Pharmaceutical** during 2005–07. It failed to evaluate the company's accounting of '*sales returns reserve*', overstating sales and not accounting for probable return of goods sold earlier. The firm was fined $2 million in February 2012. 'The fine underscores the severity of the audit failure and sends a message to the profession', said a board official.

DELOITTE & TOUCHE

Misconduct and Lack of Autonomy: Firm Banned for One Year in New York State

'I scratch your back if you scratch mine culture and stunning lack of independence', stated the Superintendent of New York's Department of Financial Services while commenting on Deloitte's performance in its consultancy work. The assignment pertained to Deloitte's faulty review of anti-money laundering practices at **Standard Chartered Bank**, where misconduct, violation of the law and lack of autonomy had been observed. Deloitte agreed to a one-year suspension from engaging in consulting work for financial institutions and paid a fine of $10 million. The allegations pertained to Deloitte aiding StanChart's deception in hiding transactions linked to Iran. This was a great embarrassment for the firm.

Consistent Poor Audit Quality Provided by Partner

An audit partner of Deloitte, James Fazio, was perceived as having conducted poor quality audits in the past. However, Deloitte still entrusted audit of **Ligand Pharmaceutical** to Fazio, even when the firm knew him to be a substandard auditor. The Public Company Accounting Oversight Board imposed a penalty of $1 million on Deloitte. The firm agreed to pay the penalty without admitting or denying the allegations. What did Ligand do? The company over-reported sales during 2003–04, which helped keep its stock price high. Sales were being made with purchasers given the right to return the goods if they did not sell. This did not constitute *sales* under accounting principles. What did Deloitte do? It ignored basic accounting rules and allowed its client to over-report its revenue, an accounting mischief.

Misstatement: Debt and Equity

'Deloitte did not do its job, plain and simple', complained the SEC. The audit firm failed to detect significant misstatements in **Adelphia Communication**'s annual report of 2000. According to the SEC, Adelphia understated its subsidiary debt by $1.6 billion, overstated its equity by at least $368 million, improperly netted related party receivables and payables, and failed to disclose the extent of its related party transactions. Deloitte paid a $50 million penalty into a fund to compensate the investors in April 2005.

Insider Trading

A former Deloitte Partner, Thomas Flanagan and his son Patrick, had a whale of a time by trading in shares of Thomas' clients at least on nine occasions, based on non-public information. Walgreens, Best Buy, Sears and Motorola were among Deloitte's clients who were affected by their misconduct. From 2005 to 2008, the Flanagans would buy and sell the shares of these companies to profit from their earnings. They knew the companies' figures in advance, being their auditor, and sometimes helped them to prepare investor presentations. Thereby, they could profit from information to which the general public did not have access. After being caught, Thomas and Patrick agreed to pay back the profits they had earned with interest and penalties. The SEC director said, 'The insider trading violated one of the most fundamental rules of public accounting. All audit firms should learn from this unfortunate episode'.

Poor Bank Audit: The Cause for a Financial Crisis

The common man is generally unhappy with banks for creating the global financial crisis. Some believe that banks sell dreams, take too much risk and are solely guided by their own interests. The auditors have also come in for some flak. In October 2011, the Public Company Accounting Board held the auditing community responsible, and Deloitte in particular, for not conducting proper bank audits in 2007. They felt that the auditors should have been more careful in looking into banks' books; they should have asked more questions on their loan books, drilling into the quality of provisioning made in their accounts, and carefully examined the valuation of mortgage-backed securities and loans they were selling like hot potatoes, and not relied mainly on bank-management certifications. The Accounting Board drew these conclusions after inspecting over 60 of Deloitte's audits, which the firm had completed by

November 2007. These were mainly bank audits of 2006 results. The firm has denied all the allegations. Post-inspection, the board made scathing observations on Deloitte saying, '…a firm's culture that allows, or tolerates, audit approaches that do not consistently emphasise the need for an appropriate level of critical analysis and collection of objective evidence, and that relies largely on management representations'.

PwC

Dereliction of Duty: Non-verification of Cash Balance

'PwC routinely failed to follow the most basic audit procedures' reported the SEC while penalising the firm on the Satyam fiasco. In early 2009, **Satyam Computer Services**, listed in India and USA as a software outsourcing company, admitted to a $1 billion accounting fraud in which it had overstated its sales, profits and cash balance over a period of time. Two of PwC's partners, along with eight others including Ramalinga Raju, the former Chairman of Satyam, have been sentenced to seven years in prison. What was PwC India's failure? It failed to verify the company's bank balance of $1 billion from the concerned bank. In reality, based on the confession of the company's chairperson, its cash balance was only $66 million. PwC based its audit opinion on the company's management's confirmation of its bank balance without verifying this independently. It ignored basic auditing procedures.

Misstatement: Overstating of Inventory

Warnaco Group, the apparel company, overstated its inventory (implying overstating profits) between 1996 and 1998 by $145 million. Had its inventory been disclosed accurately, this would have resulted in its having to restate its accounting information for the past three years. Its management decided to restate its accounts, which would entail correction of its past over-statement. Even with this august motive, the company carried out further accounting fraud. They falsely characterised the *inventory over-valuation* reinstatement as '*write off of deferred start-up costs*'. Though the costs would go up (implying profits would get reduced as inventory over valuation would be corrected) it was an incorrect disclosure. It is very wrong to attribute correction of over-valuation of inventory to writing off start-up costs. PwC was the auditor and failed to object to the company misclassifying its inventory. The firm had to pay a penalty of $1.4 million.

Misstatement and Theft

The symbol of corporate excess was **Tyco International**. Its then CEO Dennis Kozlowski and CFO Mark Swartz looted the company of $180 million for their personal use. This included items such as umbrella stands worth $17,000 and birthday parties costing $2 million. They also made $430 million by manipulating the company's share price by falsifying accounting information. PwC remained a mute spectator to these con games and excesses from December 1999 to June 2002. The firm was penalised $225 million to settle Tyco Investors' claims.

Failure to Safeguard Client's Assets

The British regulator imposed a fine of £1.4 million ($2.1 million) on PwC for failing to safeguard its client's assets in **JP Morgan**'s securities business. The firm failed to notify that the bank had not separated client's money (of more than $8 billion) from bank's own money in filings with the Britain's Financial Service Authority from 2002 to 2008. The British authority cracked down on this separation issue of the client's money and the bank's funds after the post 2008 debacle of Lehman Brothers, where similar issues arose. JP Morgan reported the mistake made by it in 2009 and had to pay a fine of £33 million ($50 million) fine in 2010. Britain's Accountancy Discipline Board observed, 'PwC had committed misconduct in respect of each allegation ... the misconduct in this case is very serious'.

Tailpiece

While there have been several hiccups in the role of auditors, there are numerous instances where they have fought for proper financial reporting and good governance.

Avant Corporation, a software-maker, fired its auditor KPMG in 2001, when it reported the company's ineffective internal controls. Sometimes auditors drop poky clients—E&Y moved out of **Vascular Solutions**, a medical device company, in 2005. Deloitte & Touche, auditors for **General Motors**, sounded alarm bells in 2009 that bankruptcy seemed imminent unless the company initiated significant restructuring steps. When AF Ferguson, Kabul Bank's auditors, warned about siphoning of funds and kickbacks in 2009, it fell on the deaf ears of Afghanistan's Central Bank—**Kabul Bank** had a run due to this in 2010. In its audit report in April 2014, PwC raised the alarm on questionable transfer of funds by the Indian commodity exchange **MCX** to its parent, **Financial Technologies**. Such instances abound. Not all audits get poor grades. Only a few do.

George Burns once said, 'In business, the key word is honesty. Once you have learned to fake that, the rest is easy'. A possible retort from Nicholas Butler, 'An expert is one who knows more and more about less and less'. One wonders whether there is anything to do with auditors in these age old comments!

Morale of the story of this section is that even the police need to be policed sometimes for proper policing.

'SELFIE': HOW CAN CORPORATES DETECT FRAUD?

'Catch the thief before he catches you' goes a Romanian proverb.

In several cases, auditors have not been able to detect wrongdoings in their client companies. This has been already detailed in this chapter. However, the nature of most of the audits discussed constituted *statutory* audits, implying that these were necessitated by prevalent legal provisions. *Internal* audits, on the other hand, are conducted by companies' employees or specialised firms, auditing on behalf of management to ensure its compliance with their internal control systems. These audits are sometimes known as management audits.

How can an enterprise detect wrongdoings? Auditor reports are obviously a possible way out. However, just like a 'selfie' or smartphone self-photo, self-detection is a good way to fight against economic deception.

With or without the help of auditors, detection of corporate fraud involves different methods employed by enterprises to discover whether economic crime has been committed in their operations.

Possible fraud-detection methods could be the following:

1. Internal corporate controls including internal audit, fraud risk assessment, electronic and automated suspicious transaction analysis and reporting (also known as forensic audit) and job rotation.
2. Corporate practice and culture, including a whistle-blowing system involving internal and external tip-offs.
3. Accidental reporting, beyond the influence of the board or management, which includes fortuitous tripping over incidences, enforcement of law or investigative media reporting.

Traditionally, internal audit was perceived to be the main source of fraud detection. This is no longer true, since in most parts of the world, staffing of the internal audit function has either been curtailed or fewer people are being asked to do more due to budgetary constraints.

Whistle-blowing mechanisms are yielding good results. Jiri Urban of PwC Forensic Services, once said, 'An effective whistle-blowing system not only increases the likelihood of preventing wrongdoing and criminal behaviour, it also sends a positive signal to business partners and the public at large and reduces the risk of a negative reputation'.

There is, however, no substitute for a proper risk-assessment system to identify potential red flags and plug loopholes.

Tailpiece

The main deterrent of fraud is the fear of getting caught. Risk assessment, prevention and prompt action taken on potential red flags are the keys to unlock fraudulent acts or intent to perpetrate fraud.

A Russian proverb aptly states, 'It is not for the stealing that you are punished, but for getting caught'. There is an Indian saying on similar lines—'Theft is a good vocation till one gets caught'!

8

Do Pharma Companies Care? Do Medicines Heal? Are Doctors Concerned?

Faith, trust and hope prevail when we take medicines to cure our ailments. We take medications prescribed by a medical practitioner as we have confidence and belief that the pills and tablets will be good for us. Therefore, we unquestionably accept that recommended drugs would have been tested on similar symptoms, pharmaceutical companies have found that the drug works, the doctors testing were qualified to do so, drug research reports were based on real-life studies.

What if I were to tell you that none of these may be true in many cases? How would you feel if I tell you that some drugs may not be better than just placebos (tablets or capsules without any active ingredients) or may be sometimes worse than that? Unbelievable as this may sound, it is true.

Companies manufacturing and marketing medicines have failed on certain occasion in their august duty to protect the interest of humanity for dollops of extra profits.

This does not however mean that the next time you suffer from pain and pop in a *paracetamol* (an analgesic) tablet, it will not work. You must have had many pills till now, and most must have worked. But there are a few that do not. That is the problem.

Few instances will now be discussed in the chapter to throw light on some of the ills by which the medical system is plagued. It will help us to be more aware and careful.

I SCRATCH YOUR BACK, YOU SCRATCH MINE: DOCTORS, DRUG MAKERS, ET AL.

Did you ever get the eerie feeling of inappropriateness when your doctor asked you to get diagnostic or pathological tests done for a relatively minor ailment? Did you not feel that testing centres are charging similar amounts amongst them for the tests? Did you know that your doctor may be getting kickbacks for his recommendations? Exasperated, the Health Minister of India brought out these issues of the doctor–laboratory nexus in the Parliament in July 2014.

Medicine is our lifeline in many cases. In spite of this, gory stories of unethical practice and prevalence of human and corporate greed abound. *Conflict of interest* has been found time and again in the medical profession.

Federal investigators in the USA have recently revealed that 'conflict of interest' is not even clearly defined, and government officials do little to police the nexus among doctors, medical experts, pharmacists and drug-manufacturing companies who ultimately make decisions on what is good for people to remain pain-free, fit and healthy.

Interested Doctors Providing Guidelines

Doctors prescribe medicines based on research and guidelines published. There are guideline panels with select groups of experts assigned to evaluate health science independently and advise doctors on correct clinical practice. Doctors usually follow their advice in treating their patients, prescribing medicines as well as on insurance coverage. However, it was found that in several cases, doctors were members of some of the panels that wrote the guidelines on cardiovascular health in recent years.

The *Financial Times* reported that a study published in the Archives of Internal Medicine found that conflict of interest was reported by 56% of 498 persons who helped to write 17 guidelines for the American Heart Association and the American College of Cardiology between 2003 and 2008. Furthermore, 81% of the leaders of the groups formulating these guidelines had a personal financial interest in companies affected by the guidelines. Similarly, it was found that experts serving on an advisory panel to evaluate vaccines for flu and cervical cancer in 2007 had potential conflicts of interest. In its report of December 2009, the Centre for Disease Control and Prevention of USA admitted that it did not screen medical experts for financial conflicts with drug companies when they hired the experts for advising on vaccines and its safety.

How can such guidelines and advice be the objective evaluation of science when evaluators are only interested in recommending solutions so that the products of companies in which they have a financial interest are recommended by doctors? The matter is further complicated, since many research studies on drugs are funded by pharmaceutical companies, which expect recommendations to be in their favour.

Drug Companies as Teachers

When drug-makers teach doctors, what does this lead to? Doctors prescribe what they have been taught—that the drug companies' products should be prescribed. Clearly, their prescriptions may not be in the best interest of their patients, although they serve the purpose of the drug companies. Education thus doubles-up for advertisement. Training then tantamounts to virtual indoctrination of medical practitioners and constitutes sheer conflict of interest.

Teaching and training doctors have become a part of drug companies' overall marketing strategies. Almost half of continuing medical education in the USA is funded by drug companies, up from one-third earlier. Crucial information pertaining to the dangers of certain drugs and their downsides are played down by the drug companies when doctors are taught.

To cite some examples, in the case of the *Avandia* disaster, **GlaxoSmithKline** sponsored educational courses to teach and promote the benefits of Avandia over other drugs, without discussing one of the drug's significant side-effects of increasing levels of lipids associated with heart disease. In the case of another drug, *Vioxx*, **Merck** promoted the brilliance of the drug for treatment of arthritis through continuous education. It did not highlight the potential danger of patients taking the drug developing cardiac problems. Vioxx was responsible for 140,000 cases of serious heart diseases between 1999 and 2004 until it was withdrawn from the market.

Research Papers Written by Ghost Writers

Prominent doctors are often paid to be listed as authors of articles published in medical journals, whereas the articles, in reality, are articles written by ghost writers. This has been documented in a court trial of **Pfizer**.

In many cases, content is rarely developed by the experts whose names appear in a publication. It is usually developed by unknown medical communication companies that are paid by sponsoring drug companies. Basically, communication companies are paid by pharmaceutical companies to prepare research papers and medical guidelines, and then well-known doctors are asked by the former to deliver their findings in public talks or articles. This is also a 'back door' way of paying doctors to say good things about a product!

Merck, for instance, had sanctioned dozens of research studies (written by ghost writers) on Vioxx in 2007–08, and then attributed prestigious doctors' names to these before they were published. According to *Infuse*, a US Senate investigation, **Medtronic Inc.**, the maker of heart-rhythm devices, had ghost writers write articles for medical journals under its tutelage on behalf of doctors to promote its *bone-growth products* after spinal surgery.

Sponsored Speakers

From 2008 to 2011, there were issues of conflict of interest among the health panel members of the committee set up in the USA with the objective of developing guidelines on leading causes of cardiovascular disease. Many of the panel members were found to have received speakers' fees from drug companies.

It has been revealed that several members of obesity, cholesterol and hypertension panels have received fees of up to $400,000 as speaker or other fees for their work. For instance, **GlaxoSmithKline**, the maker of *Alli*, an over-the-counter obesity product; **Allergan Inc.**, the maker of the *Lap-Band stomach device*, and **Nestlé** have all paid some of the recommending-panel doctors either as speaker fees or other modes.

Involvement of Journalists

In the quest to increase their profits, pharma companies have not spared the media. Apart from being a conduit to channelise medical education to doctors and carry advertisements on medical journals, press constitute an important vehicle to carry news of medical successes—rightly or wrongly. Awards presented for journalism and sponsored trips are some of the journalistic tie ups which help to keep the media on the right side.

The *Embrace Award*, presented to journalists for reporting on *urinary incontinence*, sponsored by **Eli Lilly** and **Boehringer Ingelheim**, included fully paid foreign trips. Similarly, awards for *cancer treatment* stories, sponsored by **Eli Lilly**, included weeklong foreign trips for two.

The drug companies do not end their financial niceties to journalists with awards only. They also fund journalism training, education programmes and professorships. To keep media happy, the possibilities are endless.

Doctors' Interest Conflicting with Insurance Coverage

Medical insurance provides reimbursement for medicines bought in part or in full as well as for the cost of treatment for patients covered under these schemes. Conflict of interest arises between doctors, pharmacists and insurance companies regarding the type of drugs that should be covered under insurance policies. Many countries have a list of drugs and treatments that are covered by medical insurance. Not all drugs and not all types of treatments are covered for reimbursement.

Who decides on insurance coverage? Doctors and experts are frequently the decision-making authorities.

Millions of dollars are at stake every year when decisions are taken about whether a drug is to be covered by the insurance system—in the USA, this is known as the 'Medicare drug plan'. In many cases, the insurance system does not even verify whether the panel members have a financial interest in the drug companies.

It is important that the insurance system of any country should include a wide range of medications for various diseases, and not just a few drugs from influential drug companies.

Panels have experts and doctors, who have conflicts of interest with drug companies. And yet, they continue recommending what you and I should consume, and what the insurance companies should pay when there are medical requirements. Can these recommendations be correct in all cases?

FRAUDULENT MARKETING OF DRUGS

Unbelievable as it may sound, drugs can be killers. In Germany, **Grunenthal** apologised for its crime in September 2012 after 50 years of developing and marketing *thalidomide*, a drug that caused birth defects in 10,000 children around the world. It was sold in the 1950s as *Contergan* in Germany and *Distaval* in other countries as a cure for morning sickness in pregnant women worldwide. It was withdrawn in 1961 after it was linked to children being born with problems such as missing or shortened limbs to women who consumed thalidomide. Germany, Britain, Japan, Canada and Australia were among the countries that were the most affected. The company claims to have paid €500 million ($625 million) to the victims.

Let us consider another instance. News headlines flashed for weeks in mid-2013 on **GlaxoSmithKline**'s Chinese unit being accused of bribing doctors and medical officials, funnelling $490 million payments to them through 700 travel agencies for over six years. According to the company's Sales Manager in the country, its representatives had 'established good personal relations with doctors by catering to their pleasures or offering them money in order to make them prescribe more drugs'. This was reported by the official Chinese news agency Xinhua (quoting *The New York Times*).

Drug companies' practice of unethical marketing is endemic. They sometimes promote drugs for unapproved uses. Pharmaceutical companies sometimes minimise or conceal the dangers associated with the use of drugs for particular purposes. Medicines are sold without safety data being clearly mentioned on them. Bribing doctors is another popular method used by pharmaceutical companies to fraudulently market drugs. They keep doctors in good humour by reimbursing them in cash and kind.

It is well known that the drug industry's spending on advertising and marketing is double that of their research budgets.

Examples abound in the area of inappropriate marketing of medicines. It is sometimes hard to believe the sort of roguish misconduct which certain renowned multinational outfits can engage into.

The British drug giant **GlaxoSmithKline**'s dishonest marketing activities have been continuing for a long time. In June 2012, Glaxo pleaded guilty and paid a penalty of a massive $3 billion for marketing its bestselling antidepressants for unapproved uses and for failing to report safety data about its top diabetes drug. It also paid fines for marketing *Paxil*, *Wellbutrin* and *Avandia*. 'The company was aware that its own research on *Avandia* demonstrated a health hazard, but failed to warn the physicians or patients', stated

Dr Steven Nissen. In the case of Paxil, the company apparently used several tactics that aimed to promote the use of the drug on children. It also helped to publish a medical journal article that misreported data from a clinical trial. According to four of the company's employees, who were whistle-blowers, Glaxo engaged in improper practices from the late 1990s to the mid-2000s.

Glaxo dismissed its Quality Control (QC) Manager because she pointed out that certain drugs being manufactured in the country's Puerto Rico plant had possible health hazards.

The company agreed to pay $750 million as penalty in October 2010 after complaints were made about it knowingly selling 20 contaminated drugs manufactured in its Puerto Rican unit. The drugs included *Bactroban*, an ointment; *Coreg*, a heart drug and *Tagamet*, a drug to treat acid reflux. Incidentally, the QC Manager became a whistle-blower.

'Loving-moments with families' is the tagline of **Johnson & Johnson**'s ads. Contrary to this ever-caring image, the pharmaceutical giant paid several fines for improper marketing of drugs. In November 2013, the company was fined $2.2 billion for marketing an antipsychotic drug, *Risperdal*, by minimising or concealing the dangers associated with it. Risperdal, approved for treating schizophrenia, bipolar disorder and behavioural problems in teenagers and children with autism, did not highlight the side effects of weight gain, increased risks of diabetes, and in older patients, the risk of strokes. The US Attorney General said the company had 'recklessly put at risk the health of some of the most vulnerable members of our society—including young children, the elderly and the disabled'.

Johnson & Johnson's illegal marketing saga has been going on for some time. In April 2011, the company was fined $70 million after it admitted to bribing European doctors to market its *knee and hip implants* in countries including Greece, Romania and Poland. Johnson & Johnson offered cash incentives to surgeons for using its products.

Johnson & Johnson's two subsidiaries, its **Ortho-McNeil-Jansen Pharmaceuticals** unit and **Ortho-McNeil Pharmaceutical**, pleaded guilty and were fined $81 million in April 2010, for illegal promotion of a drug, *Topamax*, to treat epilepsy and for psychiatric use. The drug was cleared by drug regulators for treating migraine headaches and epilepsy.

Not learning from past mistakes is unpardonable. **Pfizer** has over the years paid several fines for illegal marketing of drugs. In September 2009, the company agreed to pay a whopping $2.3 billion to settle allegations of illegal marketing of its painkiller *Bextra*, which has since been withdrawn.

Neurontin, an epilepsy drug, was illegally marketed by Pfizer, The company was fined $430 million in 2004. The drugs were not approved for their intended use. Pfizer was levied a further fine of $142 million in 2011 for making insurance companies believe that Neurontin could work on migraines and bipolar disorders. According to Kopchinski, a senior manager in Pfizer, 'The whole culture of Pfizer is driven by sales, and if you don't sell drugs illegally, you are not seen as a team player'.

Bribing doctors and healthcare workers from Bulgaria to Italy and Russia to China is not easy. But that is what **Wyeth** (acquired by Pfizer in 2009) did to increase sale of its drugs. The company agreed to settle allegations made against it by paying a fine of $45 million in August 2012. **Pfizer H.C.P. Corporation** agreed to pay a $15 million penalty to settle a similar case. The Chief of US market watchdog, SEC, said, 'Pfizer had bribery so entwined in its sales culture that it offered points and bonus programs to improperly reward foreign officials who proved to be its best customers'.

Eli Lilly pleaded guilty to criminal conduct and paid a $1.4 billion fine in January 2009 for illegally marketing its antipsychotic drug *Zyprexa* for unapproved purposes such as treatment of dementia or dementia-related psychosis.

A pharmaceutical company selling unapproved drugs for the elderly with dementia is heinous act. This is precisely what **Abbott Laboratories** did between 2001 and 2006. It marketed the drug *Depakot* to treat schizophrenia and agitated dementia although it was only approved for treatment of seizures. It agreed to pay a fine of $1.6 billion in May 2012.

Doctors often have a field day! **AstraZeneca** allegedly paid kickbacks to doctors to market its products for unapproved use for children, the elderly, veterans and prisoners. The drug involved was schizophrenia drug, *Seroquel*. The company agreed to pay a fine of $520 million to settle the marketing-related investigations.

Even cancer patients are not spared. **Amgen** was promoting (by giving kickbacks to doctors and clinics) the use of *Aranesp* to treat anaemia in cancer patients 'not undergoing chemotherapy', although the drug had only been approved for patients receiving chemotherapy. The biotechnology giant also illegally marketed its anaemia drug for unapproved uses, even when the Food & Drug Administration specifically ordered it not to. Amgen agreed to pay a penalty of $762 million after pleading guilty in December 2012.

Who has not heard of *Botox*, the wrinkle-killer? Can you believe that **Allergan**, the maker of the immensely successful Botox, settled lawsuits by agreeing to pay a penalty of $600 million in August 2010 for illegal marketing of the drug's usage as a *cure for migraine*? The company agreed that it misbranded Botox between 2000 and 2005 before the Food & Drugs Administration could clear Botox for severe migraines.

Who does not want to elevate one's mood? **Elan** took advantage of this innate desire. The Irish drug maker illegally marketed *Zonegran* as a mood elevator and a drug for weight loss although Zonegran was approved as an anti-seizure medication. The company agreed to pay a fine of $203 million in September 2010.

Which man does not want six-pack abs? Taking advantage of customers' gullibility, **GNC** and **Vitamin Shoppe**, retailer of dietary supplements, marketed certain workout-booster and fat-burning products. It was warned to stop marketing some of its advertised products in April 2013, since they could be hazardous for users. *Jack3d* (pronounced 'Jacked'), developed by USP Labs, and *Oxy-Elite Pro* were the brand names of these products. They contained dimethylamylamine (DMAA), which is a stimulant that does not qualify for use in legal dietary supplements and can raise blood pressure and cause heart attacks. An instance of selling dream bodies fraudulently!

Can a pharma company be subjected to manslaughter and consumer fraud? **Laboratoires Servier**, a private French drug manufacturer, is precisely facing such an investigation. The maker of *Mediator*, the diabetes drug, created the greatest public health scandal in France after the drug's withdrawal from the market in 2009. According to reports, around 2,000 users died and thousands were hospitalised due to cardiac valve damage and pulmonary hypertension, allegedly linked with the drug. What did the company do? It influenced doctors to prescribe the drug as a diet aid to boost sales.

Popular global drugs can be killers! Vioxx, meant to treat rheumatoid arthritis, was withdrawn from 80 countries in 2004, since it enhanced the risk of heart attacks, strokes and death. **Merck** agreed to pay a fine of $950 million and pleaded guilty for illegal marketing of the painkiller in November 2011. Not learning from its previous misconduct in 2007, the company paid a massive sum of $4.8 billion to settle 27,000 lawsuits brought against it by people who claimed to have suffered injury (or the death of relatives) after taking Vioxx.

Even HIV victims were not shown mercy. The AIDS drug *Serostim* was illegally marketed by **Serono Labs**, a Swiss biotechnology company, by concocting dubious medical tests. It offered doctors paid trips to France to prescribe the drug. Serostim was supposed to reverse the effects of 'HIV wasting syndrome' or profound weight loss. In order to prove 'HIV wasting', even in cases where there was no weight loss, the company developed false medical tests that ostensibly would determine 'body cell mass'. Serono pleaded guilty and agreed to pay $700 million as a fine in October 2005.

Tailpiece

The saga of corrupt marketing practices in the pharma sector continues in spite of imposition of penalties in millions of dollars. This clearly displays the wider problem in the industry of the prevailing disease of unethical practices. Seems pharma behaviour cleansing through drug-therapy is yet a far cry!

MARKETING TRIAL ON HUMANS GOING WRONG

Under the garb of marketing 'approved drugs', pharmaceutical companies carry out 'market seeding' (their objective being to make doctors familiar with new drugs). This involves selecting doctors, asking them to recruit subjects and administering the drugs to these. Doctors are usually paid per subject recruited. These episodes go horribly wrong in many cases, since either they are not conducted systematically or without adequate precautions.

Parke-Davis (taken over by Pfizer) conducted a research study on *Neurontin*, a drug to treat seizures, on 2,700 subjects in the early 2000s. The investigators were inexperienced and untrained, and the design of the study was flawed. This resulted in the death of 11 patients and 73 experienced 'serious adverse incidents'. Similarly, **Merck** conducted a seeding trial for its pain reliever Vioxx. A litigation report compiled in 2008 indicated that the study was managed by the company's marketing department. Three subjects died and five more experienced heart attacks due to administration of the drug. These were utter unethical ugliness!

TAMPERING WITH DRUG TEST TRIAL DATA

How will a drug-maker know that its medicines work? The only way is to test the drugs, first on animals and then on humans. Multiple trials need to be carried out over years.

Manufacture of sub-standard drugs and submission of false data are harbingers of cheating. **Ranbaxy**, a subsidiary of the Japanese pharmaceutical company **Daiichi Sankyo**, with two plants in Paonta Sahib and Dewas in India, pleaded guilty of such falsifications during 2002–05. The company agreed to pay a fine of $500 million to resolve the allegations in May 2013. Ranbaxy acknowledged that it had failed to conduct the requisite safety and quality tests for several generic drugs such as *gabapentin* (known as *Neurontin*) for treatment of epilepsy and nerve pain, and the antibiotic *ciprofloxacin*. Dinesh Thakur, a former director in Ranbaxy's research information division, was the whistle-blower who pocketed $49 million as a reward in the settlement.

Unapproved drugs are sometimes prescribed by doctors. In May 2012, the Indian Parliamentary Standing Committee on health and family welfare shook the country by revealing the existence of a nexus between some doctors from distinguished medical colleges and pharmaceutical companies. *Pirfenidone* of **Cipla** was approved by two doctors in 2010, although the drugs had been apparently only clinically tried in Japan at that time.

There have been instances where drug-related data has been either (i) not released, (ii) delayed or (iii) hidden.

Non-release of Drug Trial Data

Drug-makers are supposed to conduct numerous tests on new drugs or for new use of existing ones.

What happens when test reports are held back for years?

This means that something is not right with the test data. However, you and I will never get to know that a pharma manufacturer is receiving negative reports on drugs. Common sense demands that it should make this information known to at least doctors, so that they can take appropriate steps before the drugs are prescribed to treat patients. But many a time they do not.

Roche, manufacturer of anti-influenza drug *Tamiflu*, used to treat 'swine-flu' in 2009, refused to publish internal test data to prove its claim that the drug was effective for treating influenza-related complications. Independent verification was necessary to disprove doubts about the efficacy of the drug. However, even after years, Roche did not publish its research data although it had earlier agreed to do so. Professor Peter Doshi, a research scientist at Johns Hopkins University's School of Medicine, claimed that his study in 2012 found that 'Tamiflu is no more effective than aspirin'.

Delayed Release of Unfavourable Drug Study Results

Pharmaceutical companies spend millions of dollars on conducting research on molecules and various types of tests, compiling research reports and results, and then marketing drugs for human use.

If research indicates either negative results or areas of negative health fallouts in a drug launched in the market, this information needs to be made known to the public. Not releasing or delaying the release of unfavourable study results is unacceptable.

Merck and **Schering-Plough**, which jointly marketed *Vytorin*, delayed the release of unfavourable study reports for its cholesterol-lowering drug. Allegations were settled by the companies by their agreeing to pay a fine of $688 million without admitting their wrongdoing. Investors filed suits against them on grounds that the test results were held back by two years till 2008. Clinical trials apparently failed to show that the drug was any better than statin drugs (low-cost generics known to reduce risk of heart attack) or that it helped to limit build-up of plaque in arteries. The stock price of the companies declined significantly after the poor test results were made public.

'Per Senior Management request these data should not see the light of day to anyone outside of GSK' was **SmithKline Beecham**'s dictum through internal emails in 2001. The company, while testing whether its drug Avandia was safer for the heart than the competing pill *Actos* made by **Takeda** in 1999, the results proved to be disastrous. Not only was Avandia no better than Actos, it was riskier for people with heart ailments. *The New York Times* reported that instead of publishing the report, the company tried to cover up its findings for the next 11 years.

It was found in 2004 that **GlaxoSmithKline** had withheld data, which revealed that its antidepressant *Paxil* led to children and teenagers having more suicidal thoughts and behaving accordingly. The company settled the lawsuit by paying a fine.

Telling half-truths is useful if it sells. This applied to **Forest Laboratories**, which was charged in February 2009 by the US

Justice Department for illegal marketing of antidepressants *Celexa* and *Lexapro* for their unapproved use in teenagers and children. It was alleged by the federal prosecutors in the USA that the company had concealed for several years a clinical study which revealed that the drugs were not effective in children, and it might induce suicidal conditions in them. Between 2001 and 2004, Forest promoted the results of another study it had financed without highlighting the negative trial results to the researchers and not giving physicians the full picture.

Hiding Unfavourable Test Data

Whenever any study is undertaken, unless the full findings are made known, a judgement cannot be made on its content. Until both the pros and cons are disclosed, a report has no meaning. However, picking and choosing of reports have occurred in many cases. It seems that drug-makers' follow the creed of not communicating bad news—only the good.

How can any sense be made of drug research findings when it omits negative ones?

Pfizer disclosed a part of the research data while reporting on the effectiveness of *Reboxitine*, an antidepressant drug. Reboxitine, dubbed as 'ineffective and potentially harmful' by a German research group in 2010, accused Pfizer of only publishing evidence on 1,065 patients, overstating benefits of the drug and understating its risks, and not publishing the findings on 3,033 patients. According to the *British Medical Journal*, this 'was the latest in a series of cases where manufacturers buried unfavourable evidence'.

DRUG TRIAL WITHOUT LONG-TERM PATIENT TRIAL

Drugs that are often heavily prescribed are frequently not backed by adequate long-term research data that they actually cure the ailment being treated or improve the condition of the patient.

Many medicines are approved on the basis of what scientists call 'surrogate end-points'. For example, a study may indicate that a drug reduces cholesterol, but does not show improvement in disease or reduction of death, or that a cancer drug reduces the size of tumours, without proving that the patient can live longer.

Let us look at some instances to make this point clearer.

Adequate proof does not exist to indicate that patients live longer or avoid heart attacks by using **Merck and Schering-Plough** product *Zetia* or as a combination medicine with *Vytorin*. Either drug is taken every day by more than three million patients. Worse, a few studies showed that by the use of Vytorin instead of sugar pill, the patient had 40% higher chances of dying of cancer. The findings could just be a coincidence, but the matter remains that the trial results were inadequate.

Glaxo's drug for diabetes, *Avandia*, was approved by drug administrators for helping to reduce blood sugar in 1999. However, in 2007, 44 clinical trials of the drug proved that it increased the risk of heart attacks. It revealed that earlier trials were inadequate.

In another example where larger samples helped, was the lung cancer pill *Iressa,* made by **AstraZeneca**. It was approved by drug authorities in 2003, based on a small trial. This indicated that the drug helped to shrink tumours in around 10% of patients who had run out of other options of therapy. However, subsequent trials showed that it did not prolong the lives of lung cancer patients. The drug was withdrawn for new users in June 2005.

The answer to all the problems mentioned above is for pharma companies to 'get more data' for longer period. Unless there are enough trials on humans, the effect of the drug is very difficult to understand. Moreover, unless there are enough trials on humans, the effect of a drug is difficult to gauge. Short cuts may create shorter lives for short-changed patients!

Tailpiece

'A drug is that substance which, when injected into a rat, will produce a scientific report', goes a saying. No wonder Earl Wilson, an American columnist once commented, 'You may not be able to read a doctor's handwriting and prescription, but you'll notice his bills are neatly typewritten.'

LACK OF HUMANE TREATMENT OF HUMANS IN TESTING DRUGS

Before launching a drug in the market, it is first tested on animals. If found efficacious, it is then tested multiple times on humans. However, human procedure needs to ensure that the negative effects of the drug are minimised. Sometimes, tests on human subjects are carried out without taking adequate precautions.

In the USA, **Parexel** tests new medicines for drug-makers. A new immune stimulant, *TGN1412* (trade-marked *superMABS*), manufactured by a small Germany company, **TeGenero**, which had never been tried on humans, was tested on six healthy young men. The method of testing went horribly wrong. After the first subject was tested and there were negative reactions, the other men also went through the same tests without the company taking into cognizance the negative reactions of the earlier test. Concurrent tests impaired the immune systems of all the six human subjects—a negative implication of a very poor execution of the testing on humans.

Eli Lilly applied on a 19-year-old student, larger than therapeutic doses of *Duloxetine,* a drug it proposed to introduce as an antidepressant. The girl was one among 25 healthy subjects who killed herself in 2004 due to depression. Four other patients, who had been administered the drug during an earlier trial, also committed suicide—an instance of a misstep in testing drugs on humans without adequate preparations.

A new drug *Trovan*, an antibiotic, was tested by **Pfizer** during a meningitis epidemic in Kano in Nigeria in 1996. Eleven children died, five after being given Trovan and six after taking an older antibiotic used for comparison in the trial. The issue here was that Pfizer did not inform the parents of the children that this drug was at an experimental stage, giving the parents the opportunity to opt out of the treatment. In 2011, Pfizer paid $175,000 to the parents of the four children who had died. It was another example of mishandling of clinical trial procedures.

BAD ADVERTISEMENTS FOR DRUGS

Pharmaceutical companies are generally forbidden from advertising their products to ordinary consumers in most countries. Specialist medical and drug journals can, however, be used as a vehicle for pharma advertisements. The advertisers, thus, need to be careful to not over-claim or give an incorrect picture of a drug and its uses. And this is what happens sometimes.

Bayer advertised its contraceptive pill *Yasmin*. The advertisement claimed, 'Yasmin, it's for more women than you might imagine'. It also wrongly stated that it works for acne, fluid retention, hirsutism and premenstrual symptoms. The company also underplayed its side effects. The pharma industry's self-regulatory body reprimanded Bayer for its aggressive marketing in advertising the contraception pill for health problems beyond contraception.

WRONG PRICING OF DRUGS

Most jurisdictions in the world have drug-pricing norms. Some are on a cost-plus basis and some have pricing guidelines on maximum mark-ups or profits. In some countries, the cost to the insurance company should be lower than the market price. Whatever be the rule, drug companies need to abide by them. However, they do not comply with these norms on many occasions.

The antibiotic *Cipro* was wrongly priced by **Bayer**. The Germany-headquartered drug giant pleaded guilty and agreed to pay a fine of $257 million in April 2003. The fraud involved Bayer selling Cipro to Kaiser Permanente (a healthcare organisation) at a price that was lower than that it was charging Medicaid, a government-funded insurance scheme. Legally, Medicaid was to be charged the lowest price. Buyer planned a cover-up, but this did not work—bottles of Cipro sold to Kaiser were re-labelled with Kaiser's name and a different drug identification number.

Cipla, an Indian drug-maker, was fined by the National Pharmaceutical Pricing Authority in late 2009 for increasing the prices of drugs above the Government's recommended pricing guideline. The drugs included *theophylline*, *ciprofloxacin*, *norfloxacin* and *doxycycline*. The company was levied a fine of INR 7.4 billion ($120 million).

Tailpiece

Nothing like getting affordable medicines that cure our ailments. It will help to make the best fashion statement—having a healthy body.

INVESTORS CAN SUE

Investors are the 'owners' of companies, even if an entity holds one-hundredth or even less in a company. They have the right to know about key developments in the companies so that they can decide whether they wish to keep or withdraw their investments in them.

In March 2011, the highest court in the USA decided that investors could sue a company if it fails to disclose reports of the adverse effects of an over-the-counter drug even if the sample size falls short of having a statistical significance. The matter pertained to **Matrixx Initiatives**, the maker of *Zicam*, a nasal spray and gel, which was sold as a homoeopathic remedy. It was alleged that the company received scattered reports of users losing their sense of smell, medically called anosmia, from 1999 to 2004. Matrixx failed to disclose the reports. A TV programme disclosed this linkage in 2004, and the company's share price crashed. It recalled the product in 2009. The Supreme Court decided that Matrixx not sharing material information with its shareholders made the company liable to wrongdoing.

ARE IRRESPONSIBLE EXECUTIVES NOT RESPONSIBLE?

It has been a long-standing demand from members of the public that while drug companies are penalised for their misdemeanours, this should also apply to their executives? Drug companies are legal entities. They cannot think or work on their own. It is their people who do their work.

In a rare move, the Justice Department of the USA charged Laurence Stevens, a former Vice President and top lawyer in **GlaxoSmithKline**, in November 2010 for making false statements and obstructing investigations into illegal marketing of antidepressant *Wellbutrin* for weight loss.

Penalties and fines have been levied of late on pharma companies on grounds of alleged bribery and their over-aggressive marketing activities. However, the *back-bench* people are still hiding behind the corporate shield and are not being touched.

There are moves in the pharma sector towards self-regulation and an effort to meet higher ethical standards. Only time will tell whether the industry will be more responsible and humane in caring for people in the future.

Tailpiece

Instances of medical chicanery get mainly reported in the developed world. Drugs made in these countries are usually sold globally, even though a few of these may be dubious in their effect on humans.

The *Financial Times* reported that the USA, the UK and Germany dominate enforcement of the pharmaceutical anti-corruption measures. Doubts exist whether Russia, India and China would enforce with the same vigour against its own companies. Hence, European and American companies are perhaps at a disadvantage, compared to their counterparts in other countries that are less concerned about pharma-related corruption. One Chinese businessman said, 'This is our competitive edge.'

9

'The Last Word' on Fraud Yet to Be Revealed

Several business entities have either practised fraud or have themselves been victims of deception. But with enhanced awareness and imposition of penalties, is the world of deceit and deception changing? Is it becoming a worse place to do business? What should we do to prepare ourselves to deal with, if not prevent, corporate mischief?

Let us look at the ever-changing face of fraud and scams in the corporate world.

Situation continues to be grim within the banking system—place where your and my money is kept—the fulcrum on which the world's economy functions. In 2014, Banks created a new world-record—not the sorts we would like them to achieve. Globally, for several wrongdoings they paid a total fine and legal settlements surpassing $56 billion, almost similar to the GDP of Uruguay, Sudan or Bulgaria. This is terrible news. The Bank of England Governor in late 2014 summarised the situation as 'the succession of scandals mean it is simply untenable now to argue that the problem is one of a few bad apples—the issue is with the barrels in which they are stored'.

Skeletons keep tumbling out of the closet of banks' tax-evasion schemes. After **UBS** and **HSBC** were castigated for playing ducks and drakes with clients' taxes, in February 2014, a US Senate panel rebuked **Credit Suisse** for helping around 22,000 Americans conceal $10–12 billion worth of assets from US tax authorities between

2001 and 2008. The bank's CEO admitted that 'a small number of employees were involved in actively recruiting American clients and helping them hide money offshore'.

Banks continue to deceive. **American Express** misled its credit card customers with hidden fees and supposed 'add-on-products', for example, by promising to excuse them from making minimum monthly payments if they lost their jobs. In reality, the benefit was limited to 2.5% of customers' outstanding balance. American Express was penalised $75 million for its nefarious practice, which it perpetrated between 2000 and 2012 on 335,000 customers. Fraud in the 'add-ons' market is fairly common. The UK's financial watchdog intervened in the insurance market in March 2014, when customers were being overcharged up to 20% for products sold along with cars and home insurance.

The reputation of banks has been severely tarnished, since they have not only rigged Libor rates, but even manipulated foreign-exchange rates. Record fines of over $4 billion have been imposed by UK, US and Swiss regulators on **UBS**, **Royal Bank of Scotland**, **JP Morgan**, **HSBC**, **BofA** and **Citigroup**. Britain's financial regulatory body FCA found that the banks did not exercise effective control in the spot foreign exchange market between January 2008 and October 2013. This meant, even after getting pulled up for the libor scandal, the banks continued with their transgressions long after they were supposed to clean up their act.

Alternatively, currency did not escape pilferage. *Bitcoin*, a virtual currency, an alternative to traditional money so that transactions can take place anonymously, has been subjected to theft. In this Internet-based 'crypto-currency' domain, rumours of 750,000 Bitcoins going missing and unnoticed for years led to shutting down of its website in February 2014 at Mt. Gox, one of the largest trading platforms of the currency. The theft involved 6% of the 12 million Bitcoins in circulation, which was significant enough to shake Bitcoin's investors' confidence.

Even legal firms take the illegal route at times. **Dewey & LeBoeuf**, once a high-flying global law firm, was *cooking up* its accounting books from 2007 to paint a rosy picture of its financial position, when it was in fact unable to pay the bills of its expensive lawyers. Eventually, it filed for bankruptcy in 2012.

Insider trading is a malady. People and organisations find ingenious ways to gain an undue advantage. **BlackRock** systematically sought advance information from analysts studying companies even before they had published their findings. Doubts have been expressed that BlackRock, the US fund giant, may have pressurised analysts to give them their advance views to gain an early unfair advantage over other investors. BlackRock was forced to close the programme in January 2014.

Rolls-Royce, the British jet engine-maker, is alleged to have paid bribes in Indonesia, China and India. It acknowledged that its investigations had identified 'matters of concern in these and in other overseas markets'. **Novartis** faces criminal trials in Japan for allegedly falsifying clinical data and claiming additional heart-related benefits in advertising Diovan, a popular blood pressure medicine. The company has acknowledged its employees' involvement in this scam.

Cyber criminals are always on the prowl. Debit and credit card data of 70 million customers was stolen from the big US retailer *Target* in December 2013. Its sales suffered and customers were frightened.

Cyberattacks are reigning havoc. Retail trade is becoming increasingly vulnerable. Hackers broke into *Abode* in October 2013, stealing 38 million records of its customers' usernames and passwords, including intellectual property in the form of the source codes of its most widely used products such as Acrobat and Photoshop. Corporates continue to be susceptible. In December 2014, unprecedented but well-planned cyberattack took place on *Sony Corp*'s Hollywood studio damaging its network and wiping out PCs, with fingers of suspicion pointed at North Korea. The bad news is that cyberattacks are on the rise—rising by 14% in 2013 over 2012 according to Cisco. Stealing intellectual property by entering corporate networks, especially those in the pharmaceutical, mining and electronics sectors, seems to have become the norm today.

Making profits through stock and commodity exchanges is an ongoing process. A scam was unearthed in India at NSEL, promoted by the **Financial Technologies** group. It was supposed to be a commodity exchange, providing a platform to trade commodities, based on physical deliveries. However, none of this took place. Members gambled and illegally tampered with forward contracts. The warehouse did not have the physical commodities. Traders sold commodities without depositing these in the warehouse. It was a hoax. There was a INR 54 billion ($900 million) default in payment. Several arrests were made and assets found and frozen. Greed had overtaken rationality.

Lack of record-keeping is a disease. In December 2013, the US regulator finally held **Barclays Capital** responsible for not maintaining its electronics records properly between 2002 and April 2012 and fined it $3.75 million. Barclays failed to maintain basic transaction data including orders, trade confirmation, account records and other data in non-alteration forms.

Greed is unending. Even after numerous Ponzi and Pyramid schemes lead to investors losing millions of dollars, its dirty heads keep rearing over and over again. **Rose Valley** firm in West Bengal is turning out perhaps six times bigger scam than the infamous **Saradha** ponzi fiasco. In November 2014, the Indian Enforcement Directorate reported INR 150 billion ($2.5 billion), collected over 18 years under the garb of advances against real estate projects from thousands of small investors, are unlikely to be paid back.

Royal Twinkle Star Club, running a so-called time-sharing scheme, was banned by SEBI, the market regulator in India, in March 2014 after it collected INR 7 billion ($110 million) from 368,000 gullible investors.

Art market is booming, and so it seems. In 2014, *Christie*'s global sales hit a record of $8 billion, and *Sotheby*'s auction sales alone a whopping $6 billion, up nearly 20% over previous year. Art is sometimes a camouflage for money laundering and tax evasion. Why else should Chinese clients buy $1 billion in 2014 of art across the world? The beauty of art is often a gray and shady business.

Royalty also cheats. The King of Spain's younger daughter was formally named as the prime suspect in money-laundering and tax evasion. State heads also cheat. Former President of France, Nicolas Sarkozy, was charged with corruption and influence-peddling.

The fraud-saga is unending.

The intensity of deceit and dishonesty continues to increase. In February 2014, the European Commission reported that corruption was having devastating effect on business with €120 billion ($145 billion) being lost every year in tax revenues and foreign investment. However, the business-politician nexus continues. To top it all, around 70% of the businesses surveyed revealed that bribing and exploiting political connections are among the easiest ways of obtaining certain public contracts. The Kroll Report on Global Fraud 2013/14 concluded that fraud is on the rise with every kind of fraud covered in the survey showing an increase and procurement-related fraud and conflict of interest registering the steepest upsurge. And the worse news is that over two-thirds of companies reported that they were affected by fraud.

Making gains on the sly in the world of business has come a long way. Entering and cancelling orders in the blink of an eye has changed the rules of profit-making in *high-frequency* commodity and stock market trading. Technological breakthroughs in the cyber world have opened up new avenues of economic crimes. Sophisticated equipment such as 'Google eyes' has made eavesdropping common in corporate espionage. Rigging of international benchmark rates such as Libor, forex and gold by falsifying data has an adverse impact on almost everyone in the world. The list is never-ending in the world of unfair profit-making.

Although corporate wrongdoing keeps rearing its head, some encouraging signs of change and awareness are evident. As business entities manage their affairs to maximise profits, the means to achieve this goal may or may not be through integrity. Needless to say, most companies do not perpetrate fraud, although some may cut ethical corners from time to time. It is the shades of grey in corporate activities that increase our difficulty in understanding human behaviour in business.

The good news, however, is that baby steps are being taken to eradicate corruption in some parts of the corporate world. *GlaxoSmithKline,* the British drug-maker, has stopped paying doctors for promoting its products and remunerating its sales representatives, based on the number of prescriptions written by doctors recommending its drugs, from December 2013. *AstraZeneca* no longer pays doctors to attend international conferences.

Even God's own bank is cleaning up its stables. The *Vatican Bank,* after years of dilly-dallying, is closing numerous accounts for the first time to weed out potential money-launderers and tax evaders. If the Holy See cleanses itself, why can't lesser mortals like us do the same?

Hefty penalties are being imposed and recalcitrant executives are being shamed. JP Morgan has been fined a hitherto unthinkable amount of $13 billion for improper sales of mortgage securities; more and more executives are being put behind bars, for example, the top honchos of India's recent perpetrators of a Ponzi scheme, the **Sharada Group**. Similarly, India's Sahara Group's flamboyant chief Subrata Roy was imprisoned for months over **Sahara**'s failure to comply with a court order to refund billions of dollars invested in illegal bonds. However, just because some people are going to prison, this does not guarantee eradication of economic crimes. Public awareness and anger is helping in cleansing the system. Brazil's state-run oil company **Petrobras** lost $2 billion between 2004 and 2012 as the firm's executives took bribes to award inflated contracts to suppliers. The company is now being forced through public opinion to get its acts together fast. Enhanced awareness and proper checks and balances within businesses are what will help.

Another development which is likely to discourage institutional corruption is the increase in laws against corporate bribery, like America's Foreign Corrupt Practices Act, Anti-bribery legislations and so on have been enacted in various regions including Britain, Germany and South Korea. China and Brazil have also jumped onto the bandwagon of late. Indian laws are being strengthened. These steps will make many companies think twice before greasing palms to win business.

What should be done to reduce if not eliminate the menace of corporate fraud? Time-bound investigations, disclosure of the modus operandi, increased penalties, jailing of corrupt executives, making auditors independent from their clients and barring fraud-guilty companies from doing business for a length of time would be a good starting point.

Since it is doubtful that such far-reaching steps will actually be taken, it is important to be aware of the maxim—'knowledge is power'. Strong internal controls, management audits and providing incentives to whistle-blowers would go a long way in making the corporate world anti-fraud ready.

Tailpiece

Corruption and dishonesty are prevalent around the world. It is the degree that varies. According to the National Fraud Authority, 'Fraud is a hidden crime. Fraud reported to the authorities is a small proportion of the fraud detected, which in turn is a fraction of fraud that remains out of sight'. Angus Kidman summarises the phenomenon in 'Lifehacker—Australia' by saying, 'the unpleasant reality: many people are dishonest and will try and scam you or your loved ones. Awareness is your biggest defence'.

Index

Abacus Federal Savings Bank, 71
Abbott Laboratories, 273
Abercrombie & Fitch Co., 248
Absolute Poker, 96
accounting fraud
    accounts prior, manipulation of, 235
    affiliates, 194–195
    AOL, 169–170
    bad investment, 203–204
    banks' failure, 199–201
    bill and hold, 164–165
    Biovail, 221–222
    bogus sales, 173–174
    book phony revenue, 180–181
    booking false vendor rebates, 182–184
    camouflage poor performance, 233
    capitalising normal revenue expense, 197–198
    cash flow, 232–233
    channel stuffing, 165–167
    Comp-U-Card (CUC) International, 235–236
    contractual obligation, sales pending fulfilment of, 156–157
    controllable subsidiaries, 224–227
    creating sales out, 175–176
    deceptive barter system, 173
    enhance revenue, 161–162
    Enron, 211–212
    excess or obsolete inventory, 201–202
    expenses incurred, 205–206
    fake sales, 174–175
    first in first out (FIFO) method, 208–209
    fixed asset, 209–210
    fudging operating income and losses, 191–194
    GE, 170, 215–216
    generally accepted accounting principles (GAAP), 155
    Hewlett-Packard–autonomy, 237–238
    Hospitality Franchise Systems (HFS), 235–236
    incorrect lease accounting, 160
    inter-company expenses, 196
    inventory to generate profits, 208
    JVs, 194–195
    Krispy-Kreme, 213–214
    last in first out (LIFO) method, 208–209
    lax internal control, 241–243
    loans, 181
    manipulating profits, 186–187
    McKesson-HBOC, 236–237
    Microsoft, 214–215
    multiple products, revenue allocation method for, 163–164
    non-accounting red flags, 247–249
    non-collectable debtors, 202–203
    non-consolidating subsidiaries, sales of, 171–172
    non-existent cash-in-bank, 227–228
    of derivatives, 217–219
    off-balance sheet financing, 219–220
    Olympus corporation, 222–224
    one-time income, 188–189
    Parmalat, 229–230
    pay tax, 234–235
    peregrine financial, 231
    PNC financial service, 221
    providing cash to buyer, 167–169

pushing loans, 220–221
record and report depreciation, 207
red flags, 243–247
reduce cost, 204–205
Reebok India, 178–179
reserves and illusory profits, 210–211
revenue recognition policy, 159
round tripping, 167–169
sales recognition policy, 184–186
sales without despatching goods, 176–177
Satyam Computer Services Limited, 228–229
Sham Insurance Premium Income, 179–180
shifting non-operating income, 191–193
shifting operating losses, 193
shoddy accounting, 239–241
slow down depreciation cost, 189–190
special earnings, 187–188
stretch accounting period, 157–158
subsidiaries, 194–195
Sunbeam Corporation, 212–213
Syntax-Brillion Corporation, 177–178
time warner, 169–170
tricky sales revenue booking, 155–156
Tyco International, 171
understating cost, hiding problems by, 197–208
Adani Power Ltd., 8
Adelphia Communication's annual report of 2000, 248, 258
Afghan Bank—Bank of Kabul, 79–80
Agape World Inc., 115
Ahold NV, 182
AIG, 69, 75
Allen Stanford—Stanford International Bank, 110
Allergan Inc., 269, 274

Alliance Data, 94
Amazon, 43
Amber Gold, 77
Ambit Capital, 19
American Express, 286
American Home Products, 30
Amex, 80–81
Amgen, 5, 274
Andrx, 30
Antonveneta Bank, 83
AOL, 169–170, 197
Apple, 30–31, 38, 44
Arcelor Mittal India Ltd., 8
Arthur Anderson, 253
AstraZeneca, 274, 280
Atherstone Capital Markets Ltd., 133
AU Optronics Corp., 32
AutoChina International, 136
autonomy, 17
AutoZone, 40
Aventis Pharma Limited, 30
Axis Bank, 67–68

Baan Company NV, 256
Baan Corporation, 157
bad investment, 203–204
BAE Systems, 1
Baidu.com, 140
Bain, 31–32
Bally Total Fitness, 251
Bank of America, 61, 70
Bank of Credit and Commerce International, 96
Bank of India, 90
Bank of Saderat, 100
BankAm, 80–81
Banks
    camouflage and concealment, 82
    commit fraud, 58–59
    dangerous banks, uninsured or unlicensed, 76–77
    endless possibilities, 83–85
    failures in internal control, 89–90
    faulty security, 98–99

fraud in banks, 85–89
fraud perpetuated on, 91–96
fraud stories, 101–107
fraudulent loan, 79–82
in India, 75
ITSY-BITSY bank fraud, 99–100
Libor scandal, 59–64
miss-selling by, 69–76
money laundering, 64–68
obtain debts, 96–97
pay back loans, 97–98
sham deals, 78
Banque Indo-Suez, 80–81
Barclays Bank, 78
Barclays Capital, 288
Barclays, 5, 60, 76, 85
Barings Bank, 87
BASF, 33
Bayer, 282
BBA. *See* British Banker's Association (BBA)
BBC, sex, lies and videos, 53–54
BDL Gulf, 51
Beetal Livestock & Farm (P) Ltd., 113
Bernard Madoff, 109–110
Bhushan Steel Ltd., 8
Biotor Industries, 97
Biovail, 221–222
Black Box Corporation, 39
Blackstone, 31–32
BNP Paribas, 50
Boehringer Ingelheim, 269
BofA, 286
Boshiwa International Holdings, 134
Brazil banks, 81
Bristol-Myers Squibb Company (BMS), 165
British Aegis Group, 175
British Bank of Middle East, 80–81
British Banker's Association (BBA), 59
British Petroleum (BP), 3
Broadcom Corporation, 38

Cadbury, 55

Cardinal Health, 191, 242
Carlyle Group, 31–32
cash balance, non-verification of, 260
cash flow, 232–233
Cegetel, 202
Cendant Corporation, 257
Central Bank of India, 90
China Construction Bank (CCB), 74
China MediaExpress, 135
China Medical Technologies, 136
China Natural Gas Inc., 138
ChinaCast Education Corporation, 140
Chunghwa Picture Tubes Ltd., 32
Cipla, 283
Cisco Systems, 217
Citi, 44–45, 80–81
Citibank, 74, 81
Citic, 74
Citigroup, 60, 61, 70, 72, 82, 88, 286
City Limousine (India), 114
clever north America-listed Chinese companies
assets, diversion of, 138–139
false declaration, non-existent cash, 136–137
funds, diversion of, 138
inadequate corporate governance, 135–136
market manipulation, 136–137
overstatement of assets, 139
shareholding, false sense of, 139–140
CNS-Israel, 180
Coalgate scandal, 7–8
Coca-Cola, 167
Collins & Aikman, 184
Comptronix Corporation, 209
Comp-U-Card (CUC) International, 235–236
Computer Associates (CA), 158
ConAgra, 234
conflict of interest, 256, 265
corporate charlatan
Apple, 30–31, 44

Bain, 31–32
Blackstone, 31–32
bribery and kickbacks, 5–12
buying back share, 39–40
bypass rules, 18–19
Carlyle Group, 31–32
Coalgate scandal, 7–8
conflict of interest, 24–29
contract rigging, 5–12
Daimler, 6
Delhi airport scam, 10
Enron, 16–17
extortion provides easy money, 21–24
Facebook, 44–45, 48
food, 54–56
Freeport, 27–28
General Electric (GE), 45
Goldman Sachs, 28, 31–32
Google, 47–48
greedy corporate, 3–4
2G telecom scam, 9–10
Hachette, 30–31
Harper Collins, 30–31
Hewlett-Packard (HP), 17, 44–45
Hilton hotel, 14
Indonesia, journalists in, 23–27
Intel, 44–45
Ireland, 44–45
Japan Tobacc0, 29
KKR, 31–32
lies, damn lies and statistics, 15–18
Linkedin, 44–45
Macmillan, 30–31
MF Global, 14–15
Microsoft, 7, 44–45
Penguin, 30–31
Pfizer, 44–45
phone hacking scandal, 52–53
political or economic sanctions, 49–50
press, 51–54
price fixing, 32–34
privacy, 46–49
Ranbaxy—Daiichi Sankyo, 17–18
reliance power, 10–12
Reuters, 28
Samsung Electronics, 21
SAP, 13–14
Siemen, 6
Silver Lake, 31–32
Simon & Schuster, 30–31
Starbucks, 45–46
stock option, 34–39
Symantec, 23
taking labour for ride, 19–21
Tata Consultancy Services (TCS), 20–21
taxes, 40–44
theft, route to instant gratification, 12–13
TPG, 31–32
Walmart, 7
WhatsApp, 49
corporate cybercrime, 144
corporate organisations under attack, 150–151
corporates detect fraud, 263–264
Credit Suisse, 61
cyber fraud, 145
cyber security world, 147–149
cybercrime, 142–143, 145–146
    preventive actions, 151–152

Daelim, 50
Daiichi Sankyo, 276
Daimler, 6
Daiwa Bank, 88
Daniel Sebastian, 114
Daqing Dairy Holdings Ltd., 135
David Lerner Associates, 129
DB Power Ltd., 8
DB Realty, 90
debt and equity, 258
Delhi airport scam, 10
Dell Inc., 51, 187, 205, 210
Deloitte & Touché, 248
Deloitte Haskins & Sells, 253

Delphi Corporation, 181
dereliction of duty, 255
Deutsche Bank AG, 84
Deutsche Bank, 34, 60, 80–81
Dewey & LeBoeuf, 286
doctors providing guidelines, 266–267
Dollar General Corporation, 188
drugs
    bad advertisements for, 282
    companies, 267–268
    fraudulent marketing of, 270–275
    test trial data, 276–277
    trial without long-term patient trial, 279–281
    wrong pricing of, 282–283

E&Y, 256–260
Edelweiss Financial, 19
Elaf Islamic Bank, 49
Elan, 274
ElectraCardSystems, 91
electronic fraud, 145
Eli Lilly, 269, 273, 281
ENI, 50
Enron, 16–17, 211–212
EnStage, 91
Epsilon, 94
Ernst & Young (EY), 251
Essar Power Ltd., 8
Essel Group, 21
Etisalat, 9
Exxon Mobil, 209

Facebook, 44–45, 48, 130
Fannie Mae, 69, 200, 242
falsification
    bogus expense claims, 254–255
    IPO document data, 254
    over-reporting of profit, 254
Federal Bank, 80–81
financial fraud, 144
Financial Technologies group, 262, 288
Fincare Financial & Consultancy Services, 133

Fine Indisales Pvt. Ltd., 115
first in first out (FIFO) method, 208–209
fixed asset, 209–210
Forest Laboratories, 278
Freddie Mac, 69
Freeport, 27–28
fudging operating income and losses, 191–194
Full Tilt Poker, 96
Furukawa Electric, 33
General Electric (GE), 45, 170, 215–216, 246
General Motors, 249, 262
generally accepted accounting principles (GAAP), 155
Geodesic, 244
ghost writer, 268
Glaxo, 280
GlaxoSmithKline, 268, 269, 270, 278, 283
GLC Ltd., 114
global crossing, 175
GMR Energy, 8
GMR Group, 10
GNC, 274
Golden Forests, 111
Goldman Sachs, 28, 31–32, 105–106
Google, 43, 45, 47–48
Grindlays, 80–81
Grunenthal, 270
GVK Power Ltd., 8

Hachette, 30–31
hactivism, 144
HannStar, 32
Harper Collins, 30–31
HCA, 254
HDFC, 67–68
HealthSouth Corporation, 176
Hewlett-Packard (HP), 17, 44–45
Hewlett-Packard–autonomy, 237–238
Hilton hotel, 14
Hindalco Industries, 8

Hindustan Construction, 90
Hindustan Zinc Ltd., 8
Hontex International Holdings, 133, 254
Hospitality Franchise Systems (HFS), 235–236
HSBC, 64, 66–67, 76, 80–81, 106–107, 242, 285, 286
Huaxia Bank, 74
Hunan AVA Dairy Industry Co. Ltd., 55

IBM, 166, 176, 188
ICAP, 60
ICICI, 67–68
IKEA, 4
improper tax shelter products, 256
Indonesia, journalists in, 23–27
ING Bank, 50, 61
Innolux Corporation, 32
insider trading, 259
insurance coverage, doctors' interest conflicting with, 270
Intel, 44–45
internet attacks, terrorists, 145
Internet banking, 94–96
Internet, societal intrusion, 144
Interpublic Group of Companies, 196
Iranian banks, 99
Ireland, 44–45
Italian Bank, 83–84

J&J, 44–45
James Risher, 114
Japan Tobacco, 29
Jim Donnan, 114
JM Financial, 19
Johnson & Johnson, 5, 272
journalists, involvement of, 269–270
JP Morgan Chase Bank, 60, , 61, 69, 70, 85, 103–105, 242, 261, 286
JSW Steels Ltd., 8
JVs, 194–195

Kabul Bank, 262

Karvy Stock Broking, 131
Kellogg's, 55
Kendall Square Research Corporation, 245
Keyuan Petrochemicals, 138
KFC, 54
Kidder, 89
KKR, 31–32
Knight Capital Group Inc., 130
KPMG, 133, 251, 254–255
Kraft Foods, 54
Krispy-Kreme, 167, 213–214
Krupp, Thyssen, 2
Kuehne & Nagel, 34

Laboratoires Servier, 275
Lanco Group Ltd., 8
Larsen & Toubro (L&T), 18
last in first out (LIFO) method, 208–209
Lauren, Ralph, 5
Lehman Brothers, 82
Leoni, 33
Level Global Investors, 122
LG Display, 32
Liberty Reserve, 77
Libor scandal, 59–62
LIC Housing Finance, 90
Ligand Pharmaceutical, 258
Liliput Kidswear, 240
Linkedin, 44–45
Lloyds, 76
Longtop Financial Technologies, 137

Macmillan, 30–31
Marriott International, 183
Matrixx Initiatives, 283
McAfee Inc., 38
McCann Erickson, 196
McKesson-HBOC, 236–237
MCX, 262
Medaphis Corporation, 205, 239
Medicis Pharmaceutical, 1, 257
Medtronic Inc., 268
Merck, 268, 275, 276, 278, 280

Merrill Lynch, 78, 128
Mesco Group, 99
MF Global, 14–15, 88–89
Microsoft, 7, 33, 44–45, 214–215
Mideast Integrated Steel Ltd., 99
misconduct and lack of autonomy, 257–258
misreporting of profits, 257
misstatement
    overstating of inventory, 260–261
    and theft, 261
Money Matters Group, 90
Monsanto Company, 248
Monster Worldwide, 38
Morgan Stanley, 72
mortgaged-backed securities, 69–72
Motilal Oswal Securities, 19, 128

Nestlé, 269
non-accounting red flags, 247–249
non-collectable debtors, 202–203
non-existent cash-in-bank, 227–228
non-release of drug trial data, 277
Nortel Networks, 164
Novartis, 5, 286

off-balance sheet financing, 219–220
OfficeMax, 183
Olympus Corporation, 222–224
Onelife Capital Advisors, 133
Oracle India, 11
originator, 149–150
Ortho-McNeil Pharmaceutical, 272
Ortho-McNeil-Jansen Pharmaceuticals, 272
overstating of inventory, 260–261

Panalpina World Transport Ltd., 34
Panasonic, 32
paracetamol, 265
Parexel, 281
Parke-Davis, 276
Parmalat, 97
Peabody & Co., 89

Penguin, 30–31
PeopleSoft's, 256
Peregrine Systems, 158, 173, 239
Peregrine, 166
Petrobras, 50, 290
Pfizer H.C.P. Corporation, 273
Pfizer, 5, 44–45, 268, 273, 281
pharming, 142
Philips, 32
Philips–LG JV, 32
Phishing, 93–94, 142
PNC financial service, 221
PokerStars, 96
poor audit quality, 258
poor bank audit, 259–260
Postal Savings Bank of China, 11
Posterscope, 175
Precise Consulting & Engineering, 133
Proton Bank, 81
Puda Coal, 138
Punjab National Bank, 90
PwC, 254, 260

quick-rich financing schemes
    Credit Development Corporation (CDI), 119
    Koscot, 118
    money-making racket, 108–116
    Philipino scheme, 118–119
    Ponzi scheme, 109–111
    Ponzi Schemes in India, 111
    Ponzi Schemes in Russia, 112
    pyramid scheme, 116–120

Rabobank, 5, 60
Rana Plaza, 19
Ranbaxy, 276
Ranbaxy—Daiichi Sankyo, 17–18
ransomware, 142
Reebok India, 178–179
Reliance Industries Ltd. (RIL), 122
Reliance Petroleum Ltd. (RPL), 122
Reliance Power Limited, 11
Rent-Way, Inc., 201, 204, 207, 246

Repsol, 50
Republic Bank's, 96
research in motion, 38
Reuters, 28
Rex Venture Group, 116
Roche, 277
Rogue Trader, 85–86
Rolls Royce, 11, 286
Rose Valley, 288
Royal Ahold, 172
Royal Bank of Scotland (RBS), 5, 60, 76, 63–64, 286
Royal Dutch Shell, 50
Royal Twinkle Star Club, 288

SAC Capital Advisors, 130
safeguard client's assets, 261–262
SafeNet, 193
Sahara Group, 111
Sahara, 290
Samsung Electronics, 21, 32
Sanchayani Savings & Investments, 111
Sanchayita Investments, 111
SAP, 13–14
Saradha Realty Ltd., 110–111, 288, 290
Satyam Computer Services Limited, 228–229, 260, 244
scams, corporate world, 285
Schering-Plough, 30, 278, 280
Serono Labs, 275
Sham Insurance Premium Income, 179–180
Shaw Group Inc., 248
Siemen, 6
Silver Lake, 31–32
Simon & Schuster, 30–31
Sino-Forest Corporation, 139, 251
SinoTech Energy, 135
SK Foods, 54
SmithKline Beecham, 278
snooping, 144
social activism, 144
Société Générale, 5, 60, 86, 242

Softbank, 164
Sohu.com, 140
Spain—Bankia, 84–85
SpeakAsia, 115
sponsored speakers, 269
Stan C, 80–81
Standard Chartered Bank, 21, 50, 74, 257
Starbucks, 45–46
State Bank of India, 81
Statoil, 50
Stiefel Laboratories, 15
Stock Market Swindles
    brokers, 127–129
    clever north America-listed Chinese companies, 134–140
    deceitful listing, 131–133
    Galleon Group, 124
    insidious insiders, 121–123
    KPMG, 124–125
    Martha Stewart Living Omnimedia, 125
    Nomura, 126
    Polaris software labs, 125–126
    rapid trading, 129–131
    SAC capital advisors (SAC), 123–124
Stockguru, 111
Sumangal Industries, 113
Sumitomo Corporation, 89
Sunbeam Corporation, 212–213
Susi Emu Farm, 113
Symantec, 23
Symbol Technologies, 38
Syndicate Bank, 99
Syntax-Brillion Corporation, 177–178, 244

Takeda, 278
Tata Consultancy Services (TCS), 20–21
Tata Sponge Iron Ltd., 8
tax evasion schemes, 72–73

tax shelter products, 255
TD Bank NA, 100
Technicolor, 32
TeGenero, 281
Telenor Group, 9
Tenet Healthcare Corporation, 4
testing drugs, humans in, 281–282
Thomson Reuters, 130
ThyssenKrupp AG, 34
TISCO, 8
Toshiba, 32
Total, 50
Toy "R" Us, 30, 217
TPG, 31–32
Trafigura, 4
Transaction Systems Architects Inc., 159
Trident Microsystems, 39
2G telecom scam, 9–10
Tyco International, 171, 206
Tyson Foods, 5

UBS, 5, 60, 62–63, 83, 86–87, 101–103, 285, 286
UCO Bank's, 131
Ulticom Inc., 180
Ultratech Ltd., 8
unfavourable drug study results, 278–279
unfavourable test data, 279
United Parcel Services, 34
UnitedHealth Group, 39
Upsher-Smith Laboratories Inc., 30
US Foodservice, 182

Vascular Solutions, 262
Vatican Bank, 65–66
Vestas Wind Systems, 184
VIPshop, 140
Vitamin Shoppe, 274
Vivendi Universal, 195, 202, 232

Wachovia, 64
Walgreen Company, 242
Walmart, 7, 242
Warnaco Group, 245
Warner Technology & Investment Corporation, 140
wealth management, 74–75
Weavering Capital, 42
web activities, violence and combat-related
    terrorism, 145
    warfare, 145
Wegelin Bank, 73
Wells Fargo, 70
WhatsApp, 49
Wyeth, 273

Xerox Corporation, 160, 254

Yazaki, 33
Yes Bank, 90
Yum Brands, 54

ZeekRewards.com, 116
Zenith InfoTech, 12
Zenith Technologies, 12
Zions Bank, 57

Scan QR code to access the
Penguin Random House India website